# Forming Deacons

# Forming Deacons

*Ministers of Soul and Leaven*

EDITED BY William T. Ditewig
WITH Michael J. Tkacik

Paulist Press
New York/Mahwah, NJ

Cover design by Joy Taylor
Book design by Lynn Else

Library of Congress Cataloging-in-Publication Data

Forming deacons : ministers of soul and leaven / edited by William T. Ditewig with Michael J. Tkacik.
    p. cm.
Includes bibliographical references.
ISBN 978-0-8091-4497-6 (alk. paper)
1. Deacons—Catholic Church. I. Ditewig, William T. II. Tkacik, Michael J.
BX1912.F667 2010
262´.142—dc22

2010017893

Published by Paulist Press
997 Macarthur Boulevard
Mahwah, New Jersey 07430

www.paulistpress.com

Printed and bound in the
United States of America

This book is dedicated to the Ditewig and the Tkacik families—
and their endless amounts of patience.

## Acknowledgments

The editors of this volume would like to thank Kevin Carrizo di Camillo, our editor at Paulist Press.

"Let them be tested first;
then, if they prove themselves blameless,
let them serve as deacons."

—1 Timothy 3:10

# Contents

Foreword: The Deacon and His Relationships
    *Most Rev. Wilton D. Gregory, Archbishop of Atlanta*.............ix

Introduction
    *William T. Ditewig*...............................................................1

**PART ONE: Background**
1. The *National Directory for Deacons* and How to Read It:
   Implementation Strategies
       *William T. Ditewig* .......................................................11
2. A Purpose-Driven Formation
       *Theodore W. Kraus*.......................................................28
3. Lessons from Priestly Formation in Integrating the
   Dimensions of Formation
       *Paul J. Langsfeld*...........................................................41
4. The Basic Standards for Readiness: A Commentary
       *Stephen Graff and William T. Ditewig* ......................49

**PART TWO: The Human Dimension**
5. Ecclesial Ordinations: Baptism, Marriage, and Orders
       *Michael G. Lawler* .......................................................61
6. The "Gift" of Formation at Midlife
       *Ann Healey* ...................................................................82
7. Priests and Deacons in Partnership: Thoughts on the
   Role of the Priest in the Ongoing Renewal of the
   Diaconate
       *Timothy J. Shugrue*....................................................100

**PART THREE: The Spiritual Dimension**
8. The Spiritual Formation Path: The Vision and Hope of
   the Director
       *David Dowdle*..............................................................121

# Contents

9. Themes for a Canonical Retreat: The Spiritual Apex of
Diaconal Formation
*James Keating*................................................................134

**PART FOUR: The Intellectual Dimension**
10. The *National Directory* and the Educational Formation of
Deacon Candidates
*Michael J. Tkacik* ........................................................151

**PART FIVE: The Pastoral Dimension**
11. The Deacon as Preacher
*Marshall Gibbs*.............................................................171
12. The Deacon's Ministry vis-à-vis the Laity and Parish Life
*John R. Alvarez*............................................................193

Notes .................................................................................217

Bibliography....................................................................233

Contributors...................................................................240

# The Deacon and His Relationships

## In Service of Christ's Church

### *Most Rev. Wilton D. Gregory,* Archbishop of Atlanta

> He emptied himself and took the form of a slave.
> —Philippians 2:6–7

The figures speak for themselves. In 1967, Pope Paul VI renewed the permanent diaconate. On July 4, 2004, I was privileged to meet with hundreds of deacons from every part of the United States, as they gathered in Baltimore for the fourth National Catholic Diaconate Conference. Deacons from other parts of the world were also present, giving the occasion an even broader significance. I was asked on that occasion to speak about the various relationships of the deacon in the Church, and it is appropriate to introduce this book addressing the formation of deacons for the contemporary Church with a similar focus. The sacrament of Holy Orders is all about relationships, and this is certainly evident in the diaconate. This means that every facet of diaconal formation—from selection to aspirancy, candidacy, and postordination formation—must revolve around the nurturing and strengthening of the myriad relationships of the deacon.

During that gathering on the Fourth of July, we remembered that we were not simply there to celebrate this Independence

Day as an act of national patriotism. Rather, we view human freedom, responsibility, service, and sacrifice as values we hold as Catholics and, in particular, as responsibilities we bear as ministers of the Church. The many relationships of the deacon, when viewed through these lenses of faith and service, thus take on renewed significance. Indeed, they help us to realize the very public identity deacons have as the Church's front line of response to the needs of others.

# Deacons and the Servanthood of the Church

Pope Paul VI provided us with a wonderful insight about the work of the Second Vatican Council. On December 7, 1965, the day before the solemn closing of the Council in St. Peter's Square, the Council Fathers celebrated Mass together with the pope in St. Peter's Basilica. During his homily, the pope offered a reflection on the ultimate significance of the Council's work:

> We stress that the teaching of the Council is channeled in one direction, the service of humankind, of every condition, in every weakness and need. The Church has declared herself a servant of humanity at the very time when her teaching role and her pastoral government have, by reason of this Church solemnity, assumed greater splendor and vigor. However, the idea of service has been central.[1]

As every deacon knows well, this same pope would later refer to the renewed diaconate as a "driving force" for the Church's own *diakonia*. Deacons may take heart, then, that the renewal of the Order of Deacons by the Second Vatican Council was not simply one historic act among many at the Council; rather, it was seen—certainly by the pope who would eventually implement the Council's decision—as a sacramental embodiment of the most central idea of the entire Council!

The contemporary diaconate is grounded on the balanced exercise of the threefold ministry of word, sacrament, and charity. All disciples are called by baptism to proclaim their faith before all; through confirmation they are more strictly obliged to spread the Gospel in word and deed.[2] Through his ordination, the deacon serves as a public and permanent sign of the unity binding these three dimensions together. His particular role is to remind the Church of its own servanthood and of its responsibility to be a "sign and instrument" and "leaven and soul" in creating a more just world.[3]

# The Bishop and His Deacons

No one—bishop, priest, or deacon—is ordained in a vacuum or for his own personal spiritual fulfillment. The purpose of any ordination is to help build up the Body of Christ, and deacons are ordained to this task by their bishop in a special and powerful way. Through the deacon's ordination, his relationship with Christ is forged anew. The *Directory for the Ministry and Life of Deacons* from the Congregation for the Clergy reminds us:

> The primary and most fundamental relationship [of the deacon] must be with Christ, who assumed the condition of a slave for love of the Father and mankind. In virtue of ordination the deacon is truly called to act in conformity with Christ the Servant.[4]

It is precisely this relationship that enables and empowers the deacon to serve as the sacramental focus for the diaconal ministry of the entire community. It is why one text on the diaconate can say, "A parish, which is a local incarnation of Church and of Jesus, is not sacramentally whole if it is without either priest or deacon."[5]

Because it is the bishop who ordains the deacon and brings the deacon into a permanent sacramental participation in his own apostolic ministry, the relationship of the bishop with his deacons is particularly close. From the earliest days of the

Church, deacons have been linked sacramentally and pastorally with their bishops, serving as the bishop's "eyes, ears, heart, and soul." One ancient writer even said that the bishop and deacon should be like two souls in one body.

This historic relationship is a cornerstone of the contemporary diaconate, reflected in the teachings of every pope since the Second Vatican Council and in major documents from the Holy See. Liturgically this relationship is expressed most pointedly when, during the ordination of a deacon, only the bishop lays hands on the ordinand. The deacon, from the moment of ordination, is given a participation in the bishop's own ministry. One often hears of the special sacramental relationship that binds the bishop with his body of priests. There is a similar sacramental relationship between the bishop and his deacons, and this relationship is a foundational theme of the *National Directory for the Formation, Ministry, and Life of Permanent Deacons in the United States*, which the bishops of the United States promulgated in 2004. The *National Directory* features prominently in the various chapters of this book, and rightly so: the bishops, in their document, want to stress the centrality of the relationship they enjoy with their deacons, and to let that relationship serve as the basis of their formation.

# Deacons and Mission

The 1998 *Basic Norms for the Formation of Permanent Deacons* says that "we must consider the diaconate, like every other Christian identity, from within the Church which is understood as a mystery of Trinitarian communion in missionary tension." I would like to focus for a moment on the last part of this description: that this Trinitarian communion is lived "in missionary tension." One's sacramental identity, in other words, finds its concrete expression through mission. But what is this mission? Cardinal Roger Mahony of Los Angeles once observed that "it is not so much that the church has a mission; it is rather more that the mission has a church." This mission is that of Christ Himself:

Jesus' mission is to announce the time of God's favor, the coming of the reign of God. Jesus proclaimed the reign of God as the fulfillment of God's hope, desire and intention for the world now and to come. In God's reign, truth, holiness, justice, love and peace will hold sway forever. Jesus established the church to continue and further this mission....This mission is so central to the word and work of Jesus that the Second Vatican Council affirmed and emphasized that *mission* defines the church. The church in every dimension of its life and practice exists for mission: to proclaim in word and deed the reign of God to people in every culture, time and place.[6]

Mission "defines the church." If this is true for the entire Church, for all of the baptized, think what ramifications it has for those who are the Church's ministers! Sacramental ordination, as an act of the Spirit working through the Church, provides the Church with the graces of leadership and strength that are "supremely necessary for the life of the Church."[7] The deacon is a minister filled with the Spirit, established in the Order of Deacon by his bishop, to be an instrument of Christ and of the Church that Christ established to carry on His mission.

The way in which deacons carry out their exercise of the Church's mission is unique. Diaconal ministry revolves around servant-leadership: leadership that inspires, enables, and empowers; leadership that models for other members of the Church what servant-leadership can mean in living the demands of Christian discipleship in the contemporary world.

Cardinal Walter Kasper, writing both as a bishop and as a theologian, has given considerable thought to the deacon and his ministry. He has written that the basic attitude of the deacon must include "a perceptive eye for those suffering distress, illness, or fear. The task is to bring a healing that sets free and empowers them to trust and so to serve and love others in their turn."[8] He continues, "The goal of diaconal activity is not simply help, but the empowering of life, so that those who lie prostrate may get to their feet....In some situations, the deacon can and must become the public advocate of the weak and powerless and of all those who have no other voice or lobby."[9]

Notice how servant-leadership forms the basis of Cardinal Kasper's insights. The deacon not only takes responsibility for taking concrete steps to meet the needs of others; the deacon also becomes a "public advocate" on behalf of the powerless. While most people, including many deacons, might prefer to work quietly "behind the scenes" to effect change, sacramental ordination demands a willingness on the part of the ordained to risk having a public role on behalf of others. The deacon does so both in the person of Christ and in the name of the Church. Cardinal Kasper describes the deacon as the obvious and public "contact partner" for all those in need, to whom they know they can look confidently for help. As the official representative of the community, "he is the obvious contact person" for regional Catholic charity organizations and health centers.

Cardinal Kasper outlines the various contexts in which the deacon ministers. The parish forms a base for the deacon's other ministries, suggesting that it would be a good idea to provide at least one deacon for every parish so that the sacramental nature of the parish might be complete. He writes:

> Each parish has to make sure that *diakonia* is realized. This means that faith and preaching, as well as the Eucharist and liturgy must be oriented to *diakonia*. Faith without diakonia is not a Christian faith. Preaching without *diakonia* is not Christian preaching. A non-diaconal parish celebrating the Eucharist may express its faith, but its faith remains dead; in the final analysis it cannot find God, as they miss the point that God reveals himself in the people, especially in the poor.[10]

Kasper writes that deacons should also be considered for assignments with an even broader scope of city, deanery, and region. A national study on the diaconate in the United States found that deacons have been well-received in parish-based ministry, but that one of the primary challenges for the future would be "to broaden its ministries in order to be model, animator and

---

*Most Rev. Wilton D. Gregory*

facilitator of charity and justice" within the diocesan church.[11] To this end, a number of bishops now give their deacons a dual assignment: one to a parish and another to a diocesan or regional institution for service. Cardinal Kasper suggests how this might work, when he observes:

> I am thinking here of hospitals, homes for the elderly, spiritual care in places of work, in prisons, in refugee shelters, etc. I also include co-operation in the leadership of a diocese in those regions, where the main question is that of diaconal leadership. In this context, I would like to point out that for the bishop the community of deacons of a diocese can be a welcome panel of advisors. The deacons can act as the eyes and ears of the bishop in identifying areas of need and can help him in his task of being father to the poor.[12]

In this description we find echoes of the ancient diaconate expressed in contemporary terms. Finally, at the even broader level of more regional, national, and international ministries, we turn to Pope John Paul II:

> A deeply felt need in the decision to re-establish the permanent diaconate was and is that of greater and more direct presence of Church ministers in the various spheres of the family, work, school, etc., in addition to existing pastoral structures.[13]

Deacons can and should exercise leadership in community-based service initiatives. Such service can take many forms, depending upon the deacon's own skills and qualifications, the sociopolitical structures of the society in which he lives, and the needs to be met.

It must not be forgotten that the object of Christ's *diakonia* is humankind. Every human being carries the traces of sin but is called to communion with God. "God so loved the world that He gave His only Son, so

xv

that all who believe in Him might not die but have eternal life" (John 3:16). It was for this plan of love that Christ became a slave and took human flesh. The Church continues to be the sign and instrument of that *diakonia* in history…Growth in imitation of Christ's love for mankind—which surpasses all ideologies—is thus an essential component of the spiritual life of every deacon.[14]

As the renewed diaconate continues to mature in the years since the Second Vatican Council, opportunities and challenges abound across the whole range of diaconal ministry. It remains for all of us to explore creative, courageous, and collaborative models of ministry across the spectrum of possibilities.

# Conclusion

Those who are involved with the formation of deacons—bishops, their staffs, lay experts, religious, priests, and other deacons—need to be committed to not only the renewal of the diaconate as such, but also to the diaconate in its varied relationships. May we be renewed in our commitment to service and to the challenges our ministry demands. May we accept, in freedom and in obedience, new challenges that may be demanded of us. Above all, the proper exercise of ministry calls us to constant renewal in Christ.

The late Pope John Paul II, during the Jubilee Day for Deacons, spoke about the mission of deacons in his address to the assembled deacons and their families:

Dear deacons, be active apostles of the new evangelization. Lead everyone to Christ! Through your efforts, may his kingdom also spread in your family, in your workplace, in the parish, in the diocese, in the whole world! This mission, at least in intention and zeal, must stir the hearts of sacred ministers and spur them to the total gift of themselves.[15]

In a remarkable passage full of pastoral concern and experience, the pope continued:

> Dear deacons, perhaps some of you are tired because of the burden of your duties, because of frustration due to unsuccessful apostolic projects, because many misunderstand you. Do not lose heart! Throw yourselves into Christ's arms: he will refresh you. May this be your Jubilee: a pilgrimage of conversion to Jesus.[16]

These words could easily serve as a vision statement for the formation of deacons, and the chapters of this text, in one way or another, concern themselves with this goal of ongoing conversion.

Pope John Paul II also reminded the bishops to be "true fathers" to their deacons, encouraging them in their ministry.[17] A brother bishop once remarked to his deacons, "When you were ordained for service to this diocese, you were ordained to share in the concerns of my heart for the people. Today I want to share what's on my heart, so it can be on yours." This bishop understood both his relationship to his deacons, and their participation in his own pastoral responsibilities. Regardless of the specific ministries deacons exercise in support of the Church's mission, they do so in sacramental communion with their bishop.

Those who are involved in the formation of deacons have a most important ministry to perform for the Church. This book was written in support of that ministry. All of the authors are experienced and knowledgeable, and many of them served the bishops directly as advisors and consultants in the preparation of the *National Directory for the Formation, Ministry and Life of Permanent Deacons in the United States*. I pray that in the pages that follow, you will find valuable insights and information to aid you in this ministry.

*Most Rev. Wilton D. Gregory,*
*Archbishop of Atlanta*

# INTRODUCTION

## William T. Ditewig

The Church serves as a leaven and as a kind of
soul for human society as it is to be renewed in
Christ and transformed into God's family.

*Gaudium et Spes*, no. 40

Deacons likewise must be serious, not double-
tongued, not indulging in much wine, not greedy
for money; they must hold fast to the mystery of
the faith with a clear conscience. And let them
first be tested; then, if they prove themselves
blameless, let them serve as deacons.

1 Timothy 3:8–10

The rubrics for diaconate ordinations in the Catholic Church
begin with the instruction *Omnibus rite dispositis*, usually trans-
lated "when everything has been properly arranged." While these
words refer to the proximate readiness for the ordination ceremony, their meaning might easily be expanded to include the
total formation and preparation of the candidates for ordination.
The readiness of the ordinands to assume the mantle of ordained
ministry is the concern of the diocesan bishop and those with
whom he collaborates on the candidates' human, spiritual, intellectual, and pastoral formation. This formation flows from a systematic understanding of a theology of the diaconate within the
broader framework of a theology of ministry in service to the
Church. Although this book focuses on the actual formation of
deacons, this Introduction provides a short overview of the theology foundational to formation. Only with such a foundation

can "everything be properly arranged." In the words of the 1998 *Basic Norms for the Formation of Permanent Deacons*, promulgated by the Congregation for Catholic Education, "The effectiveness of the formation of permanent deacons depends to a great extent on the theological understanding of the diaconate that underlies it. In fact it offers the co-ordinates for establishing and guiding the formation process and, at the same time, lays down the end to be attained."[1]

What is the "end" to be attained? The Church seeks ministers who will work together to build up the Body of Christ[2] so that the Church—as the People of God, the mystical Body of Christ and the Temple of the Holy Spirit—may carry out its mission to be, in the famous words of the Second Vatican Council, "a leaven and a kind of soul for human society as it is to be renewed in Christ and transformed into God's family."[3] The deacon must be understood within this overarching ecclesial framework of serving this mission of the entire Church within the modern world. It is for this reason that we have echoed the theme of "soul and leaven" in the subtitle of this work.

Although deacons have been a part of the life of the Christian Church from its very beginning, a substantive theology of this ministry, however, has not. Furthermore, how deacons were to be prepared for ministry remained largely unspecified for two millennia. The First Letter to Timothy, cited above, offers the only insights to diaconate formation found in scripture, and then, with rare exception, silence descends on the matter. Once the diaconate became simply a transitional step on the way to ordination as a presbyter, the question of the formation of deacons became rather moot, since the end of holy orders was found in the presbyterate, and the diaconate became defined and described within the context of the priesthood. Vestiges of this can still be seen today, as the Church continues to ordain seminarians—who are discerning possible vocations to the presbyterate—to the order of deacons. The formation of these future priests is not at all about service as deacons, and yet they are ordained to this ministry prior to their ordination as priests. As I have written elsewhere, there was simply no need for a fully realized theology of the diaconate during this lengthy period of history, since the diaconate was simply understood as a phase that one passed through to get to the ultimate goal of priesthood. What theology that existed vis-à-vis the diaconate was therefore priestly in nature.[4]

And then came the Second Vatican Council. By permitting the possibility of a renewed diaconate that could be lived as a permanent vocation, not leading inevitably and inexorably to presbyterate, suddenly there was a need for work in theology, canon law, and in formation theory and practice. An autonomous diaconate demanded a new kind of theology and a new kind of formation. While the content of formation for ordained ministries might be similar, the context in which formation needed to be carried out would be significantly different.

The question of a theology for the renewed diaconate was examined by the Congregation for Catholic Education in its 1998 *Basic Norms for the Formation of Permanent Deacons*. As would also be the later experience of the United States Conference of Catholic Bishops' Committee on the Diaconate and of the International Theological Commission, the Congregation realized that crafting a systematic theology of the diaconate was simply not possible at that time. In a section entitled "Reference to a Sure Theology of the Diaconate," the Congregation states:

> The almost total disappearance of the permanent diaconate from the Church of the West for more than a millennium has certainly made it more difficult to understand the profound reality of this ministry. However, it cannot be said for that reason that the theology of the diaconate has no authoritative points of reference, completely at the mercy of different theological opinions. There are points of reference, and they are very clear, even if they need to be developed and deepened.[5]

The theological reference points listed by the Congregation in paragraph 4 include:

- *Trinitarian* and *Ecclesiological.* The diaconate is compared to "every other Christian identity" in that it must be understood from within the Church, "a mystery of Trinitarian communion in missionary tension." In their ministry, deacons "necessarily depend on the Bishops," and "they are placed in a special relationship with the priests, in communion with whom they are called to serve the People of God." Upon ordination, "the deacon is incardinated into a particular Church or personal prelature…[or] into a religious institute of consecrated life or a clerical society of apostolic life." Incardination is "a constant bond of service to a concrete portion of the People of God....This entails ecclesial membership at the juridical, affective and spiritual level and the obligation of ministerial service."

- *Pneumatological* and *Christological.* The diaconate is conferred through ordination, "a special outpouring of the Spirit," which conforms the deacon specifically to Christ, "Lord and servant of all."
- *Sacramental.* "The *matter* of diaconal ordination is the laying on of the hands of the Bishop; the *form* is constituted by the words of the prayer of ordination, which is expressed in the three moments of anamnesis, epiclesis, and intercession." As part of the sacrament of orders, diaconate "imprints a character and communicates a specific sacramental grace."

At almost the same time that the Congregation was preparing its own document on diaconate formation, the Bishops' Committee on the Diaconate was beginning its own task of developing what would become the *National Directory for the Formation, Ministry, and Life of Permanent Deacons in the United States*. One of the first decisions the bishops made was to construct the *National Directory* in two major segments. The first segment was to be entitled "Foundations" and the second was to be "Formation." A subcommittee of bishops was created to focus on the foundational elements of the diaconate: theology, spirituality, and ministry. A second subcommittee would focus its work on the various aspects of formation itself. While the final form of the *National Directory* no longer includes these two subdivisions formally, chapters 1 and 2 constitute the foundational section and the remaining chapters are the formational section. It is critically important, when studying and implementing the *National Directory*, to first master the foundational material before moving into the formational.

Throughout the next few years of the *National Directory*'s development, the committee and its consultants studied, reviewed, and debated the subject of the doctrinal foundation of the diaconate. Various drafts examined different approaches to a theology of diaconate, but all were found lacking, simply because the Church's experience with diaconal ministry had rarely been the subject of substantive and systematic theological reflection. Furthermore, official documents on the diaconate were almost nonexistent until 1967 (when Pope Paul VI implemented the decision of the Second Vatican Council concerning the diaconate by promulgating *Sacrum Diaconatus Ordinem*); but even after that, official documents were rare until 1998, when the aforementioned *Basic Norms* for diaconal formation and the *Directory for the Ministry and Life of Permanent Deacons* were promulgated by the Holy See. It was decided that the *National Directory* would not attempt to break new theological ground, but rather summarize critical theological points that were foundational for the diaconate.

In chapter 1 of the *Directory*, "Doctrinal Understanding of the Diaconate," the bishops quote the Vatican's *Basic Norms* regarding the "reference points" of diaconal theology, and then proceed to ground their presentation in the sacramental nature of the Church herself. They then review the decision of the Second Vatican Council to renew a permanent diaconate in light of the needs of the time and in terms of the Church's mission of evangelization. The chapter concludes by describing the deacon's participation in the Church's triple ministry (*munus docendi, munus sanctificandi, munus regendi*) as having an "intrinsic unity" and by stating that no one should be considered for ordination who is not prepared to exercise all three ministries in some way. It is significant that the bishops of the Second Vatican Council also spoke of the intrinsic unity of the traditional "triple *munus*" when they describe the ministry of the bishop (in teaching, sanctifying, and ruling) as "a true service, which in sacred literature is significantly called "diakonia" or ministry."[6] In this way, while the bishops are offering, in large part, a commentary on the "reference points" proposed by the Holy See, they also provide a strong ecclesiological and pastoral understanding upon which to consider both the deacon's ministry itself and, ultimately, the formation necessary to prepare candidates for such ministry.

Perhaps even more significant, the ministry of the deacon is clearly articulated as a participation in the bishop's own ministry. This most fundamental relationship of bishop and deacon is evident in scripture, throughout all of the patristic literature, and most recently in the documents of the Second Vatican Council and in the postconciliar papal and ordinary magisterium. The intimate bond between bishop and deacon is a key theme throughout the *National Directory*, and this is done intentionally. The deacon is consistently linked with the bishop, not only in scripture and patristic evidence, but also in current documents: when the council fathers took up the debate on the diaconate on October 4, 1963, it was in the middle of their own debates over the nature and ministry of the episcopacy; the bishops' renewal of the diaconate was tied to their even more fundamental renewal of the episcopacy itself.[7]

In 1967, when Pope Paul VI reinstated a permanent diaconate in accordance with the wishes of the council fathers, few people in the world had a clue about how to provide adequate formation for these new ministers. While significant steps had been taken in Germany, especially following the Second World War, these efforts were largely unknown outside of Germany. Not only was there no practical experience available on which to build, there was not even much of a theoretical framework! After all, none had been needed until then.

Over the past forty years, all of this has changed. The Church has gone from zero permanent deacons to a worldwide total as of this writing of more than 35,000 deacons, with nearly 17,000 in the United States alone. Formation programs that began in the United States as early as 1967 have now matured with experience. The bishops of the United States have published three increasingly sophisticated regulations for the formation of deacons, and in 1998 the Holy See itself offered two valuable documents, one on the formation of deacons, which was cited above and which had been heavily influenced by the experience gained in the United States. The *National Directory*, promulgated in December 2004, was the result of more than eight years' work by the U.S. bishops and their collaborators, and it built upon the experience gained over the previous decades, the two previous sets of national guidelines, and the documents from the Holy See.

The goal of this book is to provide bishops and their formation staff with a resource to assist in the formation process. While this text is not properly a commentary on the *National Directory for the Formation, Ministry, and Life of Permanent Deacons in the United States*, the *Directory* is its foundation and touchstone. A number of the authors assisted the bishops with the *National Directory*'s preparation and provide invaluable insights into the context within which the *Directory* was prepared. Rather than being a commentary, this text consists of a series of thoughtful reflections on the process of diaconate formation, written from a wide variety of perspectives. Our hope is that the very diversity of this material will serve to inspire ongoing reflection on the nature of the diaconate and its renewal in the contemporary church.

The material is organized in five sections. Part 1 consists of background material on the nature and history of the *National Directory*, as well as reflections on the dimensions of formation and the model standards that form a major contribution of the material prepared and promulgated by the bishops in 2004. Part 2 focuses on aspects of the human dimension of diaconate formation, part 3 on the spiritual dimension, part 4 on the intellectual dimension, and part 5, the pastoral dimension.

As the renewed diaconate moves into its fifth decade within a renewed Church, the formation of men and women in the Church's various ordained and lay ministries will continue to be a matter of increasing interest and sophistication, as the Church seeks to offer all her members the best prepared and deeply spiritual ministers. As such, it is hoped that this book can make its own modest contribution to this effort.

# PART ONE
# Background

# CHAPTER 1

# The *National Directory for Deacons* and How to Read It

## Implementation Strategies

## *William T. Ditewig*

> According to the prescripts of the conference
> of bishops, those aspiring to the permanent
> diaconate are to be formed to nourish a spiritual
> life and instructed to fulfill correctly the duties
> proper to that order.
>
> *Code of Canon Law*, c. 236

With the December 2004 promulgation of the *National Directory for the Formation, Ministry, and Life of Permanent Deacons in the United States* (hereafter, the *National Directory*), the Catholic Church in the United States moved into a new phase in the development of the diaconate. This document, when seen in context, reflects the growing maturation of the renewed diaconate flowing out from more than thirty-five years of pastoral experience, as well as the impact of recent documents (promulgated in 1998) from the Holy See.

This chapter is arranged in three parts. First, there is a brief historical sketch of the role of the United States Conference of Catholic Bishops (hereafter, the USCCB) in the development of

11

the diaconate in the United States. The *National Directory* is, after all, a document of the episcopal conference and is issued under its authority. It is, therefore, necessary to understand something of document's nature and responsibility vis-à-vis the diaconate. Second, we will review the development of the *National Directory*. The promulgation of the document was the result of a dynamic process, and the process itself is illuminating and helpful in interpreting the text. Finally, I will offer six suggestions concerning the implementation of the *National Directory*.

# The USCCB and the Diaconate

Not surprisingly, the specific responsibility of episcopal conferences for the diaconate finds its source in the Second Vatican Council. The *Dogmatic Constitution on the Church* (*Lumen Gentium*, no. 29) says simply, "It pertains to the competent territorial bodies of bishops, of one kind or another, with the approval of the Supreme Pontiff, to decide whether and where it is opportune for such deacons to be established for the care of souls."[1] On June 18, 1967, Pope Paul VI implemented this conciliar decision through *Sacrum Diaconatus Ordinem*. In establishing the first norms for the renewal of the diaconate, the pope picked up on this responsibility, writing, "It is the task of the legitimate assemblies of bishops of episcopal conferences to discuss, with the consent of the Supreme Pontiff, whether and where—in view of the good of the faithful—the diaconate is to be instituted as a proper and permanent rank of the hierarchy."[2]

This national responsibility for the renewal of the diaconate is something that the bishops of the United States have taken quite seriously. For forty years, from 1967 to 2007, the bishops maintained a committee of bishops and a staff secretariat that focused on the growth and support of the diaconate throughout the United States. (Beginning in January 2008, responsibility for the diaconate was absorbed into the new Committee on Clergy, Consecrated Life, and Vocations.) This level of commitment has not been the practice in other parts of the world. I believe that this constant and consistent dedication to the diaconate by the

USCCB is one of the reasons that the diaconate has flourished as it has in this country.

Immediately after Pope Paul VI promulgated those first norms, five episcopal conferences requested and received authority to ordain permanent deacons: Germany, France, Italy, Brazil, and Cameroon. These countries had been discussing the possibilities of a renewed diaconate for many years and were ready and eager for the diaconate.[3] After receiving the approval of the Holy See, these countries moved immediately into preparations for ordination, with the first ordinations being celebrated in 1968 in Germany and Cameroon.[4]

I want to focus briefly on the first of these ordination classes. On April 28, 1968, five men were ordained deacons for Cologne, Germany. They ranged in age from thirty-five to forty-seven, and had been in formal preparation for eight years. With the appearance of the first "deacon circle" in 1951 in Freiburg, Germany, many men had pursued formation on the remote possibility of eventual ordination at some vague point in the future. In the case of these five men, they began formation in 1960: before the Council had even begun, before the decision was made to renew the diaconate, and certainly before Pope Paul VI implemented that decision. In addition to being a marvelous act of faith, service, and prescience, their formation began when they were aged twenty-seven to thirty-nine: *all* of these men were still working in secular occupations (although one was a full-time diocesan official) and were married with families.

I point this out because a current issue in this country is the aging of the diaconate, where the average age of deacons is now at least sixty-two, and the average age at ordination is around fifty-five. Elsewhere in the world, the average age of deacons remains about forty-two. This is not the time or the place to address this issue, but certainly bishops and directors of diaconate formation programs need to consider the age of applicants closely. It also underscores a point made quite sharply in the *National Directory*: that formation for the diaconate should involve the entire family, as appropriate. This is how formation is handled in many parts of Europe: the entire family comes to formation, with teams of qualified youth ministers caring for the children while their parents are in class; during meals and prayer times, however, the families are together. Several United States dioceses are now following this same approach, allowing younger families the opportunity to participate in formation.

While the diaconate in Europe and Africa was moving ahead smartly in 1967 and 1968, here in the United States, the USCCB moved a bit more deliberately, since there had not been the same level of theological and pastoral discussion here about the possibilities of the diaconate. When our bishops gathered in 1967, they discussed Pope Paul VI's document. Based on this conversation, they commissioned a research study to be done by the Catholic Theological Society of America (CTSA) on what a renewed diaconate might contribute to pastoral life in the United States. They also appointed a new ad hoc Committee on the Permanent Diaconate to oversee this whole process. In 1968, the CTSA completed their report and recommended to the committee that the USCCB *should* move forward with a request to the Holy See to renew the diaconate in the United States. The full body of bishops agreed, and the letter to the Holy See was prepared and submitted in April 1968. The Holy See quickly granted permission in August 1968. Therefore, at the November 1968 general meeting of the full body of bishops, they approved the transition of the ad hoc Committee on the Permanent Diaconate to the status of a standing (permanent) committee, with a supporting secretariat. This structure remained in place until the major USCCB restructuring of January 2008.

At the November 1968 meeting, the full body of bishops approved the first four training centers for diaconate formation: two national sites and two diocesan sites. Two things are significant in this regard: First, many dioceses and institutions are exploring again the possibility of regional models for formation (in addition to diocesan models), and thus some insights can be gained from these early national projects. Second, the pattern was established whereby the episcopal conference was to serve as the approval authority for each and every diocesan diaconate formation program established in the United States.

The first permanent deacon ordained in the United States was Michael Cole, ordained on June 1, 1969, by Archbishop Fulton

J. Sheen in Rochester, New York. Deacon Cole was a former Episcopalian priest who had recently been received into the Church. It was determined that, since he already had extensive theological and pastoral experience, no additional formation was necessary. The year following his diaconal ordination, he resumed his former ministry in the Anglican Communion and assumed a pastorate in Canada. The next permanent deacon ordained in the United States was Paul McCardle in Kansas City–St. Joseph. He was ordained on May 24, 1970, by Bishop Charles Helmsing. Deacon Paul became the first deacon ordained following a period of formation designed for him.

In 1971, the first large classes of deacons were ordained in several dioceses. It was also in 1971 that the Bishops' Committee on the Diaconate issued its first guidelines on formation. When the *Code of Canon Law* was revised in 1983, new canons that were related to the diaconate needed to be reflected in diaconate formation. Specifically related to the topic at hand—the responsibility of the episcopal conferences for the renewal of the diaconate—canon 236 directed that

> according to the prescripts of the **conference of bishops**, those aspiring to the permanent diaconate are to be formed to nourish a spiritual life and instructed to fulfill correctly the duties proper to that order....Men of a more mature age, whether celibate or married, are to spend three years in a program defined by the **conference of bishops**. [*emphasis added*]

Once again, it is to be the various episcopal conferences that set the standards for formation, and the USCCB issued new formation guidelines in 1984.

In addition to setting formation standards, the conference, as seen above, also approved each new diaconate formation program established throughout the country. However, with the incredible explosion of new programs throughout the 1970s, that task soon became impossible to administer. As a result, programs started springing up everywhere with no formal approval from the bishops' conference. In those salad days, the executive director of the Secretariat for the Diaconate would gather informally with the directors of formation programs to discuss formation issues. However, as the number of formation programs grew, this became impractical, and the National Association of Diaconate Directors (NADD) was formed in 1976. At least officially, USCCB's approval of diaconate formation programs was required until the promulgation of the new *National Directory* in December 2004. What is now strongly recommended, however, is that whenever a diocese initiates diaconate formation or significantly changes an existing program, a *formal* evaluation be requested from the Bishops' Committee on Clergy, Consecrated Life, and Vocations, which absorbed the responsibility for the diaconate in the conference restructuring of January 2008 (an appropriate move, since deacons are members of the clergy). Unless and until the conference modifies this committee's responsibilities in the future, the responsibilities formerly exercised by the Committee on the Diaconate have been assumed by the new committee on clergy and its related staff secretariat.

Paragraph 296 of the *National Directory* outlines the responsibilities of the USCCB for the diaconate. Six particular areas are identified:

1. To provide information on the diaconate to the bishops of the United States
2. To establish national norms for the selection, formation, placement, ministry, and life of aspirants, candidates, and deacons
3. To provide formal evaluation of formation programs
4. To initiate resources for a "structured catechesis" on the diaconate
5. To initiate national studies of the diaconate
6. to maintain a current statistical database on deacons in the United States

In the past, these items were handled directly by the secretariat. However, given the vast growth of the diaconate, many of these issues (such as national studies or the maintenance of a national statistical database) are now *directed* by the USCCB but *carried out* by professional research organizations, such as the Center for Applied Research in the Apostolate (CARA), located at Georgetown University.

Paragraph 297 describes the relationship of the former Bishops' Committee on the Diaconate and the various national associations related to the diaconate. At the time of the *Directory*'s promulgation, there were seven national diaconate organizations:

1. The National Association of Diaconate Directors (NADD)
2. The National Diaconate Institute for Continuing Education (NDICE)
3. The National Association of Diaconate Organizations (NADO)
4. The National Association of Hispanic Deacons (NAHD)
5. The Native American Deacon Association (NADA)
6. The National Association of African American Catholic Deacons (NAAACD)
7. The National Association of Asian Pacific American Deacons (NAAPAD)

In the same paragraph, regarding these associations, the *Directory* specifies that, "at the invitation of the Bishops' Committee on the Diaconate, the executive officers of the national associations serve as advisors to the committee." This advisory role "promotes the accountability of each association to the committee…In addition, these associations bring unique perspectives to the committee's deliberations." While this was the process in place for a number of years, it was changed with the implementation of the new conference structure; now, only the National Association of Diaconate Directors (NADD) serves as an institutional consultant to the Committee on Clergy, Consecrated Life, and Vocations.

In summary, from the very beginning of the renewed diaconate at the Second Vatican Council, it has been the responsibility of the various conferences of bishops to oversee and provide the overall leadership for the development of the diaconate. In the United States, this responsibility has been exercised by the USCCB through its various committees and secretariats, normally through the promulgation of various documents regarding the formation of deacons in the United States, along with the preparation and support of a variety of studies and other resources supporting the development of the diaconate throughout the United States. A new phase of this relationship has been in place since the intensive conference restructuring of 2008, and it remains to be seen how this new structure will exercise these responsibilities as new relationships and responsibilities are identified.

# The Development of the *National Directory*

Three principal factors precipitated the development of the new *National Directory*. First, the pastoral experience gained since the 1984 guidelines had significantly dated them and revisions were clearly in order. Second, the nature of pastoral ministry in the United States had grown increasingly complex, with a growing shortage of priests and expanding involvement of lay ecclesial ministers; these realities required an even more sophisticated understanding of the nature and mission of the diaconate itself. Third, the Holy See had become even more involved in the renewal of the diaconate, and it is on this point that I wish to offer a few observations, due to their significant influence on the development and content of the *National Directory*.

In 1995, the Congregation for Catholic Education and the Congregation for Clergy promulgated two documents on the formation, ministry, and life of presbyters. Upon their release, these two dicasteries announced that similar documents would be developed on the diaconate. On February 22, 1998, the *Basic Norms for the Formation of Permanent Deacons* and the *Directory for the Ministry and Life of Permanent Deacons* were promulgated jointly by these congregations, along with a "joint introduction."

The *Basic Norms* was issued by the Congregation for Catholic Education. It asserted a strong level of authority, declaring that it was a *directive* and not merely a *guideline*. Furthermore, episcopal conferences are to use this document in the preparation of their own norms for formation. The *Directory* was promulgated by the Congregation for the Clergy, and it refers to itself as a "general executory decree." In both cases the Holy See is quite clear: these texts are *not* merely advisory; they are *directives* to be followed by conferences of bishops preparing their own norms for the formation, ministry, and life of deacons. If one closely examines the endnotes of the *National Directory*, it is easy to see just how significantly these two texts have influenced it.

The production of the *Directory* involved dozens of bishops, and many more dozens of deacons, wives of deacons, priests, and lay persons; the work extended over seven years of time and at least seven drafts. It spanned three different committees of bishops. Considerable consultation was done with many groups of experts in many fields and with a variety of agencies and associations, especially the NADD. The full body of bishops reviewed the entire document on several occasions, and it was reviewed twice by a number of dicasteries of the Holy See. It is hard to envision a document being given more care and scrutiny in its preparation.

Once the actual work began on the preparation of the *Directory*, an important consideration by the bishops was the juridical and magisterial character that their own document should possess. Whereas previous United States documents had been guidelines, the new document required a stronger character, especially given the nature of the Vatican documents themselves. Since the Second Vatican Council, a new genre of ecclesiastical document has developed, known as a "directory." A directory is a document comprehensive in scope that provides foundational theological and theoretical bases for extensive principles to be used in the development and implementation of a pastoral concern. Directories may also contain specific application of current law and convey new particular law. The intent of a directory is to offer a common vision without imposing rigid uniformity. The *National Directory*, therefore, is intended as a document that implements many of the universal principles found in the documents from the Holy See, while at the same time offering its own principles for further implementation at regional and diocesan levels. Most people are familiar with documents such as the *General Directory for Catechesis* and its United States counterpart, the newly promulgated *National Directory for Catechesis*. One may also point to directories on ecumenism, liturgy, and the pastoral ministry of bishops.

As may be inferred from this observation about the nature of a directory, one must always keep in mind the sheer scope involved with the *National Directory*. This document covers much more than the formational aspects of preparing candidates for possible ordination. It attempts to situate (however briefly) the diaconate itself within its broader sacramental and ministerial context in the life of the Church. I wish to stress this point, since it may seem tempting simply to turn to those chapters dealing with the details of formation. To do so without first internalizing the foundational sections on the theology, spirituality, and ministry of the deacon would be a grave mistake. The formational sections of the document are grounded deeply within those foundational sections and should not be considered apart from them.

In short, what authority do the bishops of the United States give to this document? Paragraph 14 directs, "This *Directory* is prescribed for the use of the diocesan bishop, as well as those responsible for its implementation. The specifications published in this *Directory* are to be incorporated by each diocese of the conference." Paragraph 15 addresses the objective and the interpretation of the document, stating clearly that "This *Directory* is normative throughout the United States Conference of Catholic Bishops and its territorial sees....[It] will guide and harmonize the formation programs drawn up by each diocese of the conference that 'at times vary greatly from one to another.'"

# Six Elements for Implementation

I want to conclude by offering six essential elements to consider when beginning to implement the *National Directory*. There could undoubtedly be many more, and these here are offered merely as suggestions to spark additional thought and creativity. These six components involve interpretation, context, scope, content, attitude, and resources.

# 1. Interpretation: *By* Bishops, *For* Bishops

In my opinion, one the most critical things to understand about this document is that it was written *by* bishops, *for* bishops. Time and time again during the drafting process, the bishops mentioned this fact. They were constantly concerned that the document should say precisely what they felt their brother bishops needed to read about the diaconate. This means that the text was *not* prepared primarily for the deacons (or priests for that matter) of the country; the principal audience is the college of bishops and those who assist those bishops in carrying out the norms of the document. This fact should be borne in mind whenever reading or studying the text. If there is an overarching theme of the *Directory*, it is to stress the sacramental relationship that binds the deacon in a special way to the apostolic ministry of the bishop himself. This provides a foundational hermeneutic for understanding everything that follows.

# 2. Context: Link between Relationships and Structures

The sacramental relationship between the bishop and his deacons provides the context for the integration of the order of deacons into the pastoral life of the diocesan church. Consider first the theological basis of chapter 1, grounded as it is in an ecclesiology of *communio*. In chapter 2, the *Directory* moves directly from this presentation into the ministry and life of deacons, offering twenty-one paragraphs on the relationships of deacons that are brought about by ordination, beginning with several very strong paragraphs on their relationship with the bishop. For example, paragraph no. 41 says:

> The deacon exercises his ministry within a specific pastoral context—the communion and mission of a diocesan Church. He is in **direct relationship** with the diocesan bishop with whom he is in communion and under whose authority he exercises his ministry....It is therefore a **particular responsibility** of the bishop to provide for the pastoral care of the deacons of his diocese. The bishop discharges this responsibility both **personally** and through the director of deacon personnel. [*emphasis added*]

Given the fact that the bishops who wrote this document are addressing their brother bishops, this is a particularly strong tone. In chapter 8, paragraph 257, notice the linkage between the role of the bishop and the role of the deacon in an overall pastoral plan for ministry in the diocese.

> The establishment or renewal of diaconal ministry within a diocesan Church needs to be conceived and established **within an overall diocesan plan for ministry** in which the diaconate is seen as an **integral component** in addressing pastoral needs. In this way, deacons, who are ordained for service to the **diocesan Church**, will have a richer and firmer sense of their identity and purpose, as will those who collaborate in ministry with them. [*emphasis added*]

Many dioceses *still* do not have a pastoral plan for ministry: perhaps this is a particular service in which deacons might provide leadership. Certainly, the bishops are reminding themselves that deacons are a critical component of whatever pastoral planning is necessary. I would also point out that in the last national study on the diaconate conducted directly by the USCCB (reported in 1996), one of the major concerns that surfaced was that deacons were being wonderfully received as parish ministers, but that people were not yet recognizing the fact that deacons are ordained for service to the *entire* diocesan church. It is clear in the *Directory* that the bishops want there to be *no* confusion on this issue: deacons serve the bishop in the whole diocesan church.

## 3. Scope: Diocesan Church

This theme of service to the entire diocesan church and the communities in which that church finds itself provides the scope of the document itself. I mentioned above that chapter 2 of the *Directory* offers twenty-one paragraphs on the various relationships effected by the sacrament of orders. The categories sketch out the ecclesial breadth of the *Directory*. Paragraphs 41–47 address the relationship with, and the responsibilities of, the diocesan bishop. Paragraphs 48–49 refer to the diocesan church in general; paragraphs 50–53, diocesan presbyters; paragraph 55, the religious in the diocese; paragraphs 56–57, the laity; paragraph 54, those men in formation for possible ordination; paragraphs 58–60, society at large. Finally, paragraph 61 highlights an essential unity in all pastoral activity, and the deacon is involved in all of it.

You will notice that I have *not* mentioned some of the most important relationships of all for deacons, especially those who are married; namely, his relationships with his wife and family! These relationships are certainly addressed, and at some length, in the text. What I am highlighting here, however, is the scope of relationships brought about by the act of ordination itself. This is *not* meant to minimize other sacramental relationships, but to see *all* of them in context.

## 4. Content: Current Process, Law, Policy

As diaconate formations are reviewed and evaluated, especially with a view toward a fuller implementation of the *Directory*, it is important to know and appreciate what is already being done. Keep in mind that, when the Holy See began its work on the two documents released in 1998, Cardinal Dario Castrillon-Hoyos, then prefect of the Congregation for Clergy, frequently remarked that their work was heavily influenced, in a quite positive way, by the experience of the Church in the United States with the diaconate. So, the first step of implementation of the *Directory* ought to acknowledge the positive contributions of the current formation program: what is already being done of value that the diocesan bishop does not want to lose. Nonetheless, the evaluation of the current formation program and processes must be honest, thorough, and comprehensive. The key here will be to integrate the strengths of the existing experience into whatever modifications the diocesan bishop and his staff decide to make. Furthermore, ways must be found to even more systematically integrate the diaconate into the various pastoral structures of the diocesan church in light of the *Directory*. For example, regarding those persons who might be assigned to provide pastoral leadership to parishes in the absence of a priest (c. 517.2), what diocesan policies already exist? This issue is addressed within the *Directory*, and so existing diocesan policy needs to be reexamined. Similar reviews may, for example, involve the incorporation of deacons into diocesan liability insurance coverage.

Some other possible starting points for a program review include the norms provided at the ends of chapters 2 through 8; the particular law provided in chapter 2; chapter 8's discussion of existing diocesan structures; and, finally, the "secondary document" provided at the end of the book, which offers a self-evaluation instrument that may be used to great benefit. Program reviewers will find that some of what is already being done is fine as it is, while other areas will be in need of greater reform. This systematic review process, however, will give you a valuable template with which to operate.

## 5. Attitude: Creativity, Continuity, Consistency

As we all know, the attitude with which one approaches a task can have a great influence on the results of that task. I am suggesting that our attitude with regard to implementing the *Directory* ought to be "we are going to implement this document fully and completely." In other words, we should not lightly assume that certain parts of the document do not apply to us, because they *all* do!

A measure of diocesan adaptability may be seen in the notion of "basic standards for formation" in the first place. When approaching the notion of diaconal formation, the bishops *could* have simply directed, for example, that all deacon candidates obtain a college degree; they deliberately chose not to do so. They *could* have simply designed a national curriculum to be implemented throughout the country; they deliberately chose not to do so. They *could* have simply said that each diocese should design its own formation programs, using its own formation standards; they deliberately chose not to do so. What the bishops *did choose to do* was develop a set of national standards to be used by every diocese, while leaving specific curriculum design, development, and assessment to each diocese. With this in mind, we must have an attitude of creativity, continuity, and consistency.

## a. Creativity

Your creativity will be stretched as you consider, for example, how "assessment" will be constructed and implemented throughout your formation program. How will the "basic standards" be adapted? If a basic standard seems, on first reading, not to be applicable to your diocese, I suggest you reread it with a view to finding out how it *does* apply. Remember, the standards are to be implemented and adapted *as necessary*, but they are not to be ignored or disregarded. Finally, what resources are available to you? Think creatively: traditional resources may or may not be available, such as schools, institutes, and so on. However, what other resources *are* available, such as high technology? What *can* be used to help design and "deliver" the formation experience to candidates in your diocese?

## b. Continuity

After your diocesan self-assessment is complete, consider these questions about continuity: What components of your *current* formation program and *current* diocesan structures may be continued as they are, or with only modest adaptation? And for those changes that are necessary, how will they be *transitioned* into existing structures, curriculum, and policies?

## c. Consistency

How does diaconate formation relate to other ministry formation programs in the diocese? How might they be integrated (or not)? How may resources be shared? How is the formation program documented? Key query: If your staff were to leave suddenly, could the program be replicated? Documentation of *every* aspect of the program is essential, not only for accurate record-keeping, but so that it can also be shared with others. Finally, documentation is critical because of the need for greater transportability of diaconal formation programs. Deacons and deacon candidates tend to be quite mobile since they are frequently moved by their employers. This has been a particular challenge in the past. The bishops are hopeful that the challenges presented by deacons and candidates moving from one diocese to another will be minimized by a consistent, well-documented application of the basic standards across the country.

# 6. Resources

This last element speaks to the need to look beyond "deacon specific" resources in the formation of deacons. For example, who else is doing similar work in formation? One example: a key contribution of the process of preparing the *National Directory* involved the preparation of a set of "model standards" for formation. These model standards, often referred to as "competencies," were developed from earlier work of the National Association of Lay Ministry (NALM) and other national organizations. These organizations and their contributions are valuable resources for diaconate formation as well. Another resource that might be tapped is the National Organization for the Continuing Education of Roman Catholic Clergy (NOCERCC). This organization has for many years focused on the continuing formation of priests, but in recent years has realized that it has, by its very nature, a responsibility for continuing education of deacons as well. Yet another trove is the USCCB itself. The staff in Washington can provide immeasurable help and support with specific aspects of diaconate formation: liturgy, social justice and peace, family, youth, pro-life activities, and religious education and catechesis. Finally, there are the many Catholic colleges, research universities, and institutes that are often looking for opportunities for collaboration.

The message of this component is simple enough: always look beyond the obvious resources and see how we might collaborate with all the expertise and experience that is out there, waiting to be tapped. This is also a great way to familiarize these other institutions and agencies with the nature and work of the diaconate itself; all can benefit from this mutual interaction and collaboration.

# Conclusion

The *National Directory* on the diaconate provides a good framework for the formation of deacons. As a document of the bishops of the United States, it is a powerful statement of the bishops' understanding and appreciation of the ministry of deacons, and, as such, can offer valuable insights into their formation. To implement the *National Directory* optimally, it is important to understand the context in which it was prepared, as well as its content. This chapter has been an attempt to sketch the broad outlines of that context.

# CHAPTER 2

# A Purpose-Driven Formation

## *Theodore W. Kraus*

## Introduction

Taking my lead from a paradigm for ministry proposed by Rick Warren in his books *The Purpose-Driven Church* and *The Purpose-Driven Life*, I have entitled this chapter "A Purpose-Driven Formation."[1] The bishops of the United States describe a similar paradigm in their *National Directory for the Formation, Ministry, and Life of Permanent Deacons in the United States*: "One who will serve as deacon requires a formation that promotes the development of the whole person. Therefore, the four dimensions of formation (human, spiritual, intellectual, and pastoral) should be so interrelated as to achieve a continual integration of their objectives in the life of each participant and in his exercise of ministry."[2]

## The Question

A diaconate formation program, prior to its implementation, is required to identify its screening and ongoing evaluation processes—its academic, spiritual, human, and pastoral components—all in conformity with the *National Directory*. But how the specific objectives for each dimension will purposely drive (that is, will be consciously programmed) "to achieve [their] continual integration…in the life of each participant and in his exercise of ministry" is rarely described or exemplified. Yet this integration, the bishops mandate, should drive the entire formation experience.

# Insights

In a parallel text issued nearly fourteen years earlier than the *National Directory*—"Guidelines for Doctrinally Sound Catechetical Materials"—the bishops enumerated two formation principles that are as insightful as they are challenging: Christian formation must *"be authentic and complete,"* and *"the mystery of faith is incarnate and dynamic."*[3]

The *National Directory* and its supplement, *National Standards for the Formation and Ministry of Permanent Deacons in the United States*, provide guidance for an "authentic and complete" formation of a candidate and deacon. For each path in formation, objectives for the four dimensions are specified. The competency skills to be realized in each level of formation and the methods for assessing a participant's successful appropriation of them are also clearly delineated. Those responsible for formation must reference both documents to ensure the "authentic and complete" formation of each participant. Equally important is the bishops' statement that "the mystery of faith is incarnate and dynamic." The age, ability, and experience of the one being formed, the bishops state, reveal the candidate's areas of need and his potential for development. Classical theology proposes a similar reminder: *"grace grows on nature."* But how might these theological insights be transformed into a process, a method, a model to promote and nurture the core, driving purpose of formation—a holistic, integrated life and ministry?

All aspects of formation begin subjectively. Diaconate formation is premised on a conviction that the aspirant/candidate enters the formation process already formed as a disciple, already in "grace." His culture, family, and age; his psychological and physical health; his educational opportunities and work environment; his civic, social, and ecclesial engagements—all these have already molded his character, his personality, and his manner of being. His strengths and limitations, his comprehension and appreciation of diverse points of view, his capacity to be challenged and transformed will be exposed through a subjective exchange with the program's formators—administrators, faculty, mentors, spiritual directors, and other participants. Actually, in this formation environment, there is no artificial boundary between the one who is a student and another who is a teacher. Here, each person is both. Here, the lived experience of the individual and the gift of the community's diversity meet, and formation begins.

The primary task required of those who guide the formation process is to ensure the creation of a communal environment in which individuals can experience an authentic invitation to "acquire and perfect a series of human qualities which will permit them to enjoy the trust of the community, to commit themselves with serenity to the pastoral ministry, to facilitate encounter and dialogue."[4]

Recently, I came upon the address given by Blessed Pope John XXIII at the end of the first session of the Second Vatican Council:

> The first session was like the slow and majestic prelude to a great masterpiece. The Fathers settled themselves to enter wholeheartedly into the very nature and purpose of their work…to penetrate the divine plan. They had come together from far and wide to this Ancient See, and obviously they had first to be acquainted. To understand one another's hearts, they had to look at each other squarely. To achieve a balanced and profitable interchange of views on pastoral matters, they had to describe their own experiences, gleaned under the most varied conditions of the apostolate in differing parts of the world. Understandably, in an assembly of this magnitude, time was needed to arrive at an agreement on matters about which there existed, in all charity, a sharp divergence of views. Such difference of opinion can be disturbing at times, but it was providential, for it served to clarify issues, and to demon-

strate to the world the existence in the Church of the holy freedom of the children of God.[5]

Pope John XXIII is describing a formation community and the formation process. This is not a new model. It is essential to Jesus' mission, as well as to that of the early Christian Church. The Gospel of Matthew emphasizes that "Jesus told the crowds all these things in parables; without a parable he told them nothing." all this Jesus said to the crowds in parables; indeed he said nothing to them without a parable" (Matt 13:34). The use of parables in each teaching, or formation, situation *asserts* that Jesus understood that *contact between God and a human occurs primarily within the everyday world of human experience.* "Whether spoken to confront opponents or to encourage disciples, the parables take up the world of the hearer....The participants recognize their own values and ethos and can identify with the situation and characters; yet their familiar values are transformed....In couching his message in parables Jesus challenges people to a free response and risked rejection."[6]

The formation community and a narrative praxis is, also, the transformative model of the early Christian community. Recall the Pentecost experience:

> Now there were devout Jews from every nation under heaven living in Jerusalem. And at this sound the crowd gathered and was bewildered, because each one heard them speaking in the native language of each. Amazed and astonished, they asked, "Are not all these who are speaking Galileans? And how is it that we hear, each of us, in our own native language?...What does this mean?" (Acts 2:5–8, 12)

This scripture manifests the integrity and commonality that we, as humans, share in spite of linguistic, cultural, racial, and ethnic diversity. Aristotle, in his work *On Interpretation*, observes: "Spoken words are the symbols of mental experience and written words are the symbols of spoken words. Just as all men [*sic*] have not the same writing, so all have not have the same speech sounds, but the mental experiences, which these directly symbolize, are the same for all, as also are those things of which our experiences are the images."[7] Andrew Greeley, in our time, offers a similar comment especially in relationship to religious faith-formation: "I do not want to deny the importance of intellectual religion. I am merely saying that religion takes its origin and its raw power *from experiences, images, stories, community and ritual, and that most religious socialization takes place in conceptual, analytic form.* Religion must be intellectual but *it is experiential before it is intellectual*"[8] [*emphasis added*].

The bishops direct that "the four dimensions in formation (human, spiritual, intellectual, and pastoral) should be so interrelated as to achieve a continual integration of their objectives in the life of each participant and in his exercise of ministry."[9] The achievement of this goal, I propose, "takes its origin and its raw power from," and is sustained by, each participant through sharing "*experiences, images, stories, community and ritual.*" An integrated formation process begins and is sustained through stories that describe the contact between God and humans within their ordinary, everyday world of experience.

Narrative praxis, *narrative theology*, has too often been dismissed as a novel, quaint approach to adult formation, to theological study. Surely, I couldn't be suggesting that we spend all of our formation sessions every year listening to one another's stories? After all, when would we get down to the business of doing theology, doing ministry, doing formation, becoming spiritual? On one level of understanding, however, that is exactly what I am suggesting.

# An Imaginary Conversation

I invite you into an imaginary conversation among several significant educators, formators, spiritual authors, theologians, and teachers to whom a narrative community and narrative praxis is the method leading to an integrated, holistic formation.[10] Our speakers include Carl Jung, a Swiss psychologist; Dr. Choan-Seng Song, an Asian theologian; Raimundo Panikkar, proponent of intra-religious dialogue; David Bosch, Chair of Missiology at the University of South Africa; as well as holistic educators Maria Montessori, Rudolph Steiner, and Paulo Freire.

*Moderator*: Dr. Jung, you wrote in *Psychology and Alchemy*: "Christian education has done all that is humanly possible; but it has not been enough. Too few people have experienced the divine image as the innermost possession of their own soul." Are you suggesting that religious formation is incapable of leading people to a holistic experience of God within?

*Jung*: As long as formation is only an outward form, something intellectual, as long as the deeper religious function is *not truly experienced*, nothing of any importance has happened. Often a modern person does not understand how much excessive "intellectualization" of life can destroy a capacity to experience God. When people lose the true meaning of their lives, their social organization disintegrates, and they morally decay. Isn't this what we are experiencing in our world today?

*Moderator*: Are you suggesting that forming people on an intellectual level may help on that level, but it doesn't get the participant into a deeper and holistic transformation?

*Jung*: Deep inside each organism is something that knows what its true nature is, what its life-goal is. If we can assist an individual to become related to this inner Center, then a holistic person will emerge. "Individuation" is the process that moves one to become a complete, unique person. By "individuation," I mean that human, spiritual, learning experiences, and a concern for others, become one.

*Moderator*: How might this process be realized?

*Song*: In the view of those of us engaged in the reconstruction of Christian theology in the Asian world of symbols and images, our primary task is to ask: How does religious faith *affect* the life of believers? How *does it shape* the tradition and the ethos of a society? Our theological attention is directed first to *stories* of how ordinary believing women and men live their religious faith and become potential agents of change in their society and in their nation. Formation is realized and theology is possible only when we begin to experience the power of the Spirit, at work in men and women who build their life and history for themselves and for the generations to come.

*Panikkar*: There are three indispensable prerequisites for such an encounter: a deep human honesty in searching for the truth wherever it can be found; openness in the search, without conscious preconceptions or willingly entertained prejudices; and finally, a profound loyalty toward one's own religious tradition. In the past, when people lived either in isolation or in subjection, the religious quest was mainly directed toward the uni-dimensional deepening of one's own religion. But the authentic religious urge of today can no longer ignore a certain thirst for open dialogue and mutual understanding. The religion, or religious experience, of my brother and sister becomes a personal religious concern for me as well.

*Song*: We human beings are makers of symbols and images that tell who we are and how we relate one to the other, to the world, to nature, and of course to God. We have to realize that—in the world of symbols and image—the dichotomy between the sacred and profane, between the religious and the secular, is abolished.

*Moderator*: But how do we consciously construct a formation environment that fosters the human, spiritual, theological, and pastoral in such a way that they become integral to the process?

*Song*: For some people, theology has nothing to do with "mere" stories. For them, theology has become an abstract discourse carried on among theological professionals. The question seldom arises whether it reflects the sweat and labor, sighs and longings, of men, women, and children who struggle in a world of harsh realities. Theology, ironically, has become *disincarnated*. Storytelling, folktales, and narrative exchange can bring us back to the heart of the Christian faith. By reading and listening to stories, we find ourselves in a theological world that was closed to us before—the real world in which God and humanity are engaged in the search for justice, freedom, and compassion. Doing formation with and through the individual's personal story, we are taught an important lesson: stories of people, not preconceived theological ideas and criteria, lead us to deeper truths about humanity and God.

*Bosch*: As a missionary and as a theologian, I am beginning to realize that all people need one another. We influence, challenge, enrich, and invigorate each other. What I am involved with as a missionary is not just *inc*ulturation, but *inter*culturation. Our churches, worship, and formational communities have to be de-provincialized. This can happen only if vital contact with the wider Church through many diverse experiences is nurtured. Such discourse certainly leads to tension, but it can be a *creative* tension if we focus our attention to the model of unity within reconciled diversity. If we follow this road, our understanding of mission and Church will indeed be qualitatively different from that of earlier models.

*Panikkar*: I would stress, also, that we need to listen well and deeply to our own story, the one incarnated in us. Many people in all walks of life, in both East and West, have abandoned their own "religion" or religious story and turned to the "scientific" study of religion. What I see as essential is that, in my discourse with others, my life—my fidelity to my story—may offer an example of transformation that is without total rupture, and of continuity that is not mere prolongation. *To offer my own story in response to what I observe to be the plight of many seems a moral imperative to me. Each of us needs to reveal the incarnation—the Word made flesh—in ourselves.*

*Moderator*: Earlier, we repeated some of the remarks that Blessed John XXIII made to the Council at the end of Vatican II. He also said:

> The [Fathers] had come together from far and wide, as brothers to the ancient See, and obviously they had first to be acquainted. To understand one another's hearts, they had to look at each other squarely. To achieve a balanced and profitable interchange of views on pastoral matters, they had to describe their own experiences gleaned under the most varied conditions in differing parts of the world....They needed [this experience first] to arrive at an agreement on matters about which there existed a sharp divergence of views.

John XXIII is describing an educational model. We are privileged to have three distinguished educators with us. What insights, what observations, would you bring to this conversation?

*Montessori*: The human person must be at the center of education, of formation. The child is one whose dignity increases in the measure to which we see in him the builder of his own mind. Every child is guided by his inward teacher, who labors indefatigably in joy and happiness—following a precise timetable—at the work of constructing the greatest marvel of the Universe, a human being. We teachers, or formators, can only help the work already going on.

*Steiner*: A sound education and a true formation must never tear the student out of his connections in life. The point I wish to stress is to educate, to form each person so that he remains in touch with present day life, with the social order of today. And here, there is no sense in saying that the present social order is bad. Whether it is good or bad, we simply have to live in it. Hence, we must not simply withdraw our students from it. There must come a time when every detail of life becomes of interest in the formational process.

*Montessori*: The fundamental principle is *freedom to develop*. The concept of liberty in education should be understood as a condition most favorable to physiological and psychological development. A teacher who is urged on by a profound reverence for life should respect the gradual unfolding of the student's life. The life of the student is not an abstraction; it is something that is lived by each one in particular. Too often, the world of formation today is like an island, where people, cut off from the world, are prepared for life by exclusion from it.

*Freire*: I want to affirm the comments of my colleagues. Liberating education or formation consists in acts of cognition, not simple transfers of information. At the outset, therefore, the teacher-student contradiction must be resolved. Through dialogue —and through their shared stories, experiences, and backgrounds—the teacher-of-the-students and the students-of-the-teacher cease to exist. A new term emerges: teacher-student with student-teachers. The teacher, or formator, is no longer merely the one-who-teaches. He or she becomes jointly responsible for a process in which all grow. In dialogue, people share their stories, their narratives, which inform each other of their families-of-origin, their cultures, and their faith. In the dialogue, each participant is invited to reflect critically upon his life, upon what he is doing; to identify new information, seeking further resources for additional formation and training; and then together to plan their future actions. In this dialogical cycle, each participant becomes more effective in transforming his daily life and environment, as well as the life and environment of those with whom he has shared.

# Application

The implementation of a *narrative* formation model requires *creative coordination* and organization between administrators, faculty, mentors, spiritual directors, and pastoral supervisors. It's not merely an adaptation of a lecture, homily, or a conversation between the "authority figure/formator" and the "candidate," inserting a little personal story now and then. On the contrary, it is a radical administrative decision and commitment requiring formators and candidates to teach, learn, and experience together. Earlier, we said that Jesus always used parables as his teaching, his formation, method. And so it should be with us. Through the personal sharing of their human and spiritual journeys; through the presentation of theological content, not merely as articles to be believed, but as the consequence of a historical, evolving story of a faith seeking to be understood among God's people; and through a shared reflection of the impact of a particular ministry on one's life—all of this together *asserts*, as Jesus understood, that *contact between God and a human occurs primarily within the everyday world of human experience.*

The components of a narrative process include four themes: (1) the gospel story, (2) personal stories, (3) cultural stories, and (4) stories of service. The Jesus story, the gospel, is always normative. It has a higher authority than the others. It invites me to personal conversion and requires my participation in the transformation of the social structures and cultural belief systems in which I live.

The relationship between the gospel story and my own personal and cultural stories are both creative and complex. On the one hand, the gospel requires inculturation if it is to be communicated. On the other hand, the gospel also challenges cultural belief and social structures that exclude or restrict the compassion and liberation that Jesus offers. Robert McAfee Brown captures this creative tension that a formation process would hope to maintain.[11]

For example, I could choose, as far as I can, to make the Christian story my *normative* story, and to keep my masculine story, the American story, and the rest of my stories and experiences subordinate to it, so that they are defined by it, rather than the other way around. Yet, I cannot tell my story in isolation from them, nor in isolation from other stories that are not part of my original story, but which I am interwoven with—such as the black story, the Third World story, the Marxist story. All of these other stories threaten and refine, even purge my personal story. The black story tells me how much my Christian story has been tainted by my white story; the Third World story unmasks the uncritical way I have interwoven the American story and the Christian story, and so on.

Thomas Merton provides an even deeper description of the process: "That I should have been born in 1915, that I should be the contemporary of Auschwitz, Hiroshima, and the Watts riots, are things about which I was not first consulted. Yet they are the events in which, whether I like it or not, I am deeply and personally involved."[12]

Personal, cultural, and societal stories placed before the scrutiny of the gospel story, enable the formator and the candidate to pay particular attention to specific turning points, conversion opportunities. They expose the limitations imposed by one's family, culture, and society-of-origin. Allow me to suggest several texts that I have found useful in initiating this conversation: Gerald O'Collins, *The Second Journey: Spiritual Awareness and the Mid-Life Crisis*; Vincent Donovan, *The Church in the Midst of Creation*; Robert McAfee Brown, *Unexpected News: Reading the Bible Through Third World Eyes*; John Sanford, *The Kingdom Within: The Inner Meaning of Jesus' Sayings*; and Albert Nolan,

*Jesus Before Christianity*. Key theological concepts will always arise: sin, salvation, kingdom, Trinity, Jesus, Church, compassion, justice, evangelization, ministry, and so on. But they arise out of the experience of the participant and not as a theological tract imposed for a superficial study. A few examples will demonstrate what I mean.

One participant in our formation program was from El Salvador. He and his family had escaped from their homeland, leaving all to come to the United States. Jose's near-death story, which involved him and the thirteen members of his family, made the biblical story of the exodus a reality that was lived right before us. He related how his parents, siblings, wife, and children were almost killed when they were caught within a battle between Nicaraguan and Salvadorian troops. He spoke eloquently of their journey, mostly on foot, through Central America, Mexico, and finally the United States. This wasn't just history relived. This was an event happening before us in its telling. We all comprehended a basic truth that God is among his people, calling them into maturity, into a personal and communal journey to a promised land.

I had also invited the director of the Dorothy Day House to join us for that conversation. He shared how his community had become a safe haven for many who had entered this country seeking sanctuary. He spoke to the need of every Christian home being a place for people on exodus. Exodus requires, he said, a personal and communal commitment to reach out in life to those among us who walk too close to death.

A counselor from Catholic Charities, also in attendance, captured all of us with her own story of being a former drug addict. She spoke of her denial, her slow process of dying. She tearfully shared how she experienced the exodus through the kindness of her parents and family, who confronted her caringly and stood with her through her withdrawal and therapy. Another participant simply said, "Now I know what McAfee Brown meant when he wrote that 'exodus reveals that God takes sides with the poor, with those in need.' I guess I'm expected to do the same."

The contact between God and a human occurs primarily within the everyday world of human experience. To listen, to listen well and deeply, to listen theologically—to the whispers, voices, groaning, and shouts from the depths of humanity, "especially those who are poor or in any way afflicted"[13]—leads us to deeper truths about ourselves, about humanity, and about God.

Be attentive, be intelligent, be reasonable, be responsible: these descriptors from the Jesuit theologian Bernard Lonergan are developmental levels of response to the love that God has created in every human heart and that humans articulate through their lives. No one can fully attend to the story of Jesus unless he or she is drawn to it by the Father's gift of love (cf. John 6:44). No one can adequately comprehend the Jesus story unless he or she is connaturally linked with it. The Fathers of the Council express this reality in these words: "Indeed, nothing genuinely human fails to raise an echo in their hearts....That is why this community realizes that it is truly and intimately linked with mankind and its history."[14] This will not happen, however, without sharing and listening to each other's stories. Without a narrative praxis in formation, faith will not, *cannot*, obtain understanding.

I hope that the ideas and insights expressed in this chapter will stimulate your creativity and planning so that the restoration of a narrative praxis in the sanctuaries of theology and ministry training will drive all aspects of diaconal formation—enabling "the four dimensions of formation (human, spiritual, intellectual, and pastoral), to be so interrelated as to achieve a continual integration of their objectives in the life of each participant and in his exercise of ministry."[15]

# CHAPTER 3

## Lessons from Priestly Formation in Integrating the Dimensions of Formation

### *Paul J. Langsfeld*

The experience of those engaged in the formation of priests in seminaries can be very helpful to those engaged in the formation of permanent deacons. The formation program outlined for deacons in the *National Directory* is modeled on, and inspired by, the priestly formation program outlined in the apostolic exhortation *Pastores Dabo Vobis* ("I Will Give You Shepherds"; hereafter, *PDV*). The expectations of deacon candidates in the four areas of formation are very similar to those for priesthood candidates, apart from requirements that are more or less specific to one of the orders, such as celibacy for priesthood candidates. The influence of *PDV* on the formation program of deacons is evident in the number of citations of John Paul II's exhortation in the section "Dimensions of Formation" (nos. 105 through 133) in chapter 3 of the *Directory*. The *Directory*'s description of each of the four areas of formation follows closely what is laid out in the corresponding sections of *PDV*, but the exhortation provides a fuller treatment of some issues, like the meaning of affective maturity. It also places the discussion of the four areas of formation in a Christological context (par. 42), which is wanting in chapter three of the *Directory*. It is worthwhile, then, to read the section of *PDV* on the four areas of formation (nos. 42–59) as if they applied to the diaconate, for much of what is said there applies to all ordained ministers and not just to priests. Indeed, the fundamental unity of *all three* orders in *one* sacrament presupposes a fundamental unity in their responsibilities and hence also in their formation.

Our task here is not to reflect on the individual areas of formation, but to consider how their integration can be most successfully achieved. The *Directory* recognizes the need for integration: "Therefore, the four dimensions of formation should be so interrelated as to achieve a continual integration of their objectives in the life of each participant and in his exercise of ministry" (no. 105). Integration of the four dimensions of formation is one of the major challenges today in seminary formation. When asked to suggest where improvements might be made in their formation program, seminarians frequently note the difficulty in seeing connections among the various areas of formation.

Drawing on my own experience in the formation of seminarians, I will point out the dimensions where seminarians find the greatest challenge in making connections, as these are probably the same difficulties that deacon candidates will encounter. Then, I will propose a model, as well as specific methods, for facilitating greater integration of the four dimensions of formation.

Let's examine the obstacles to making connections among the dimensions of formation. Three come immediately to mind. First, the seminarians' most frequent and consistent complaint about formation is that the seminary places too much stress on the intellectual or academic component, and, as a result, they believe their spiritual development suffers. Somehow they see their academic requirements as a necessary evil, a hoop they have to jump through to get ordained, rather than an integral part of their spiritual formation. Ideally, they should be grateful for the way their studies lead them to a deeper knowledge and love of Christ and the Church, and to the ability to be effective preachers and teachers of the faith. However, they are very much products of our culture, which presupposes a conflict, and not just tension, between "heart" and "head," between theory and practice. The roots of this tension go back centuries to the conflict between rationalism and romanticism, and, because we have

42

inherited the conflict and take it for granted, we have to constantly try to show how study and intellectual rigor are not opposed to spirituality—or pastoral action, for that matter—but are essential for effective ministry and knowledge of Christ and the Church.

Second, another area where students find it hard to make connections lies in the relationship between human and spiritual formation. For too long in seminaries, the need for human formation was barely acknowledged. As long as students fulfilled the external requirements of the formation program with respect to academic, spiritual, and pastoral formation, a blind eye was turned to defects in character and personality that could seriously hinder their capacity to relate to other people and, thus, to carry out the Church's ministry. In *PDV*, there is a sentence that forcefully brings out the necessity of human formation; the sentence is partially cited in the *Directory*. John Paul II writes, "In order that his ministry may be humanly as credible and acceptable as possible, it is important that the priest should mold his human personality in such a way that it becomes a bridge and not an obstacle for others in their meeting with Jesus Christ the Redeemer of humanity" (*PDV*, no. 43). Too often, especially at a time of a severe shortage of priests, we have *not* considered sufficiently how the personality of a priest will be a liability or an asset in carrying out his ministry, and we know all too well from experience the consequences of that neglect. A true challenge for the seminary is the recognition that, by the time they arrive, seminarians are practically fully formed (humanly speaking), and there may be only limited possibilities for molding their personalities.

Seminarians need an excellent self-knowledge that would allow them to see their own human flaws that might be a potential obstacle to their ministry. But that requires an extraordinary openness to the counsel and criticism of others and a willingness to put one's being into question. It is painful to face those personal problems that need to be resolved if one is to be an effective witness to Christ, and it is even more difficult to face these issues if one realizes that it is not likely that they can be overcome because they are so deeply ingrained in the personality. An inability to deal with these issues can lead one to seek refuge and compensation in the spiritual life. Of course, we are supposed to turn to God in prayer in moments of difficulty and sorrow, but a great disconnect occurs in formation when the development of the spiritual life becomes a way of blocking out and ignoring the human issues that we find it too painful to face. A scenario that could result from such a disconnect is a seminarian who is very devout and conscientious with regard to the spiritual program he has developed for himself, but who at the same time is afflicted with serious psychological or emotional problems that emerge in his relationships with other people or even his very self. Pastoral ministry can be effective *only* where the human and spiritual dimensions are fully integrated with each other.

Third, still another area that requires integration in seminary formation is the relationship between the pastoral dimension, on the one hand, and the intellectual and spiritual dimensions, on the other. *PDV* and the *Directory* treat pastoral formation last because pastoral charity is the goal of all areas of formation. John Paul II writes, "This pastoral aim ensures that the human, spiritual, and intellectual formation has certain precise content and characteristics; it also unifies and gives specificity to the whole formation of future priests" (*PDV*, no. 57). Yet pastoral activity during the academic year is very restricted because of the demands of study and spiritual formation. Summers allow much more time for pastoral formation. Most important, future priests have a *lifetime* of pastoral work ahead of them, so the seminary years should be devoted to the study and spiritual formation that will equip them for their future ministry. The seminary can give no more than a mere taste of the whole range of pastoral responsibilities that priests have, and frequently the seminary provides little introduction to such important matters as, say, parish administration. As a result, seminarians express concern about how well the seminary formation program is preparing them to deal with the responsibilities they will actually face after ordination. Furthermore, they wonder how useful what they are doing in the classroom will be helpful in daily ministry. From the perspective of the seminary, the emphasis on study and prayer ensures that the life of contemplation will *always* serve as a foundation for the pastoral ministry. which would become a frenetic activism if it lacked a contemplative dimension.

The challenge of making connections in the seminary between the intellectual and the spiritual, the spiritual and the human, and the pastoral and the spiritual and intellectual is also a great challenge in diaconal formation for very much the same reasons. A tendency toward compartmentalization, or even opposition, among the areas of formation calls for a model for integrating them in a convincing way.

Such a model may be found in *PDV*, paragraph 42, which serves as an introduction to the four areas of formation. It describes the seminary as an opportunity to develop a "deep communion and friendship" with Christ, so that "the person who is called to the priesthood by God may become, with the sacrament of orders, a living image of Jesus Christ, head and shepherd of the Church." Though deacon candidates cannot afford the luxury of withdrawing from the ordinary obligations of daily life to spend a number of years in a seminary, the goal of their formation is identical to that of priesthood candidates. Through the sacrament of orders, deacons become living icons of Jesus Christ, not as head of the Church, but as the *servant* who has come to give his life as a ransom for the many. In each of the three orders within the one sacrament of holy orders, the *ordinandi* are conformed in a unique way to Christ. What the Catholic tradition calls the sacramental character derives from the new identity that the ordinands receive to represent Christ to the People of God. Though men are empowered by holy orders to perform certain functions on behalf of the Church, what is most characteristic of their office is not what they *do*, but who they *are*. They are ordained to represent Christ in a quite specific way, and out of this new identity, certain responsibilities flow. In the case of deacons, they represent Christ in his lowly state as *servant of all*, while the priesthood, which embraces both bishops and presbyters, is charged with representing Jesus as Lord, Pastor, and Shepherd of his people.

In *PDV*, the Christological foundation for the priesthood is given before the description of the individual areas of formation, in order to provide a rationale and principle of unity for the whole formation process. This Christological understanding of ministry applies also to the diaconate, for, without it, there is no justification for the inclusion of the diaconate in the sacrament of holy orders. Most of the functions the deacon performs, including sacramental functions, *could* be performed by lay persons as well. Certainly the works of charity, which are said to be the most characteristic of the diaconate, not only *can*, but *should* be performed by priests, bishops, and laity too. What is most decisive for the deacon's status as an ordained minister is his *Christological identity*, that is, his unique *way* of representing Christ to the rest of the Church. Hence, in his years of formation, what is most crucial for the deacon candidate is that, like priesthood candidates, he realizes that the time of formation is an occasion to grow in deep communion and friendship with the Lord, so that he might be ready to be a living image of Jesus the Deacon to the ecclesial community.

If we look at diaconal formation as a time to take on a new identity as "another Christ," we have a model for integrating the four dimensions of formation that is theologically satisfying. The goal of human formation is more than acquiring a balanced, integrated personality, but, in the words of *PDV* (no. 43), it is to reflect in oneself "as far as possible, the human perfection which shines forth in the incarnate Son of God." Just as Christ's humanity is what God looks like in human form, the deacon in his human formation aims at making his own humanity a transparent image of Christ. Intellectual formation in this perspective is not just a matter of learning the Catholic tradition in order to teach it. Rather, it involves entering into the mystery of the Word made flesh, and strengthening our friendship with Jesus by learning more about him. Our studies then have a personal purpose and not just a narrowly academic one. Through them, we get to know the person of Christ so that we can then make him known to others.

As for spiritual formation, it is through the grace that comes to us in the sacraments, in prayer, and in good works that our human lives are transformed to be ever more faithful images of Christ, the servant of all. Spirituality, then, is no longer seen as a regimen of prayers and exercises, but a living relationship with the Lord that is communicated to others.

Finally, from a Christological perspective, pastoral work is much more than a kind of ecclesial social service. It is a way of exercising the *charity of Christ* toward others, which flows out of communion with him. What *PDV* says about priests applies to deacons too. The ever deeper communion with the pastoral charity of Jesus "should constitute the principle and driving force of the priestly ministry." It is not just a matter of pastoral skills or competencies but a "way of being in communion with the very sentiments and behavior of Christ the good shepherd" (no. 57).

By interpreting the various areas of formation according to the Christological identity of the deacon, we can see them as diverse ways in which the deacon grows in his communion with Christ. The integration of these four dimensions in Christ lays the foundation for a highly personalist understanding of formation, one that goes far beyond a technical process that involves simply the fulfillment of requirements, and thus leads to ordination as a kind of glorified ecclesiastical graduation ceremony. Moreover, it is essential to achieve an integration of the four areas of formation because each brings out a different aspect of Jesus. He is the Word of God, a human being, the Son who lives in deep spiritual communion with the Father, and Pastor of God's people. Adequate formation in each of the four areas is needed in order for the ordained minister to bring out these different dimensions of Christ. By taking on a new identity at ordination, the ordained minister can say with St. Paul that "it is no longer I who live, but it is Christ who lives in me" (Gal 2:20). The four areas of formation are helps to his living out different dimensions of the mystery of Christ.

In continuity with the Christological model for integrating the areas of formation, we should also highlight the threefold office of Christ as Prophet, Priest, and Pastor as a way of integrating them. In treating the spiritual, intellectual and pastoral dimensions of formation, *PDV* stresses how each of them presupposes that word and sacrament consistently lead to service. For example, speaking of spiritual formation, the pope writes that seminarians "should be taught to seek Christ in faithful meditation on the word of God and in active participation in the sacred mysteries…to seek him in the bishop by whom they are sent and in the people to whom they are sent, especially the poor, little children, the weak, sinners and unbelievers" (no. 45). In treating intellectual formation of seminarians, *PDV* notes that scientific precision in theology should lead to a great and living love of Christ and the Church. Then it goes on to say: "This love will both nourish their spiritual life and guide them to carry out their ministry with a generous spirit." (no. 53) In both of these instances, the unity of word, sacrament, and service are set forth as essential ways of remaining in communion with Christ and representing him as an ordained minister, and they are more than mere functions that a minister performs since they spring from Christ's identity as Teacher, Priest and King.

To ensure that the Christological model works effectively in integrating the four areas of formation requires that, from the beginning of the formation process, and indeed throughout the process, the candidates are instructed in the Christological foundation of their ministry. The different areas of formation are distinct ways of being in communion with the Lord so that his ministers can make him present in his different aspects. Just as Jesus said that to see him was to see the Father (John 14:9), so too ordained ministers should be so formed in the image of Christ that God's people see Christ in them.

To help candidates see the connection between the various areas of formation, theological reflection, as recommended by the *Directory*, is most helpful. Consciously reflecting on the connections between pastoral activities and what candidates are learning in their theology courses allows them to achieve integration. It is also crucial for professors of theology to assist the process of integration by presenting their material with a pastoral purpose in mind. Furthermore, when formation mentors meet with the men whom they are directing, they should challenge them to see the connections between the areas of formation. In the annual assessment of progress, the formators should refer specifically to the way the candidates are succeeding in integrating the dimensions of formation, and the candidates should do the same in their self-evaluations.

The Letter to the Hebrews urges us to keep our eyes fixed on Jesus, "the pioneer and perfecter of our faith" (12:2). By following his advice, we will find a principle of unity for the integration of the four dimensions of formation.

# CHAPTER 4

# The Basic Standards for Readiness

## A Commentary

### *Stephen Graff*
### *William T. Ditewig*

## Introduction

The bishops of the United States faced two extremes when they began considering an updated *ratio* for the formation of permanent deacons in the United States. At one end of the spectrum was the possibility to permit each diocese to develop its own unique formation program and standards; at the other would be a kind of national curriculum to be mandated for all dioceses. Neither extreme was acceptable: certain standards are necessary to assure consistency between formation programs, especially since deacons —due to the demands of their secular employment—often move between dioceses in the course of their careers. Having a mandated national curriculum would be just as impractical, since the resources available (or *unavailable*) in individual dioceses vary considerably: some dioceses have almost no resources that could be used for diaconate formation, while others have an abundance of riches.

Therefore, as today's bishops and formation directors approach the *National Directory for the Formation, Ministry, and Life of Permanent Deacons in the United States* (hereafter, *National Directory*), care should be taken not to fall into the trap of trying to interpret its standards by either of these extremes. All of its standards are expected to be addressed in some way, and yet they should not be interpreted so rigidly that there is no room for local adaptation to need and available resources.

From its earliest draft, the *National Directory* included basic standards for readiness (in the first drafts, they were referred to as "competencies"; the term was changed by the bishops for a variety of reasons). Throughout the development of the *National Directory*, the bishops took direct responsibility for the content and form of the standards in their final approved state. Individual bishops throughout the process lauded the presence of the standards as an extraordinary and necessary contribution to the implementation of the *National Directory*.

In addition to the consultation and rewriting process carried out by the bishops and their immediate advisors, the Bishops' Committee on the Diaconate (BCD) conducted extensive consultation on the standards with professional educators, theologians, and, in particular, directors of diaconate formation programs throughout the country. In 1994 the National Association for Lay Ministry (NALM) published *Competency Based Certification Standards for Pastoral Ministers*, which served as the basis for the "model standards" for aspirancy and candidacy. Subsequently, Reverend Joseph T. Merkt, STD, and Margaret Cooper, PhD, included the competencies of the National Conference for Catechetical Leadership, as well as the National Federation for Catholic Youth Ministry, with that of the National Association for Lay Ministry in the publication of a common set of competencies, which served as the basis for the model standards for the diaconate. The reader is urged to consult the many resources on competencies available through the NALM, since they provide extremely valuable information on how to make the most effective use of competencies and especially the process of assessment.

During the preparation of the *Directory*, the bishops eventually opted to publish the model standards as a separate document. This decision was based on the fact that the model standards were too specific and too likely to be modified on a regular basis to be included in a national reference book. Nonetheless, this specificity and flexibility were seen as the very reason that the model standards should be published *in tandem* with the *National Directory* as a valuable resource both to bishops and to those who direct diaconate formation programs for program planning and evaluation.

# Model Standards in Ministry Education

## Rationale for Model Standards

Model standards do not take the place of a required curriculum. Rather, the standards are invaluable in developing the specifics of the curriculum itself. The documents of the Holy See and the USCCB—such as the Congregation for Catholic Education's *Basic Norms for the Formation of Permanent Deacons* and the *National Directory for the Formation, Ministry, and Life of Permanent Deacons in the United States*, no. 124—provide indications of specific scriptural and theological content; model standards, on the other hand, give guidance on how such content may be organized and tested.

## Uniformity and Equivalency

One important distinction necessary for the effective use of model standards is that between *uniformity* and *equivalency*. Curriculum-driven methodologies stress uniformity of experience; that is, *all* candidates take the same course and receive the same information. Outcome-driven methodologies, on the other hand, test for competency in mastering a standard, envisioning that such mastery may have been attained in a variety of ways. This puts demands on how competencies may be assessed; traditional assessment tools may or may not be equally effective.

Furthermore, creative combinations of activities may be used to assess multiple standards at the same time.

## Honoring Diversity in Ministry

We often think of diversity in ministry as referring to racial, cultural, or language diversity. In diaconate formation, there is additional diversity within the formal education backgrounds of the candidates. Model standards adapt more easily to this variation in education with the possibility for individualized programs of study.

## Specificity of Diaconal Formation

Although other ministerial organizations have developed model standards—for example, the National Association for Lay Ministry (NALM), the National Conference for Catechetical Leadership (NCCL), and the National Federation for Catholic Youth Ministry (NFCYM)—only the model standards mentioned above reflect the unique identity of the permanent deacon and the Church's ministry of word, liturgy, and charity. All standards should be interpreted through the lens of the diaconate, its nature and ministry.

# Use of Model Standards

## Curriculum and Course Design

The first and most common use of model standards is in the area of curriculum and course design; that is, designing one's program of instruction so that it includes the opportunity to learn and to demonstrate mastery of each of the required standards. A more thorough application of the model standards will also influence the methodology of instruction.

## Assessment

There is no area of standard or competency-based education that causes more concern than that of assessment. Perhaps it would be more helpful to look at assessment in the context of what we already do: discernment, both by the candidate and by the church. Again, the reader is referred to the many professional resources available online and through professional organizations, such as the NALM, to develop specific assessment instruments suitable for diaconal formation and the particular needs of the diocesan church.

## Individualized Learning and Learning Contracts

One of the principles of standard or competency-based learning is to design a program with the standards that a candidate should master, and then subtract from it that which the student can already demonstrate at admission. The remaining standards become the program of study and the subject of an individualized learning contract. Then it becomes a process of balancing individual needs, desires, and learning style with the realities of schedules, finances, and need to observe a candidate for ministry in a group setting.

## Adaptability to Distance Learning

While we acknowledge the necessity of significant group formational activities, the use of model standards makes it possible to write particular learning contracts that can be carried out in a ministry site far from any central gathering of candidates. In these situations, contact with the core formation faculty can be done by way of the Internet or by distance or computer-assisted learning.

## Ministry Placement

Having utilized a variety of learning environments, those involved in ministry placement have a much better idea of the talents and interests of the newly ordained deacon. It should also be noted that the third group of standards is for *both* the candidacy phase *and* the post-ordination phase of formation. It is presumed that formation is a lifelong endeavor; the standards recognize that not all of them will (or even *should*) be completed prior to ordination.

# Assessment and Model Standards

The process of assessment for ministry is organized around six basic principles:

1. Assessment is a natural part of ecclesial discernment.
2. Assessment is educational, not just evaluative.
3. Assessment is collaborative.
4. Assessment is progressive: once demonstrated, then it is built upon.
5. Assessment is ever more self-directed.
6. Assessment is, at its heart, a spiritual path.

In addition to the above list, please note:

1. Assessment is done differently at the initial assessment stage, at the ongoing assessment process, and at the end-of-program assessment. Care must be taken in developing suitable processes to respect where the candidate is in the formation process.
2. "Assessment of gifts must occur within the context of the discernment of the ecclesial community."[1]
3. Assessments are analogous to snapshots, examples of mastery of a standard or a behavior that are indicative of the ability to respond appropriately in a similar situation. There are multiple ways of taking this snapshot: self-assessment, faculty and mentor assessment, peer assessment, and pastoral supervisor assessment. All of these, and more, are recom-

mended. The more facets that can be assessed, the more snapshots available, the richer and more complete the portrait of the candidate.[2]

Basic to the use of model standards is the formulation and assessment of demonstrable indicators of mastery of the particular standard. These may include such academically traditional measures as tests and research papers, but they may also include the preparation of a portfolio of ministry achievements, field education reports, peer minister evaluations, and seminar participation.

# The Model Standards for Readiness for Admission into the Aspirant Path in Formation

## Introduction

The model standards for readiness for admission into the aspirant path in formation are organized in five categories, found throughout the model standards themselves and the *National Directory*; namely: the human dimension, the spiritual dimension, the intellectual dimension, the pastoral dimension, and the vocational dimension. Although the full rigor of the application *process* is required at this early stage of diaconal discernment (see the *National Directory*, nos. 174–78), the applicable model *standards* are quite modest in their requirements, looking essentially for human and spirituality maturity, a basic familiarity with the teachings of the Church, and an interest in and aptitude for diaconal ministry.

Assessment at this level is done in the context of admission documentation and interviews. More fully described in the *National Directory*, no. 179, readiness in the human dimension and spiritual dimension is usually ascertained through letters of recommendation, autobiographical statements, and interviews. Intellectual readiness is often assessed on the basis of prior experience in academic settings or through participation in a lay-ministry formation program. Readiness in the pastoral dimension, and particularly in the area of diaconal vocation and ministry, can be more complex. Here a detailed autobiography and testimony from those with whom the applicant has served in ministry would be essential. A lack of observable ministry connected to the diaconal *munera* of word, liturgy, and charity would bring the application into question, at least at this time in an applicant's life.

# Model Standards for Readiness for Admission into the Candidate Path in Formation

The model standards for readiness for admission into the candidate path in formation are somewhat more detailed than those for admission to the aspirancy path, although organized in the same five categories: human development and community-building skills; ongoing attention to growing in, and articulating, one's spiritual life; the preliminary study of theology; and pastoral skills; and the reflection on all the above in the light of a possible vocation to the diaconate.

The *National Directory* reflects very little on the content of assessment during the aspirant path, focusing rather on the process of the formal assessment conducted by the committee on admission and scrutinies (nos. 198, 200) and on the required documentation (no. 199). Given the length of time of the aspirancy path (normally one year), it is to be expected that an aspirant would move beyond the areas and methodologies of initial assessment. At this point, the director of formation, the faculty, the aspirant's pastor, and the field education supervisors would have ample opportunity to observe the aspirant's suitability for further diaconal study. Likewise, the aspirant has time and opportunity to begin the process of seeing assessment as formational and educational and so to transition to a collaborative relationship with his peers and his mentors. An examination of the model standards for readiness for admission into the candidate path in formation will show that the majority of the standards are measurements of the aspirant's attitude, rather than his knowledge. Thus it is important that conversation and observation be utilized in the assessment of the aspirant, as well as the more traditional reliance on tests.

*Note*: The intellectual dimension of the aspirancy path includes the requirement that formation methods "introduce the traditions of Catholic philosophy" (*National Directory*, no. 196). This requirement was added later in the editing process, after the model standards were completed, and therefore is not reflected in the current model standards.

# Model Standards for Readiness for the Ordination and Post-Ordination Path in Formation

## Introduction

Although still organized in the same five categories used previously, the model standards for readiness for the ordination and post-ordination path in formation are the most extensive of the three sets, consisting of twenty-seven areas of model standards, each one of which may have between four and eight separate competencies. They encompass the entire curriculum as envisioned by the *Directory*'s basic norms for the formation of permanent deacons, with detailed educational goals and individual demonstrable indicators. Presentation for ordination to the diaconate would presume a substantive mastery, although not necessarily an equal mastery, of all twenty-seven areas of study.

Some special notes on assessment: The model standards for readiness for the ordination and post-ordination path in formation demand the processes of both ongoing assessment and end-of-program assessment; that is, assessment that focuses on progressive, "once demonstrated, then built-upon" learning, as well as that focuses on whether the candidate has exhibited mastery of the standards to a sufficient degree to allow him ordination to the diaconate. As these standards also serve as the standards for continuing education, the assurance that assessment is ever more self-directed is also important. Thus, assessment that may in the earlier stages be appropriate—for example, tests and papers—would, in later stages of the program, give way to field education reports, peer evaluations, and seminar participation, to name only a very few examples.

## Notes on the Post-Ordination Path in Formation

The post-ordination path in formation is more than just everything that is "left over" from the readiness-for-ordination standards; that is, more than what didn't get mastered the first time around. Chapter 7 of the *National Directory* continues the call for growth in the five traditional dimensions of formation, with a particular area of emphasis on the social doctrine of the Church. This time formation takes place with the experience of the diaconate as a reflective filter. Life in diaconal ministry has a way of pointing out to the deacon needed areas of growth far more forcefully than any advice from a formator. Finally it is a principle of standards-based learning and assessment that "once mastered does not mean forever done." There is always greater depth to one's learning.

Throughout the entire process of the preparation of the *National Directory* the bishops stressed the lifelong commitment to formation that was to characterize the life of the deacon. The model standards offer one way to map the parameters of such lifelong formation.

PART TWO

# The Human Dimension

# CHAPTER 5

# Ecclesial Ordinations

## Baptism, Marriage, and Orders

## *Michael G. Lawler*

Some years ago, a married couple I know brought communion weekly to the sick and elderly in a nursing home. Recognizing the husband's charism for *diakonia*, their local church affirmed it as its own and ordained him to the order of deacons to continue his *diakonia* in the name of the Church. After the ordination of the husband, the couple continued their ministry in the nursing home and expanded it to include a gathering of the residents at which the husband-deacon gave a short homily on a gospel text and then both husband and wife offered communion. The gathering required that many of the elderly had to be wheeled from their rooms by the deacon and his wife. One day, as she was being returned to her room by the wife, an old woman asked, "Is he a priest?" "No, he's a deacon," the wife replied. The next week the same woman asked the same question and the same answer was given, and the next week and the next. Finally, exasperated, the wife answered, "Yes, he's a priest." To which the old woman responded with some passion: "Then who are YOU?"

It is easy to see the source of the old woman's question. Accustomed all her Catholic life to the ministry of unmarried Catholic priests, she was puzzled by this ministry she now experienced in her nursing home, a ministry offered by a husband and a wife together. It is easy to imagine the confusion. "How can this be?" she probably asked herself. "A husband and a wife ministering together? Are they Catholics, or are they a Protestant minister and his wife? And, if they are Protestants, what am I doing by sharing in their ceremonies, which I have always heard is a grave sin?" As long as she kept getting the answer, "No, he's a deacon," the questions were contained, since she didn't know what a deacon was. But once she heard, "Yes, he's a priest," the floodgates opened, and the questions came pouring out. They are good questions, flowing out of an as-yet-unanswered series of theoretical questions. What precisely is a *married* deacon? Does the fact that he is married make any difference to anything? How does his wife fit into his diaconate? What is the continuity, if any, between their unordained diaconate as a couple and his now-ordained diaconate?

These questions arise, not out of some ivory-tower theory, but out of the lived experience of married deacons. It is time, I believe, to seek answers to them. I do not believe we have final answers yet, but I do believe that we have beginning answers and that we have to make a start. I plan to do that, and only that, in this essay, by first sketching a theology of Christian marriage and a theology of ordination, and then looking at points of mutual connection between the two.

# Catholicism and Sacrament

When asked, "What is the specific of Catholicism?" Catholic theologians almost universally respond "sacramentality." Catholicism is a religion that takes incarnation seriously and believes that the gracious presence of God is embodied in common human actions with water and oil, bread and wine, and loving human relationships; in short, sacraments. To designate an action as a sacrament is to say two things: first, it is a simple human action, and, second, the human action is a sign and an instrument of the presence of God and God's Christ. A good question to ask of any sacrament is what action of the Church and of Christ is symbolized by it. An answer to that question as it relates to marriage and the order of the *married* diaconate will provide answers also to the questions raised about marriage, orders, and their potential connections.

First, a note about the foundational sacrament of baptism, for every ecclesial ministry is rooted "in the new life received in the sacrament of baptism."[1] It cannot be otherwise in the Catholic scheme of things. The New Testament is the record of the belief of those first Jewish Christians who believed that God raised Jesus of Nazareth from the dead (1 Cor 15:3–4, Rom 8:34, Gal 1:1, Eph 1:20, Acts 2:24) and made him head of a body that is the Church, the gathering or communion of believers (1 Cor 6:12–20, 12:12–27; Rom 12:4–5; Eph 1:22–23; 2:14–16; 5:22–30; Col 1:18, 24). The record explains both that believing members of the Body are "in Christ," and that they are "in Christ" through baptism. "As many of you as were baptized into Christ have clothed yourselves with Christ. There is no longer Jew or Greek, there is no longer slave or free, there is no longer male or female; for all of you are one [*heis*] in Christ Jesus" (Gal 3:27–28).

Baptism is the foundational sacrament in which Christians are ritually born. In baptism, the God who raised Jesus from the dead and anointed him as *Christos* raises to new life those who are dead in sin and anoints each of them too as *Christos*, Christians. For all its wonder, however, the ritual new birth in baptism is not enough; for baptism, the Church has consistently taught, is only the beginning of Christian life. Cyprian, the third-century Bishop of Carthage, explained to his neophytes that baptism is meaningless unless it is followed by a Christ-like life. "To put on the name of Christ," he writes, "and not continue along the way of Christ, what is that but a lie?"[2] If we have become Christ, he says, "we ought to go forward according to the example of Christ."[3] John Paul II, twenty-first century Bishop of Rome, agrees. "Communion and mission," he argues in more modern theological language, "are profoundly connected with one another, they interpenetrate and mutually imply each other. Communion gives rise to mission, and mission is accomplished in communion."[4] And the United States Catholic Bishops comment, "In the Church, we are at once brought into communion and sent on mission."[5] It simply cannot be otherwise for Christians who believe in Christ and who have sealed their belief in baptism.

Theologically paraphrasing the First Letter of Peter, "you are a chosen race, a royal priesthood, a holy nation" (1 Pet 2:9), *Lumen Gentium* teaches that "the baptized, by regeneration and the anointing of the Holy Spirit, are consecrated into a spiritual house and a holy priesthood."[6] That judgment is repeated by the American bishops. "Baptism," they teach, "initiates all of us into the one priesthood of Christ, giving us, in different ways, a share in his priestly, prophetic, and kingly work."[7] This is perfect, Catholic theological logic. Baptism ritually makes each and every believer *Christos*, and the firstborn Christ shares his priesthood with the sacramentally newborn Christ: the Church, the Body of Christ. The Church is a royal priesthood, and each and every baptized, believing member of the Church shares in the priesthood of the Church and, through it, in the priesthood of Christ. This common priesthood of believers, as it is theologically called, founds every discussion of ministry in the Church, both lay and ordained.

We need to reflect on this in a little more depth:

In baptism, as Catholic theology has held since fifth-century Augustine, believers receive a character, a spiritual power, that permanently changes their relationship to God, conforms them to Christ, and *ordains* them to act in the name of Christ[8] in a common priesthood that is a share in Christ's priesthood. Though the word has been historically reserved for the sacrament of orders, there is no need to avoid the word *ordain* here, for in official Church Latin, *ordinare* simply means "to order," "to appoint," or "to designate." To say that, in baptism, all believers are ordained to a common priesthood is simply to say they are appointed to a share in the priesthood of Christ—an appointment, *Lumen Gentium* teaches, that is made "by the Lord himself."[9] Believers are, therefore, also appointed to a common mission and a common ministry. Promoting and sustaining this common ministry are the gifts (*charismata*) of the Spirit of Christ, who "distributes special gifts among the faithful of every order [*ordo*] by which he makes them fit and ready to undertake the various tasks and offices advantageous for the renewal and upbuilding [*aedificatio*] of the Church."[10] In baptism, then, Christian believers are ordained into a common priesthood. For the vast majority of them, their common priesthood will be exercised in a Christian life in the world where they are to "participate in the work of creation, free creation from the influence of sin and sanctify themselves in marriage or the celibate life, in a family, in a profession, and in the various activities of society."[11] Christians ordained into the royal priesthood have "the special obligation to permeate and perfect the temporal order of things with the spirit of the gospel."[12] That broad task of living and acting out the gospel in the world is the first and, perhaps, most important meaning of the term *lay ministry*.

Not every Christian life, however, will be lived in identical circumstances, and we must now consider in order the two states of life that are the focus of this essay, the married life and the ordained diaconal life. In the Old Testament, we find an action-symbol known as the prophetic symbol. Jeremiah, for instance, buys an earthen pot, dashes it to the ground before a startled crowd, and proclaims the meaning of what he is doing. "Thus says the LORD of Hosts: So will I break this people and this city, as one breaks a potter's vessel" (19:11). Ezekiel takes a sharp sword, shaves his hair with it, and divides it into three careful parts: one part he burns, another he scatters to the wind, and the third he carries around the city and shreds further with his sword, explaining: "This is Jerusalem" (5:5). The prophet Agabus takes Paul's belt, binds his own hands and feet with it, and explains that "this is the way the Jews at Jerusalem will bind the man who owns this belt and will hand him over to the Gentiles" (Acts 21:11). Each prophet is careful to clarify the meaning of his action, which clarifies for us the meaning of a prophetic symbol. As Jeremiah shattered his pot, as Ezekiel cut and burned and shredded his hair, so God will shatter and burn and shred Jerusalem for its faithlessness. As Agabus bound his hands and feet, so Paul will be bound and delivered into captivity. The meaning and the reality proclaimed and concretely represented by Jeremiah is not the shattering of a cheap pot, but the shattering of Jerusalem. The prophetic symbol is a representative action; that is, an action that proclaims and represents another, more fundamental reality.

Central to the Israelite understanding of their special relationship with God was the idea of the *covenant*. Yahweh is the God of Israel, and Israel is the people of Yahweh, because Yahweh chose Israel to be, and Israel consented to be, Yahweh's people. It is easy to predict that the Israelites would seek a human image of their covenantal relationship with Yahweh. It is, perhaps, equally easy to predict that the image they would select is that other covenant, *marriage*, in which a man and woman mutually choose one another to be, and consent to be, husband and wife for a lifetime. The marriage of the prophet Hosea and the woman Gomer is, to every superficial appraisal, just like many another marriage. On a deeper level, however, Hosea presented it as a prophetic symbol, proclaiming and celebrating in representation the covenant relationship between Yahweh and Israel. The names of Hosea's two younger children reflect the sad state of that relationship on Israel's part: a daughter is named "Not Pitied" (1:6), and a son, "Not My People" (1:9). As Gomer left Hosea for another lover, so also did Israel leave Yahweh for other gods: Israel became "Not My People" and "Not Pitied." Hosea's remarkable reaction, however, reveals and celebrates the equally remarkable reaction of Yahweh. He takes Gomer back; he loves her still, "as the Lord loves the people of Israel, though they turn to other gods" (3:1). Hosea's human action is prophetic, a representative symbol of God's divine action, a steadfast and unfailing love of Israel. In both cases—the marriage of Hosea and Gomer, and the relationship of Yahweh and Israel—the covenant relationship had been violated. Hosea's action, however, images and reveals Yahweh's steadfastness. It proclaims and celebrates, not only Hosea's steadfast faithfulness. but also Yahweh's. As did Hosea, so also will Yahweh "have pity on Not Pitied" and will "say to Not My People, 'You are my people'; and [they] will say, "Thou art my God" (2:23), and both covenants will be maintained.

What should we make of the marriage between Hosea and Gomer? One basic meaning about Hosea and Yahweh is clear: Hosea and Yahweh are *faithful*. There is also a clear, if mysterious, meaning about marriage. Besides being a universal human institution, marriage is also a prophetic symbol, proclaiming and celebrating in the human world the steadfast, if somewhat troubled, union of Yahweh and Israel. From this perspective, we might say today, in faith, that marriage is a two-tiered reality: on one level, it bespeaks the mutual love of this man and this woman; on the other, this human love proclaims and represents the mutual love of God and God's people. First articulated by the prophet Hosea, this two-tiered view of human marriage becomes the Christian view of marriage we find in the New Testament, with a slight twist.

The New Testament passage that presents marriage most clearly as a prophetic symbol is Ephesians 5:21–33. It occurs within a larger context, which sets forth a list of household duties existing within a family of that time; what concerns us here is only what is said of a wife and husband. Ephesians 5:21 presents the basic attitude that is demanded of every Christian of the royal priesthood: "Be subject to one another out of reverence for Christ." Mutual "giving way" is to be practiced by all Christians, by all who are filled with the Spirit (5:18), because their controlling attitude should be that they reverence Christ. If all Christians are to give way mutually, then so too are Christian wives and husbands, and it is no surprise that a wife is instructed to give way to her husband, as she does to the Lord (5:22). What *is* a surprise—at least for the ingrained male attitude that sees the husband as supreme Lord and Master of his wife and appeals to Ephesians 5:22–23 to ground and sustain that un-Christian attitude—is what the following text says of the husband.

The text does not read that "the husband is the head of the wife," the way it is usually read and cited, but rather that "the husband is the head of the wife *as* [that is, in the same way as] Christ is head of the church." A husband's headship over his wife is an image of, and totally interpreted by, Christ's headship over the Church. That headship is unequivocally set forth in Mark 10:45: "The Son of Man came not to be served but to serve, and to give his life." *Diakonia*-service and the giving of oneself is the Christ-way of being head. Ephesians testifies that it was in this way that "Christ loved the church and gave himself up for her" (5:25). A husband, therefore, is instructed to be head of his wife by serving her and by giving himself for her. The husband is to be the "first servant"[13] (*diakonos*) of his wife, and she, in her turn, is to be his first servant. Husbands are instructed to "love their wives as [that is, for they are] their own bodies" (v. 28a). Love is always and essentially creative: the love of Christ brought forth the Church and made its members "members of his body" (5:30). In the same way, the mutual love of a husband and a wife creates such a unity between them that she may be called his body, and his love for her may be called love for his own body. Prior to marriage, a man did not have this body, nor did a woman have this head. Each receives a gift in marriage, a complement neither had before, which so fulfills both of them that they are no longer two persons but one.

The traditional biblical text that grounds this approach is Genesis 2:24: "They become one flesh." That classic Jewish statement is to be understood in its classic Jewish sense, in which *body* and *person* are understood as identical, for "'flesh' in the Jewish idiom means 'real human life.'"[14] Becoming "one body," therefore, is to be understood in English as becoming "one person." Ephesians declares that "this is a great mystery" (5:32) and that it has an eminent secret meaning that refers to Christ and the Church. Paul is well aware that this is not the traditional meaning assigned to the text, and he states this forthrightly: "*I am applying it* to Christ and the church" (5:32; Anchor Bible, emphasis added)—even while acknowledging the traditional meaning of the text that husband and wife become one body in marriage. Indeed, after going beyond that meaning to imply the other, in verse 33 Paul returns to the traditional interpretation and demands that husband and wife live up to that precise marital meaning,

Not only does Genesis 2:24 refer to the mutual union of husband and wife in a human marriage, but it also refers to the mutual union of Christ and the Church. It is a small step, then, to see a human marriage as a prophetic, representative symbol of the union between Christ and the Church. That means that Christian marriage is two-tiered. On one level, it proclaims and celebrates the union of this man and this woman. On another level, the union of husband and wife proclaims and celebrates in representation the union between Christ and the Church, a union which provides an ideal model for Christian marriage and for how Christian spouses should conduct themselves one toward the other.

Christian marriage, then, is a prophetic symbol or sacrament in the human world of the union between God and the People of God, and between Christ and the Church of Christ. On one level, Christian marriage is a human reality in which a man and a woman live into their mutual love. On another level, however, it is more; for as a Christian man and woman live into their mutual union, they seek also to reveal, by imaging and representing, the steadfast unions of God and the People of God, and of Christ and the Church of Christ. To say that Christian marriage is a prophetic symbol or sacrament is to say that it is an outward action (in this case, covenanting to one another or marrying) in which and through which a Christian man and a Christian woman make a conscious response to the mysterious God who called them in Christ in baptism, not only to "love one another" (1 John 3:11), but also to love God "because he first loved us" (1 John 4:19). The response to that baptismal call is fulfilled, of course, not in a short marriage *ceremony* but over the long haul of a married *life*. To say that Christian marriage is a sacrament is to say, therefore, not only that the wedding ceremony is sacramental, but also that the married life of the couple is sacramental. It is the same for all the sacraments in the Church. A sacramental ceremony initiates a sacramental life, and it is always the sacramental life following the ceremony that is crucial.[15]

Thomas Aquinas says of both marriage and ordination that they are "ordered to the perfection of the community";[16] that is, both are ordained for mission to the salvation of others; the believers who live in them are ordained for a ministry to others that will lead them to salvation in Christ. In marriage, the spouse's ministry or *diakonia*-service is, first, to one another and, then, to all those around them in the world. In the diaconate, the deacon's ministry is a *diakonia* to the world, solemnly authorized to be carried out in the name of the Church. As Pope John Paul II said in his talk to American deacons in 1987: "The service [*diakonia*] of the deacon is the Church's service sacramentalized.... You are meant to be living signs of the servanthood of Christ's Church."[17] There are multiple dimensions to the ministry of the deacon: he is a preacher and teacher, he has a liturgical role, and he is central in the Church's ministry of charity and justice.[18] All of these dimensions of the deacon's ministry, however, are summed up in the word from which the deacon takes his name, namely, *diakonia*-service; "servanthood" in John Paul II's own words. We must now try to explain that teaching more fully by considering the sacrament of ordination to the diaconate.

We begin by asking and answering the two questions that opened this section. First, in what sense is ordination to the diaconate a sacrament? Second, of what is it a sacrament? Our answer is this: Ordination in the Church is a sacrament in the sense that it is a prophetic symbol, proclaiming and celebrating the action of the Church and of Christ, affirming that this believing Christian stands firmly in its apostolic faith, and solemnly ordaining him to be a public representative of the Church, of Christ whom the Church reveals, and of God whom the Christ reveals. Ordination to the diaconate, and the diaconal life that follows it, is a sacrament of the *diakonia* to which the Church is called as the Body of Christ in the world. In it, believing Christians are appointed as public representatives of the diaconal Church and, because representatives of the Church, representatives also of the Christ who came "not to be served but to serve" (Mark 10:45). I must now explain those assertions.

The Second Vatican Council speaks of several modes of Christ's presence in the Church: He is present "especially in her liturgical celebrations." He is present in the Eucharist, both in the person of the minister and, especially, under the eucharistic species. He is present in the sacraments "by his power." He is present in the word that is proclaimed. He is present when the Church prays and sings, for he promised: 'Where two or three are gathered in my name, I am there among them' (Matt 18:20)."[19] The preparatory schema for the document on the liturgy was stronger theologically. It sought to establish an order in those presences, from Christ's abiding presence in the ecclesial community to his presence in word, prayer, and sacrament. That ordering effort, however, could not win enough votes in the assembly to be passed, mostly because the majority of bishops present wished to give precedence to Christ's presence in the eucharistic minister and the eucharistic bread and wine.

The central message of the New Testament is that God raised Jesus from the dead and revealed him as raised to selected witnesses (1 Cor 15:3–8). It was this act of God raising Jesus from the dead that established the eternal objective presence of Jesus for men and women. That objective presence, however, to be personally real for them, needed to be drawn into personal presence, and it was drawn into personal presence by the faith of the first believers, who believed that God had raised Jesus and had made him "Lord and Messiah" (Acts 2:36). Their personal faith in response to God's mighty act of resurrection brought into being the community of faith called Church. This apostolic faith continues to be preserved in the Catholic Church. Both ministry and office in the Church witness publicly to this apostolic faith in the name of the Church and, by so doing, maintain the Church in faith. Ordination to the diaconate in the Church establishes believing Christians in a ministry and an office of *diakonia*-service to the faith of the Church. It establishes them as official representatives of the diaconal and faithful Church and, because they are ordained as representatives of the Church, they are ordained also as representatives of the diaconal and faithful Christ.

Ordination to the diaconate is a prophetic symbol that proclaims and celebrates the appointment of this believer to act in the name of the Church and of Christ. This prophetic and sacramental ordination adds to the baptismal ordination to the royal priesthood that appointed believers to the order of Christians. It further appoints believers to the order of deacons; that is, those solemnly appointed to act publicly in the name of the Church and of Christ. *All* believing Christians in the royal priesthood are ordained for Christian *diakonia*. The deacon is ordained, not to absolve all other Christians from their responsibility of *diakonia*, but to exemplify prophetically the *diakonia* to which they are called and to summon them to it. The deacon is, in John Paul II's words, to sacramentalize the *diakonia* of the Church.

What is it, then, that happens in the sacrament of orders? The ordaining bishop—both the officially designated representative of the local Church to the universal Catholic Church, and the officially designated representative of the universal Catholic Church to the local Church—lays his hands on each individual to be ordained and prays over them the prayer of ordination:

> Lord, send forth upon him the Holy Spirit, that he may be strengthened by the gift of your seven-fold grace to carry out faithfully the work of the ministry. May he excel in every virtue: in love that is sincere, in concern for the sick and the poor, in unassuming authority, in self-discipline, and in holiness of life. May his conduct exemplify your commandments and lead your people to imitate his purity of life. May he remain strong and steadfast in Christ, giving to the world the witness of a pure conscience. May he in this life imitate your Son who came, not to be served but to serve.[20]

If its prayers are the best indicators of the meaning of a ritual, and they are, no one can be in any doubt about the meaning of the order of the diaconate: neighbor-love, service of the "underside,"[21] unassuming authority, and witness of a life in imitation of the Christ, who came not to be served but to serve.

The ordinary gesture of laying on hands and the ordinary words of prayer for the gift of the Holy Spirit are meaningful on several levels. They proclaim and celebrate the following:

1. The public verification of the faith of this believer by the one who has the office of guaranteeing the faith of the local Church, namely, its bishop
2. The public verification also of the presence in this believer of the charism of *diakonia*-service that the Church affirms as the *diakonia* to which it is called by Christ and by God
3. The public election of this believer from the apostolic Church and the public affirmation of his faith as the faith of the Church (absence of this faith automatically nullifies any sacrament)
4. The ordination or appointment of this believer to a ministry of *diakonia* in the name of the Church, an

ordination that affirms him as both a coworker with the local bishop and a corepresentative of the Church

5. The ordination of this believer also as a publicly appointed minister of Christ, so that when he proclaims the gospel, in word or in deed, or when he serves the underside that is sick, poor, and variously imprisoned, it is the Church and Christ who proclaim the gospels and who serve[22]

6. The authoritative discernment and proclamation of the presence of the Spirit of God in this believer and the invocation of this Spirit to further flood him with the charism of *diakonia*

7. The separation of this believer from the body of the laity and his introduction into the clerical order of deacons, to now stand "outside" the laity and to call forth their own *diakonia* by prophetically sacramentalizing it and inviting response to it

To clarify number 7 above, the deacon's standing "outside" the body of believers is to be understood not as total disconnection but, rather, as *further* connection, as described in Augustine's famous dictum, appropriately transposed: "For you I am a bishop, with you I am a Christian."[23]

The election of the believer to be a deacon, the verification in him of the charisms of apostolic faith and *diakonia*, his ordination in and by the Church, the proclamation of the presence in him of the Spirit charism of *diakonia*: all are done by the Church in the bishop's laying on of hands with prayer. *All* those actions of the Church are sacramental of similar actions of Christ and God. The election, the verification of faith, the ordination, the proclamation of the presence of the Spirit, the symbolic separation from the body of the Church: all of these are looked upon as *permanent* and, therefore, as not needing or even permitting repetition. This permanence is what Catholic theology underscores with its doctrine of the *character* that is received in the sacrament of orders. That character, to recall our earlier explanation, is a spiritual power that permanently conforms the deacon to the Church, to Christ, and to God; permanently alters his relationship to all three; and permanently appoints him to act publicly in the name of all three.[24] Ordination to the diaconate is a further degree of sharing in the priesthood of Christ. Of course, marriage too is understood to be an ordination for life in the Church, but it *can* be repeated on the death of a spouse. As sacrament, however, it too confers a grace that conforms the spouses to the Church, to Christ, and to God, and alters for their coupled lifetime their relationship to all three.

# Marriage and Diaconate: Relationships

Now that we have outlined our theology of both the sacrament of marriage and the sacrament of diaconate, we are in a position to reflect on two important questions. First, what does it mean that the diaconate is predominantly a *married* diaconate; secondly, what is the relationship, if any, between marriage and orders in a married diaconate? What follows is a reflection on both those questions.

When the renewal of the diaconate was first mooted by the Second Vatican Council and was described as "a ministry of service," there was no talk of marriage beyond the direction that the sacrament could be conferred "even upon those living in the married state."[25] For the vast majority of believers ordained to the diaconate since its renewal, marriage has come first. The contemporary diaconate is said to be a *married* diaconate because, chronologically, marriage comes first for deacons and *then* ordination. That superficial chronological priority, however, contains several other priorities of marriage over ordination.

Here is what happens in a Christian marriage ceremony: The man and the woman proclaim and celebrate in an ecclesial ritual their free consent to be married and to become one coupled person. They use such words as these: "I, Michael, take you, Susan, as my lawful wife, to have and to hold, from this day forward, for better, for worse, for richer, for poorer, in sickness and in health, until death do us part."[26] An ordained representative of the Church—a deacon or a priest—prays for them in words similar to these: "Father, keep them always true to your commandments. Keep them faithful in marriage and let them be living examples of Christian life. Give them strength which comes from the gospel so that they may be witnesses of Christ to one another."[27] If its prayers are always the best way to interpret a ritual (and we have already pointed out that they are), no one can be in any doubt about the meaning of the sacrament of marriage: steadfast love of God and neighbor (one another), and Christian life made manifest to the world.

The words and the gestures of the ritual, pronounced and done before the community of the joyfully gathered faithful, are meaningful on many levels. They proclaim and celebrate the following:

1. The free intention of the couple to enter into not only a marriage but also a specifically Christian marriage as we have described it

2. The public affirmation by the Church of the faith of these believers as the faith of the Church (as for ordination, absence of this faith negates any sacrament, for, as Vatican II teaches, sacraments "presuppose faith")[28]

3. The public verification of this faith by the ordained representative who shares the bishop's charism and his office of guaranteeing the faith of this local Church

4. The public verification also by the Church of the charism for mutual *diakonia*-service in these believers, a *diakonia* the Church acknowledges as its own

5. The public ordination (I use the word deliberately in its meaning of "ritual appointment") of these believers to use their charism for the creation of communion, not only in themselves and in their family—where they are meant to be the sacrament of communion—but also in the Church and the world in which they live

6. The public ordination of this couple to be a prophetic image both of the Church (a "domestic Church")[29] and of its union with Christ, whose body it is

7. The public translation of the couple into the holy

order of matrimony in the Church, with several conclusions for both marriage and diaconal ordination
following from this

An obvious relationship between marriage and ordination is
the self-gift involved in both. To commit to a partner in any marriage is to give oneself solemnly, radically, and lovingly to that
partner, and to promise to be steadfast in love and marriage for a
lifetime. To covenant in a *Christian* marriage is to do that and
more. It is to give oneself as a *disciple* of Christ to *another disciple*
of Christ, and to promise to be steadfast not only as a spouse but
also as a disciple. *Disciples* of Christ are to learn a triple mystery:
the mystery of the God who calls them to know, to love, and to
serve God; the mystery of the Christ in whom this God is incarnated and who calls them to know, to love, and to serve their
neighbors, and even their enemies (Mark 12:31; Matt 5:43–45); and
the mystery of the Church, the Body of Christ, which calls them
to communion and *diakonia*-service. As spouses ponder these
mysteries together, their Christian maturity ripens, they understand in greater depth what it means that their married life is a
sacrament, and they prepare the good ground that might produce the call to ordained service.

It is commonplace to state that personalities are shaped by
the families in which they grow up. That assertion is usually
intended of *children*, who are shaped by their families of origin,
but it is no less true of *wives* and *husbands*, who are equally
shaped by the marital family in which they mature. It is true,
therefore, for the married deacon as well. In his marriage, he can
learn self-gift to and for others; he can learn the everyday
demands of love and self-sacrifice; he can learn *diakonia*-service.
If and as he learns these lessons in his marriage, then he gradually matures into the disciple who can be called to sacramentalize the servanthood of the Church and of Christ in the ordained
diaconate. After ordination, he will continue to learn Christian
discipleship in both his marriage and his diaconate, and the two
sacramental lives will mutually fecundate each other.

The Church—which values itself as the Body of Christ, the
primary symbol of Christ's presence in the world—will of neces-

sity be interested in any other reality that it also values as a symbol of Christ. It will, therefore, be interested in both Christian marriage and ordination to the diaconate, and its interest will be to make each as effective a prophetic symbol as possible. That interest is evidenced in the preparation it requires of candidates for both marriage or ordination, however disproportionate that preparation may be at present. The apparent purpose of the course of preparation offered in each case is education; although true, this is not its only purpose. In his major statement on Christian marriage, Pope John Paul II deals with "the moral and spiritual dispositions of those being married."[30] While acknowledging that "the faith of the person asking the Church for marriage can exist in different degrees,"[31] he still decrees that, when engaged couples "show that they reject explicitly and formally what the Church intends to do when the marriage of baptized persons is celebrated,"[32] they are not to be admitted to the sacrament. The same can be said about the faith of candidates preparing for ordination to the diaconate.

The preparation required has another purpose beyond education, namely, to discover if the candidates have the required charisms for admission to the order of matrimony or the order of deacons. John Paul II mentions what Catholic theology takes to be the absolute minimum for admission to the sacrament of marriage—indeed, to any sacrament—namely, sharing in the apostolic faith of the Church. He might have also mentioned, as we have, other gifts required for both marriage and ordination, for instance, neighbor-love and *diakonia*-service. John Paul II's rule for admission to the sacrament of *Christian* marriage is a sound theological rule. If the gift of apostolic faith is discerned as present (and I would always add the gifts of neighbor-love and *diakonia*), then the Church joyfully admits the candidates to marriage or ordination, as the case may be. If the gifts are discerned to be absent, then it sorrowfully denies admission. It has to be admitted that this rule of "discernment of gifts" is applied more stringently in the case of ordination than in the case of marriage, but that does not mean that it is not equally applicable in both cases. It *is*. Commitment to both the sacrament of marriage and the sacrament of ordination is commitment to follow the way of

Christ unto salvation. Neither commitment is "more commitment" than the other; neither sacrament is "more sacrament" than the other. If the Church truly values these two states of life, then the preparations it offers for each ought to be more similar in depth than they presently are.

Because the free, mutual consent of the couple articulated in their vows is what validates marriage in the Catholic tradition, traditional Catholic theology insists that the man and woman are the ministers of marriage, and that the priest or deacon is only a legal witness of their exchange of consent. If we consider the prophetic symbolisms at play, however, we will discover the role of the Church's ordained representative in Christian marriage is more than that of a mere legal witness. Christian marriage is not just any marriage in which a woman and a man pledge their mutual love. It is such a marriage, of course, but it is also more. It is the union of a believing Christian man and woman who are disciples of Christ, and their union is a prophetic symbol of the union of God and God's People and the union of Christ and Christ's Church. In Christian marriage, a man and a woman are called to neighbor-love, to give way to one another, to be of *diakonia*-service to one another, to be the first servants of one another. A Christian husband, *qua* Christian husband, is to be deacon first to his wife and family, and a Christian wife, *qua* Christian wife, is to be deacon first to her husband and family. It is not surprising that the Church, which itself is to be imaged in marriage, is interested in whether it will be imaged well or badly in this particular marriage. It is not surprising, therefore, that it will prudently inquire into the charisms these two people bring to marriage, and then judge whether they are the gifts that will enable them to become one person and thus represent well the union of Christ and Church. When it discerns and judges that this couple has the gifts required, then, in the person of its ordained representative, it not only legally witnesses the marriage but it also blesses and designates it for its own purposes. So it does, too, in the case of ordination to the diaconate.

All believing Christians covenanting to a specifically Christian marriage, then, are ordained to a mutual *diakonia*-service in image of the *diakonia* of Christ and his Church. In baptism, they had already been ordained to *diakonia*-service, but their marriage focuses that *diakonia*; first, toward their spouses and families and, then, toward the world around them. Itself called to loving *diakonia* in imitation of the Christ, the Church is very interested in how they succeed in their *diakonia*, and how they succeed in their mutual marital *diakonia* is intimately connected with any subsequent call to ordained diaconate. In *diakonia*-service, the order of marriage comes first and the order of deacons second. The accepted guideline that anyone called to married diaconate must be one who has made a success of his Christian marriage[33] is an ancient requirement in the Church. Already in the second-century letters to both Timothy and Titus, there is stated the ancient rule that a man who aspires to the ministry and office of bishop must be a man who has made a success of his own marriage and his own family (1 Tim 3:1–7; Titus 1:6–8). The modern rule for admission to the diaconate is that ancient ecclesial rule applied to the ministry *and* office of deacon. It is as if the Church, in calling a successfully married man to the diaconate, is saying: We have seen your gift for *diakonia* in your marriage. We have seen how successful you have been at it. We are calling you now and ordaining you to expand it on behalf of the Church.

For married deacons, marriage comes first, then, not only chronologically but also essentially in terms of *diakonia*. Since his marriage essentially precedes his ordination, and in many ways provides the theological foundation for it, then in his married diaconate, *diakonia* within his domestic Church continues to be foundational for his *diakonia* within the larger Church. Married deacons must understand and adhere to this priority, for the tension created in the struggle between time given to marriage and time given to diaconate is a potential source of ongoing problems for many deacons. A recent study of the first five years of any marriage uncovered a fascinating and troubling fact, namely, that the thorniest issue in the early years of marriage is the distribution of time given to family and time given to work.[34] If he is not attentive to his marriage, the ordained deacon could easily add a third dimension to that thorny issue, namely, time given to his ministry. The best way to forestall that problem, theologically as well as psychologically, is to keep his marriage first. The neighbor-love, mutual giving-way, and mutual *diakonia* that are to characterize Christian marriage are to characterize it always, even after ordination to the diaconate. It is for this reason that the *National Directory* asserts that married deacons "bring to the sacrament of Holy Orders the gifts already received and still being nurtured through their participation in the sacrament of Matrimony."[35]

# Conclusion

I opened this essay with a story about a good Christian marriage, one in which two people learned to become one coupled person, to lovingly serve one another, and then went out to lovingly serve together as one in the local Church. Recognizing their charism for and success at the *diakonia* to which it is called, the Church called *him* to ordination to the diaconate. In the case of the couple in our story, the charism for *diakonia* was found in both partners. If the Church can recognize and ordain the diaconal gifts of the husband in this case, I believe it can and should recognize and ordain also the diaconal gifts of the wife. I do not wish to enter here into a general discussion of the ordination of women, because I do not wish to be distracted from my main focus. I do, however, wish to be on record affirming that I see no reason, neither theological, nor historical, nor cultural, for it not to do so in this case. If a couple can demonstrate, as the Church asks them to demonstrate, that they have become one, coupled, diaconal person in the order of marriage, it seems theologically unreasonable to then separate them sacramentally in the order of deacons.

I conclude this essay with a short meditation on incarnation, sacrament, and symbol:

The man Jesus of Nazareth incarnates, in his humanity, the invisible God. The communion of gathered believers called Church incarnates Jesus the Christ, who is now as invisible as the God he names Father. In the symbol of the ordained deacon, the Church incarnates itself, the diaconal Body of Christ, and Jesus the Christ, the protodeacon. In short, the Church creates another

Christ. A married diaconate takes a couple who in marriage have been successful at imaging the union of Church and Christ and ordains the husband as another Christ. I believe it is worth meditating here on the insight, which many theologians now accept as a given, that the ordained minister incarnates Christ to the degree that he first incarnates the Church. Christian theologians teach that, when a man and a woman are joined in Christian marriage, they are ordained to become one body, one person—to image the oneness of the Body of Christ with Christ. I am suggesting that, for a *married* diaconate to fully sacramentalize the Christ, who is "the last '*ad'am*" (1 Cor 15:45), it ought to be as the *first '*ad'am* and as the Church, the Body of the last '*ad'am*, both male and female.

I make this suggestion out of a deep and demonstrated loyalty and respect for the teaching of the Church, but I make it while also fully aware of what Karl Rahner called the "none too lucid argument"[36] of the apostolic letter "Declaration on the Question of the Admission of Women to the Catholic Priesthood" (*Ordinatio Sacerdotalis*), which does not remotely apply to the question of the ordination of women to the diaconate. Leaving aside the question of women priests in Catholic history, there is indisputable evidence for women deacons.[37] I also make the suggestion with hope, believing with Paul that, in the Church, "there is neither Jew nor Greek, there is neither slave nor free, there is neither male nor female; for [we] are all one person in Christ" (Gal 3:28). If a Church that is male and female together is one person in Christ, and if a Church that demands that believers in the order of marriage become one person in Christ, it is not theologically unthinkable that ordination, which creates in symbol other Christs, could be the ordination of gifted males and females.

# CHAPTER 6

---

# The "Gift" of Formation at Midlife

## *Ann Healey*

National statistics issued in 2006 by the Bishops' Committee on the Diaconate (BCD) reveal that thirty-eight percent of permanent deacons in active ministry in the United States are in midlife (ages forty to sixty).[1] In addition to men already serving the Church as permanent deacons, another three thousand are presently in formation. Of these aspirants and candidates for the permanent diaconate, eighty-one percent are in the same midlife age range of forty to sixty,[2] and ninety percent of them are married. These figures point to the importance of addressing issues of human, spiritual, and pastoral development as they surface for men in formation at midlife.

This article is the result of twenty-three years' experience as formation director for the permanent diaconate for the Diocese of Fort Worth, Texas. My awareness of these unique midlife issues for persons in formation stems from my experience with candidates and their wives. Since 1989, the Diocese of Fort Worth has ordained fifty men to the permanent diaconate. At present, we have thirty-five men in deacon formation, thirteen of whom study in Spanish. Ninety-eight percent of these men and their wives are between the ages of forty and seventy; the other two percent are between thirty-four and forty. The life issues they face and the opportunities for growth they encounter are both unique to them as individuals and common to many people their age. It is this blend of unique personal experiences and common challenges for growth as middle-aged men and women that provides opportunities for directors to guide and to minister to those in their care.

Quite practically, of course, the men found in formation programs are middle-aged because canon law mandates that a man must be at least thirty-five to be ordained a permanent deacon. While each diocese determines the upper age for ordination, chronological age has less bearing on this article than does the importance of addressing midlife developmental issues that may be experienced by each man and woman *during* the formation process. The focus here is on the events and developmental processes in individuals' lives that engender these issues, as well as strategies that can best address them and facilitate growth, leading to personal wholeness and effectiveness as deacons.

Opportunities for individuation and reconciliation at midlife seem to be "built in" to the formation process. The strategies presented in this article are designed to help men and women gain insight into their growth as individuals, as community members, and as those called to serve the Church. It is my intention and hope that the material presented in this article will be useful for directors of formation programs, for permanent deacons, for spiritual directors of candidates and their wives, for faculty members of permanent diaconate programs, and for aspirants, candidates, and their spouses.

# Midlife Tasks and the Growth Process

I've chosen to call the midlife issues "tasks and growth processes," in deference to Carl Jung, Daniel Levinson, and Erik Erikson. Although not the only researchers who address midlife development, these three are some of the earliest and most thorough. The tasks and processes they have identified include the following:

1. *Individuation*—the process of developing greater self-awareness, "definition" as an individual, and self-acceptance

2. *Inwardness*—the ability to reflect on one's motives, values, and actions
3. *Care of Self*—the capacity to make choices for one's own good, including the freedom to say "no" to some demands
4. *Generativity versus Stagnation*—the midlife task of determining the course and perspective of the remainder of one's life
5. *Life Review*—the capacity to reflect on life experiences and relationships in order to find reconciliation, healing, and meaning
6. *The Resolution of Polarities*—the process of addressing the major polarities, that is, Masculine/Feminine, Creation/Destruction, Young/Old, and Attachment/Separateness

For Jung, midlife involves a process of distinguishing the true self from the false self and, therefore, of confronting one's persona—the public self that is acceptable and pleasing to society.[3] For Daniel Levinson, defining one's authentic self involves addressing and resolving, to a greater or lesser degree, the polarities named above, in order to find greater congruency between the inner person and the "masks" he or she wears.[4] For aspirants and candidates in formation, discovering the true self through discernment of a call to ordained ministry involves confronting one's weaknesses as well as strengths, recognizing one's sinfulness as well as goodness, and acknowledging one's unworthiness in the presence of God's greatness, love, and mercy. Seeking greater congruency between the idealized self and the real self—with its gifts, but also with its limits, failures, and frailties—can seem daunting to men at midlife, especially to those who value business and personal success and for whom education, business acumen, and intellectual prowess have largely defined them—to themselves and to the world.

As Jung sees it, the struggle to live out of one's authentic self results in greater congruency between being and acting and between intention and purpose. Formation studies, especially those focused on pastoral ministry and the goal of being formed in the image of Jesus Christ, often prompt confrontation with one's "masks" and a hunger for greater authenticity. It is not unusual for men in formation to question the career paths they have pursued or the values that drive their actions and decisions, especially in light of the growth required of them as they respond to God's call to ministry.

In Erik Erikson's stages of psychosocial development, "generativity versus stagnation" is commonly associated with midlife.[5] In formation, the stage is usually encountered as the men engage in "inner work," practical studies, and service ministry. In this stage of development, the aspirant or candidate is faced with such questions as: "Do I have what it takes to do something entirely new? Am I willing to give up old ways of doing things in order to open myself to God's guidance? Can I accept that, for all my knowledge and giftedness, there are insights and skills I need to learn at this age if I am to minister to others?" In order to resolve the tension between generativity and stagnation, the individual must become willing to face the challenges of living creatively *after* midlife, rather than "settling" for a sense of incompleteness, futility, and even depression knowing that he is no longer young.

# Deacon Formation and Theories of Midlife Development

Carl Jung describes the second half of life as a time for the "Self" to develop.[6] This involves a process that he calls individuation as the personality matures and the individual becomes more self-reflective. As middle age sets in, the individual is likely to ask: "Who am I *really*?" Ultimately the answer to this question comes from within and motivates the person to move on or to settle for complacency. Self-reflection at this age is not about identity development but about the emergence of a more authentic, congruent self, capable of "pouring out" this self for the good of others.

# The "Gift" of Formation at Midlife

Many men who come to deacon formation assume that they will "learn *how* to be a deacon," and that the formation process will give them the necessary tools to "*make* them deacons." Their assumptions about formation are based on previous academic and vocational studies, in which learning meant mastering *how* to do something. In their minds, mastery of requisite skills constitutes *being* something, that is, an engineer, a nurse, a counselor, a business owner. The formation *process* poses new challenges because it focuses not only on acquisition of skills but on self-reflection (indeed, self-confrontation), character development, morality, spirituality, and a greater concern for others than for one's self.

Midlife, as well as deacon formation, is characterized by the quality and the practice of inwardness. The individuation process, like the practice of ministry itself, calls for a commitment to a life of prayer and ongoing knowledge of one's life "story" at increasingly deeper levels. Spiritual formation processes should offer opportunities to address this call to inwardness in midlife. Through studies in spirituality, scripture, prayer, and discernment, the candidates and the wives of those candidates who are married discover the uniqueness of their life experiences. Through the use of prayer journals, *lectio divina*, small-group faith-sharing, and theological reflection, they recognize the variety and richness of personal spiritualities and the depths of the faith tradition. For each man, the concept of "deacon" emerges, not as a singular identity that can be learned, but as a function or role that is defined by the unique development of each individual.

Daniel Levinson observes that, during middle age, a man is likely to experience some "culminating event" that takes on special meaning for him and that may lead him to a reappraisal of life, including reconsideration of past achievements and their meaning.[7] Immersion in the formation process, with all its opportunities for self-reflection, can provoke the culminating event that leads to an opportunity for serious life review. Levinson says that the principle task of midlife is to resolve four polarities: Young/Old, Destruction/Creation, Masculine/Feminine, and Attachment/Separateness. Rather than being qualities that an individual either has or does not have, these polarities are more likely to coexist within each individual.

As deacon formation provides an opportunity for each man to explore a new vocation, most men wrestle with these inner polarities; they are engaged, by virtue of the process itself, in evaluating goals and seeing a new "self" emerge. In the course of formation, the men are also prompted to integrate the responsibilities of marriage and service as a preparation for ordained ministry. As early as the first year of candidacy, many men describe a marked improvement in their relationships with their spouses, family members, and coworkers. They see themselves becoming more available, more patient, gentler, and less rigid and aggressive.

For the wives of deacon candidates, the formation process can be a time of significant growth as well. Carol Gilligan in her book *In a Different Voice* points out that, unlike men, women's generativity does not begin at midlife.[8] Rather, she says, women have a lifelong pattern of nurturing and sustaining relationships. What *does* change for women over a period of time is their focus: from caring for others to recognizing the importance of caring for themselves. The practices of self-care, self-acceptance, and shared community with other wives should be encouraged and facilitated throughout formation.

Initially, a woman may feel that, rather than being free to be herself, she must define herself by her husband's call and act like a "deacon's wife." The formation process should offer her opportunities to discover new ways to love, work, learn, and discover meaning for herself in midlife. Women often express with surprise and delight how much the regular gatherings mean to her because *she* is growing in self-knowledge and in her faith. Like the man, the formation process also challenges a woman's sense of herself and the roles she has been filling. She, too, is encouraged to grow in self-awareness, inwardness, and faith.

Men often begin formation with an established faith life, which may range from dogmatic to eclectic. Candidates and their wives may have spiritualities formed through Cursillo, Charismatic Renewal, and/or Marriage Encounter. There is some assumption on their part that they are well-entrenched in a given style of prayer and reflection; viewing the spiritual life as a dynamic process is often new and challenging for them. There may be a tendency on the part of most aspirants/candidates to *avoid* growth—and, therefore, the pain of growing—while at the same time recognizing that learning will involve some discomfort. Deacon formation invites them to move beyond complacency to a broader perspective.

It is important to note that because of resistance to change, several tensions can occur within formation:

1. The tension between individual and communal spirituality
2. The tension between the call to diaconal ministry and the responsibility to marriage and family, church community, workplace, and the larger community
3. The tension between fulfilling the requirements for study and engaging in self-directed learning
4. The tension between receiving evaluation from authority figures and becoming able and willing to evaluate one's self and one's peers
5. The tension between appearing and functioning adequately, and admitting one's limitations, needs, and failures

The impact of many stress-inducing (and growth-promoting) changes occurs during deacon formation, not all related to the studies themselves. Participants and their wives, as well as the formation community and staff, will experience such events as the deaths of close family members and friends, personal injury or illness, family injury or illness, job loss, job promotion, reconciliation of marital differences, retirement, the addition of new family members, changes in financial status, career changes, children leaving home, problems with in-laws, outstanding personal achievements, the start or completion of education, revision of personal habits, work-related stressors, and changes in church and/or social activities. As a result, the formation program is a "hotbed" for stress and growth.

Midlife itself is stressful and fraught with change. The stress increases when formation for ministry brings new dynamics to the lives of men and women already in middle age. A primary source of stress is the ever-present tension between caring for self and family and tending to one's work in the context of studies and service. Studies, experiences in ministry, and shared discernment demand changes in a couple's lifestyle and in their relationship together. In addition, formation usually triggers a mourning process for what will never be, for new realizations about one's limitations, and even for the yet-unexplored life of service ahead.

Since many life changes during formation produce stress and grief, a discussion of the dynamics of loss and change should be introduced in the curriculum early in the program.

On the other hand, formation also provides many opportunities for the men and women to embrace enriching and freeing changes in themselves and in their situations at midlife. In the long run, deacon formation may be a life event that itself precipitates a midlife "crisis," challenging the men and women to seek more creative and healthier coping skills for handling both personal and ministry-related challenges.

# Strategies in Spiritual Formation to Address Midlife Issues

Several strategies used in formation are relevant for addressing midlife issues. One purpose of these strategies is to assist aspirants and candidates in understanding spiritual development as an integral part of human development and, hence, essential to faith development and pastoral effectiveness.

Among other outcomes, the spiritual dimension of the program assists in the development of Jung's inwardness: the capacity to reflect on life and relationships, to identify one's motives and values, and to seek experiences that nurture growth in faith through prayer, study, worship, service, and receipt of the sacraments. The following are some specific strategies to help address areas for growth in midlife and in diaconal formation:

# Discernment

As early as the screening process, a man applying for deacon formation hears the word *discernment*. The *National Directory* states, "Any discernment of gifts and charisms must involve the ecclesial community....An individual who presents himself for ordination to the diaconate is accountable to the Church, who mediates—confirms—his vocation."[9] In deacon formation, discernment should help the man (as well as the program leadership, formation board members, and spiritual directors) to confirm or not confirm a vocation to the permanent diaconate. Furthermore, ongoing discernment enables all who are involved in the formation process—including aspirant/candidate, formators, spiritual directors, faculty, and board members—to discern the level of personal and pastoral skills that a man has to serve others through the diaconate.

Initially, a man may perceive discernment as something that happens outside himself. It is not unusual that he may even feel the discernment of others—his wife, his directors, the Church at large—to be in opposition to his will. Formation should cultivate in a man the awareness that discernment is a collaborative process. Several persons may be involved in discernment besides the man himself: the formation program director, his spiritual director, his spouse and peers, the formation board, the bishop and his staff, and the Holy Spirit. Discernment then takes place on two levels: the personal or private process, and the communal or group process.

Most men enter deacon formation on a very upbeat note (though some are timid). The formation staff accompanies each man throughout screening, inquiry, aspirancy, and candidacy—as far as he continues—to assist him to discern the will of God for him. In dialogue, the man explores with his formation directors, his spiritual director, and his spouse his reasons for seeking ordination as a permanent deacon, and whether or not he has the desirable qualities that will enhance his diaconal ministry; these are important elements in the discernment process. In addition, discernment addresses the question: Is this man "free" to be ordained? Or is he complacent and simply accommodating himself to the desires of others? Or does he want the diaconate for his own good and to enhance his ego?

About two years into formation many men report: "Something happened; something has changed for me." Some note an interior quieting, being less competitive and being more internally motivated. Some express freedom to choose the call to the diaconate with more peace, noting that even if they are not ordained, the years of deacon formation will not have been a loss.

This questioning of formation and vocation can become a crisis in deacon formation. Most of the formation participants, at one time or another, seriously ask themselves whether or not they wish to continue in deacon formation. Classes on discernment are significant at this time.

In sessions on discernment, participants learn that discernment necessitates a certain amount of self-awareness, which includes awareness about the forces of good and evil within one's self and outside one's self. Men are invited to look at the reality that good and evil are equally active in persons. A negative set of movements tends to make one more selfish, self-centered, fearful, anxious, and bored. Positive movements motivate a person to love others, beyond self.

At this juncture in the formation process, a man is likely to begin to experience the tug between the negative and positive movements and to feel an urge to reconcile the false self with the true self. A participant may also feel a sense of disintegration of all that has been familiar and dependable. Carl Jung summarizes midlife conversion as a juncture when "one cannot live the afternoon of life according to the program of life's morning, for what was great in the morning will be little at evening, and what in the morning was true will by evening have become a lie."[10]

As the men confront the tension between the false and true self, some of Daniel Levinson's midlife tasks begin to surface: reconciling the past with the present and dealing with polarities within the self, especially the polarities of Destruction/Creation and Masculine/Feminine. In order to achieve this reconciliation, the deacon formation participants have to take some risks. For example, candidates frequently recognize and seek to heal the "disconnect" between their faith life and the ways they conduct themselves in the workplace. One man expressed the need for congruency by saying, "I realized that I could no longer continue to work for the prison system, teaching others how to use firearms, and then proclaim the gospel of life on Sunday. This realization led me to leave my job and move into a different occupation."

## Life Story

Written reflections on life experiences, during the application process and throughout formation, assist the men and women to examine their life stories in light of developmental thought. As a result, they understand how growth is a lifelong process for themselves and for those they may be called upon to minister to. Reflection on one's "life story" theologically assists in learning theological reflection and understanding human development from various perspectives. The aim is to enable the men and women to gain understanding of human psychosocial and faith development and to appreciate the forces that can limit as well as encourage such growth. While studies anticipate ministry to others, they are also designed to assist the men and women to see their personal development through a broader lens and to approach the tasks of midlife in a spirit of self-forgiveness and self-acceptance.

Courses on human and spiritual development assist in the task of finding meaning in the successes and failures, joys and sorrows, of human existence in the world today. These courses are intended, not merely to impart information to be learned about God or one's self, but rather to engage the participants in a process of bringing together various perspectives on the meaning of life. Men and women continue to investigate their own experiences, with a view toward consciously integrating faith and spirituality with their humanity. They initially contribute to this process by participating in theological reflection on stages in their own life histories. An important dynamic is the community members' willingness to share examples of their personal growth-and-faith development. Small-group faith-sharing and theological reflection assist the formation program staff and spiritual directors to help the men integrate midlife growth with preparation for ministry.

# Theological Reflection

The *National Directory*, with regard to the intellectual dimension, states that "the formation faculty and staff should structure an intellectual process that includes an invitation to each participant to reflect on his adult life and experience in light of the Gospel and the Church's teaching."[11] Addressing the pastoral dimension of formation, it goes on to state that "pastoral field education fosters in general integration in the formational process, forging a close link between the human, spiritual, and intellectual dimensions in formation."[12]

The 1984 *Guidelines* suggest that "it would be useful. if, even during the period of formation, they form and take part in diaconal communities, groups in which they will be able to reflect together on the challenges and opportunities of their ministries."[13]

In order to fulfill these objectives, the men in the formation program are organized into small theological-reflection groups (five or six couples per group), with cultures and languages mixed within each group. Each group meets monthly, September through May. The theological reflection process is facilitated by formation staff to help the participants examine and reflect on their experiences of pastoral ministry.

The goal for theological reflection during deacon formation is to provide regular opportunities for the men to practice the process of reflecting on their life experiences of ministry in light of the gospel, faith tradition, personal and social values. This process also provides opportunity for each person to integrate aspects of the Christian tradition with personal experience and the influences of culture.

Theological reflection provides a context for exploring areas in which each candidate needs to grow in pastoral effectiveness, as well as in self-awareness. In light of these identified needs, each summer for three summers prior to the parish internship, candidates are given field placement assignments in community service agencies, including training, supervision, self-evaluation, evaluation by supervisors and peers, and theological reflection processes.

Every month, when the small theological-reflection groups meet, one or two men present an incident from ministry, preferably from their summer field placement, which posed some challenge for him in relation to another person or persons he intended to help. Initially in the program, before the field placement is initiated, the men may present incidents from their family life, job, or parish involvements. Each incident is then examined through the "lenses" of scripture, Christian faith, cultural attitudes, cultural messages, and pastoral theology. The purpose of this process is to facilitate each man's integration of his life and his experience of God with his style in ministry. This process also helps group members to reflect on a diversity of life experiences; to question their assumptions about themselves, others, and ministry; and to better articulate what their goals are for service to others.

For some of the men, the theological reflection process, in an atmosphere of trust and compassion, is a means for inviting transformation in both thinking and behavior. In the same way, the men also learn to affirm themselves and to receive affirmation from the group members.

## Lectio Divina and Prayer Journals

*Lectio divina*, praying the scriptures, appears in the "Basic Standards for Readiness" appendix in the *National Directory* and is a way of grounding the men and their wives in the word of God. In addition, regular use of *lectio* helps those who use this method to move from intellectual understanding of biblical passages to a deeper, regular reflection, and application of the Word in their lives. Interiority and the capacity for reflection are basic to midlife development. The use of *lectio* not only helps in this development, it also provides a prayer discipline shared among the members of the formation community, assists the men in their theological reflection process, and invites them to listen to God in the word, in ways that are relevant to their own lives, decisions, and actions toward others. The men and women are introduced to a variety of prayer styles throughout formation, beginning in aspirancy. One style is to pray the First Reading and the Gospel three times each week, in anticipation of the Sunday liturgy, using the simple pattern of *lectio divina*. Each man summarizes his reflections in a prayer journal, which is submitted monthly to the formation team for its feedback. Here are the guidelines for *lectio divina*:

**Step 1. Begin the Reading Experience**. Read each scripture passage to understand what is being said. What words, phrases, or ideas catch your attention? This first reading is an attempt to understand the meaning of the passages and your initial response to them.

**Step 2. Understand the Experience of the Scriptures**. Read each passage again. What feelings come up as you read? Are there words or phrases that affect you strongly? That comfort or affirm you? That make you resist because they challenge you?

**Step 3. Open Yourself to the Scriptures through Prayer**.

a. Read the passages a third time, slowly and thoughtfully as a prayer. Focus on a line or two (or even just a phrase or word) that catches your attention. Let the words go to your feelings. Remain in silence in the presence of God in the word.

b. Ask yourself: What is being asked of me in these texts? The word of God demands a decision that shapes our being and action. How will I put the word of God into action in my family and in my workplace in the week ahead?

**Step 4. Summarize Your Experience**. In your prayer journal for the week, write a brief summary of how God was most clearly present to you, what was asked of you in the texts, and how you put the word of God into action in your family and workplace.

The format and questions for the prayer journal may be varied throughout the formation process.

What is important is that the aspirants/candidates establish a regular pattern for prayer that includes the scriptures, which leads to a greater capacity for self-reflection and reflection on ministry, and a greater facility applying the scripture in preaching and pastoral care.

## Integration of Marriage and Ministry

The integration of ministry and marriage is emphasized throughout the formation process, thus helping the men and women to recognize and integrate the midlife polarities of masculine/feminine—all this happens as the men prepare for pastoral roles and as the women seek to affirm their own talents and ministries. One candidate described the change in his marriage through formation: "Before formation, [my wife] and I participated together with my taking the lead and she following along. Now, we are equal partners, each with distinct gifts that complement each other."

Another couple observed: "We have learned that, in order to grow in togetherness as loving persons, our individuality had to be established. We had to understand ourselves in terms of our individual spiritualities in order to grow in our devotion to each other. I have learned to think more about myself as an individual."

Finally, a wife wrote: "We are more comfortable in allowing our own uniqueness to surface—there is a greater respect for each other. Our sense of togetherness has also grown in proportion to our relationship with God."

One midlife issue addressed by many couples in formation is "the loss of the dream," that is, the growing recognition that their "idealized selves" and their ideals of marriage fall short of the realities of who they are and how they have related to each other. While couples may experience some disillusionment during formation, there is even more opportunity for experiences of *grace* as they address these issues in the context of a loving, prayerful, and accepting community.

The issue of "losing their dream" is addressed as couples explore together the integration of their dreams for themselves and their marriage with their expectations for diaconal ministry. This helps each man and woman to clarify how they had modified the dream during deacon formation. One man wrote: "I must confess that our dream of being the 'ideal' couple hasn't reached fruition. However, we are becoming a symbol to each other and others of sacramental fidelity."

As the men and women grow in their individuation and acquire a new sense of who they are before God and each other, they renew and make commitments to marriage and ministry at deeper levels. It is here that commitment to marriage is being brought into balance with the dream for ordained diaconal ministry. Men and women in deacon formation learn that if they do not attend to their individual needs, call, and growth, it may be more difficult to negotiate the integration of marriage and ministry. The goal is to try to opt for more mutuality. To do this, they learn to capitalize on their strengths, but not to deny their weaknesses. They see how each brings his or her individual gifts into the marriage and into ministry.

## Wives' Support Group

Understandably, the wives of aspirants/candidates are initially uncertain about their relationship to each other and their role in a newly formed support group. Their early concept of the "part" they might play in the deacon formation program is in support of their husbands' education and preparation for ministry. It is not unusual for women to express the expectation that the staff will "tell" them how to be "good deacons' wives." Awareness that the group exists comes as a surprise to some, yet the support, shared learning, encouragement, and prayer soon help the women to form strong bonds with each other. They learn to learn from each other's experiences and spirituality and to build trust within the community.

Often, wives of aspirants/candidates are reinforced in their roles as "deacons' wives" rather than encouraged in their own unique growth and development. Since these women also face questions of identity, meaning, resolution of polarities, generativity, and purpose, it is important to design a process that helps the women bond as a community and to grow as individuals during midlife.

During the first year, resistance among the women is high. As they gradually begin to encounter each other as unique and gifted individuals, some of their initial caution diminishes. By the third year of the formation process, the wives meet together to suggest their own issues for study and discussion. A firmer spirit of respect, as well as a greater permission to challenge and to affirm each other, takes hold. Gradually, the women grow from an awareness of themselves as wives of men preparing for diaconal ministry to a recognition of themselves as individuals, involved in a formation process in which they, too, are invited to learn to develop skills and to claim their own needs, struggles, and abilities.

While the women grow in their sense of individuals, each also moves to a more authentic level of attachment, which makes it possible for the wife to give her formal consent to the bishop to call her husband to ordination as a deacon.

## Retreats

Retreats are an important opportunity for the participants to have extended time with God, to receive spiritual guidance, and to reflect on their formation experiences. They also offer a more focused time of discernment. Studies indicate that the retreat process facilitates addressing a variety of midlife issues, including the polarities of Masculine/Feminine, Creation/ Destruction, and Attachment/Separateness. Regular retreats also contribute to the development of greater individuation in the men and women alike.

Regarding the benefit of annual retreats, aspirants, candidates, and their wives have said: "During the retreat, I began to see how God has called me ever since I was in the womb." And, "This year's retreat helped me to evaluate my life with God and to see if I would be the good servant He wants me to be." There are many more comments like that.

# Conclusion

Midlife provides profound spiritual implications for conversion. Men and women at midlife become more open to being touched by God in different ways. Some men and their wives enter deacon formation with a spirituality that is nurtured primarily by rules, rituals, and traditions. Deacon formation at midlife provides an opportunity for the men and women to expand their prayer into the inner realm or—if their prayer has been primarily private and an internal practice—into the arena of shared communal and couple-prayer. Midlife is a very creative time of life, when men and women recognize the invitation to slow down and to cultivate the call to a deeper and more genuine interiority.

# CHAPTER 7

# Priests and Deacons in Partnership

## Thoughts on the Role of the Priest in the Ongoing Renewal of the Diaconate

## *Timothy J. Shugrue*

One of the great blessings of my life and ministry as a priest has been the ten-and-a-half years I was privileged to serve in the restoration of a permanent diaconate in the Archdiocese of Newark. Although it was an unexpected development, it turned out to be an enriching and stimulating experience that resulted in an enduring interest in, and concern for, the ongoing integration of the restored diaconate in the life of the Church. It is particularly from my perspective as a priest that I continue to regard the diaconate, with a conviction that the health and relevance of its long-term contribution to pastoral ministry are closely related to its relationship with the priesthood in their mutual and complementary service to the Church. More particularly, it is from the viewpoint of a pastor, as well as a former diocesan director of the diaconate, that I now consider the conclusions I drew during those ten-and-a-half years and try to apply them in the current environment, in which more comprehensive magisterial documentation has become a definitive factor. Though not responsible for supervising the implementation of recent norms and guidelines, I believe there must be continuing dialogue between those who now do so and those of us from an earlier generation of diocesan directors.

When assigned to direct Newark's Permanent Diaconate Preparation Program in 1979, I had been a priest for a little over six years and, at age thirty-one, was younger than all of our candidates, then in their second year of formation. I was not well informed about the background of the restoration or about the theological perspectives and magisterial documents governing it. I was acquainted with some of our ordained deacons, but had not been close to any of them during their formation. The parish in which I had served did not have a deacon or candidate at that point, and the pastor was entirely unreceptive to the idea. So, when hearing of the departure of Newark's pioneering director, Msgr. Richard McGuinness, I knew the job would be a significant one, but I had no thought of proposing myself as a candidate for the post: even if I had been looking to be reassigned, I would not have thought I had any qualifications for this task. Thus, I was more than surprised to be approached about being considered as a possible successor to Msgr. McGuinness.

It was more in response to this prodding than to any confidence in my suitability for the job that I applied for consideration and met with the search committee, an experience that only reinforced my acute sense of the limitations of my knowledge and experience for meeting the position's demands. During the interview, I detected among the members of the selection panel some puzzlement as to how I could think I might be effective in the job, and I had to agree. Thus I was unprepared for the summons several weeks later to Archbishop Peter L. Gerety's office, where he informed me that I was the committee's recommended choice for director of the Permanent Diaconate Preparation Program. More than surprised, I had no idea how much my life and ministry would be affected positively and, indeed, graced by the assignment I was about to begin.

At the time, the Archdiocese of Newark counted the second-largest community of permanent deacons (after the Archdiocese of Chicago) in the United States. Large classes of deacons had been ordained between 1975 and 1978, when Archbishop Gerety placed a moratorium on the formation program and invited the Bishops' Committee on the Permanent Diaconate to conduct its first evaluation of a diocesan program. The preparation program was relieved of any responsibility for the supervision of those already ordained as deacons. My initial task was to revise the preparation program guidelines, while shepherding to ordination the forty-three candidates who had been admitted just before the moratorium began.

It was mid-December 1979 when I was appointed director, and I was introduced to the archdiocesan community of deacons and candidates at their annual St. Stephen's Day Mass on December 26. The candidates' retreat was scheduled for early January, when I would assume responsibility for their continuing progress. With the help of Msgr. Ernest J. Fiedler and Deacon Samuel M. Taub of the Secretariat for the Diaconate at the National Conference of Catholic Bishops (now the United States Conference of Catholic Bishops), I quickly acquired the existing official documentation. At that time there was not much, either from the Holy See or from the Bishops' Conference; references from Vatican II documents and postconciliar statements were very broad and even vague in describing what the restored diaconate was expected to look like and how it was intended to function. But by the beginning of 1980, there was a growing body of "learnings" from the U.S. Church's initial experience with its first permanent deacons. Most of the experience was positive and suggested the tantalizing potential of this new/old ministry's impact on the life of the Church. But there were also "shadows," revealed in anecdotes arising from negative experiences with some deacons. The same could be said from the viewpoint of the deacons themselves, who bore primary responsibility for reintroducing "permanent" diaconal ministry to the Latin Rite Church, which seemed to have done fairly well without it for a millennium.

As I studied the documents on the renewed diaconate, I was also being exposed to reports of perceived pluses and minuses in the lived experience of our local Church with its new deacons and in the lived experience of those deacons with the reality of our local Church. From both sources, I was learning that the diaconate was both a wonderful addition to the pastoral life of the

Church and a potential source of tension, both for the Church and for its deacons, as the latter were integrated into the existing structures of the former. By the time our candidates assembled for their retreat in January 1980, I was both awed by the potential of the diaconate and concerned about the issues of identity and acceptance that seemed to shadow much of the mutual experience of deacons and the Church community. What was seen as positive needed to be encouraged and fostered; what was confused or negative needed to be studied and resolved, for the sake of both the Church and its deacons.

Introducing myself to our candidates and their wives during the retreat, I was honest about my unfamiliarity with the restoration to date, but I also shared what I believed to be my one qualification for the job of director (a conviction that grew stronger as my work with deacons extended over the next decade), which was actually the reverse side of my obvious inexperience and youth: I might not know and understand much about the diaconate just then, but I had already realized that it would come to matter greatly over the course of my life as a priest. It would also come to matter very much to the Church of Newark as it encountered changing pastoral realities that could already be discerned in 1980. If, as a priest, I had the opportunity to help develop this ministerial resource so that it could positively impact the future pastoral life of the archdiocese, I felt it was a task to which I could commit myself with interest and determination.

In that conviction, I settled into a process of learning, chiefly through experience, the ingredients of which were the evidence of deacons' effectiveness and satisfaction in their ministry, and a review of the Church's response to the actual performance of our deacons. I had much assistance in this learning process, primarily from deacons and candidates, their wives and families, priests of the archdiocese, and others associated with deacons in their ministries. Significant help also came from others in deacon-formation work around the United States, channeled through the National Association of Permanent Diaconate Directors (NAPDD—now simply NADD, with the word *permanent* dropped from the name of the organization). Of particular importance to me were the insights gleaned from studies of "effective" deacons by the late

Don Clifton and his staff at Selection Research, Inc., which later merged into the Gallup Organization, especially Sr. Jo Ann Miller, OSF, and from their guidance regarding the concepts that underlay SRI's Deacon Perceiver Interview. Of great value to me was the SRI principle of respecting the talents of people by noticing and affirming them and, above all, by positioning people appropriately in roles that utilized their genuine gifts. Likewise, I was grateful for the SRI insight that recognized the significance of the recruiter or selector in determining, to an important degree, the impact on an organization of those chosen for key positions within it.

If diaconal ministry was to have its proper impact on the life of our local Church, it would derive in large measure from decisions I would be making in evaluating and selecting candidates: the importance of the necessary process of formation and education would be secondary to the selection of strong candidates. With strong candidates, the formation process could better focus and inform their essential talent for diaconal ministry; but without strong candidates, I came to realize, even a solid formation and education process could not of itself produce an effective deacon, one who would experience sufficiently the satisfaction that is vital for a pastoral minister's happiness and his optimum contribution. Also, a more appropriate selection would derive from a more accurate description of the identity of the minister known as "deacon" than was then available from official documentation and from a more modest and realistic assessment of the expectations this "deacon" would be asked to meet.

From the beginning, I considered my role in the formation program and—from 1982, with the Office of the Permanent Diaconate, responsible as well for matters affecting the life and ministry of the ordained—to be a rich opportunity for priestly ministry. First, as a priest I had a deep concern for the future quality of pastoral ministry in our local Church; I was grateful that Archbishop Gerety, and later Archbishop (now Cardinal) Theodore McCarrick, allowed a priest to serve in the capacity of director. I came to believe that the archdiocesan diaconate as an order of ministers needed a priest of its own, less for particular spiritual service than for guidance and support amid the sometimes bruising realities of integrating pastoral ministers of different types and responsibilities. I believe the diaconate benefited from having at its service one who could represent the ministerial "big brother" that was the presbyterate, at least as a resource in the mutual interpretation of identity and roles that could complicate the relationship between these two orders and their individual members. In many cases, serious complications have arisen, often to the detriment of the larger aim of pastoral ministry and often with painful results for both deacons and priests. I saw my responsibility as priest-director to be the fraternal holding of a mirror before the order of deacons, the posing of questions arising from observation of deacons' ministries and life situations, and the evaluation of processes and behaviors that were setting precedents which could, in time, prove to be either helpful or harmful. I also saw it as a pastoral service to our archdiocesan Church, our archbishop, and our presbyterate to provide an assessment and evaluation of the ministry of deacons and to represent, from a position of some objectivity, the interests of the order of deacons in its ongoing integration into the ranks of the Church's ordained ministers.[1]

Now, from a vantage point seventeen years removed from daily ministry in the service of the diaconate, questions about the relationship between priests and deacons continue to interest me—and to cause me concern. Ironically I have not, as a pastor, had a deacon assigned to my parish, more a consequence of circumstances than design. When first named as pastor of a parish that had never had a permanent deacon assigned to it (though, for a few years, "transitional deacons" served the parish, in a capacity which, I would argue, is really more "priest intern" than genuine "deacon"), I saw it as an advantage: I would have the opportunity to apply theories I had developed about the recruitment and selection of an appropriate candidate from within a parish, without having to counter any negatives from the parish's past experience with a deacon. I would be able to implement an education process about who and what a deacon is, and about what he could be expected to contribute to the overall life of the parish. I thought it necessary to observe for a while the attitudes of our existing pastoral staff members toward the possibility of a deacon being proposed, lest my own enthusiasm and conviction about the advantage of including a deacon force it on them and eventually work against acceptance of the deacon's ministerial role and possibly of the deacon himself. I also knew I needed time to become familiar with possible candidates. I knew what to look for, but realized it would take time to assess fairly a candidate's potential for actual service as an ordained deacon.[2] I considered it might take two years of my six-year term, as I got to know the parish and its members—who was who, who did what, and how they did it.

In considering potential candidates, I would look first for hands-on involvement in direct service to the poor and others in conditions of physical, emotional, or social need, and assign less significance to engagement primarily in services of a liturgical, spiritual, or catechetical nature. Time-proven participation in "service ministry," I believe, is the best predictor of solid diaconal instincts or "talent." I would also evaluate a potential candidate in light of his other strengths for ministry as an ordained deacon, and for his ability to adapt to the realities of "up close" work within the institution of the Church and with its other ministers. And I would try to develop a positive assessment of the defining characteristics of a potential candidate's marriage and family life, secular work experience, reputation for integrity, and so on. It was a tall order. One of the problems associated with some of the first deacons ordained after the restoration was their selection according to an enthusiastic but naïve belief that "anybody can be a deacon"—well-intentioned words, meant to denote a breaking of a conventional mold for those in ordained ministry, but subtly sanctioning the acceptance of men who may have had no glaring negatives but who also manifested few clear diaconal strengths. I believe a major change is required for bishops and vocation recruiters to accept the premise that a candidate for the diaconate—or, for that matter, for the priesthood—needs to demonstrate not just the *absence* of signs of unsuitability, but the *presence* of compelling indicators of suitability. I also believe that the Church should not accept for ordination someone who will require a degree of individual support or guidance that the Church cannot reasonably expect to provide and therefore should not promise. To do otherwise does not respect individuals who, while good at heart and desirous of being helpful, are likely to disappoint the expectation that an ordained minister be a responsible, "self-actualizing" leader.[3] I believe the proper way to respect people is *not* to nurture their unfounded hopes, but to help them identify their genuine strengths and find an appropriate way to make their unique contribution. For some—but only for some—this will be as ordained deacons.

After two years of watching for signs of "diaconal talent" coupled with the personal structures to render it most serviceable to the Church in ordained ministry, I learned that the archdiocese had again placed a moratorium on the acceptance of new candidates and that, when the formation program was again opened, it would be for a class composed of candidates from the Hispanic community. Our parish did not require a Spanish-speaking deacon, so I judged that recruiting a candidate from the parish should be deferred until the program again accepted non-Hispanic candidates. When that eventually happened, I was in the closing year of my initial six-year term and felt it would not be fair—either to my successor, if I were not reappointed, or to the man I might recruit for the diaconate—to initiate a move of such importance.

My appointment to a second six-year term might have revived the process, but the archdiocese continued to revise its procedures. Now I am concluding a third and final six-year term as pastor, and, although the archdiocesan program is once more accepting candidates of all backgrounds into its current five-year formation process, I am again constrained by the belief that the decision to proceed should respect the fact that another pastor will have responsibility for someone whom I will have proposed. Although a deacon is ordained for service to the diocese and not to a local parish, the reality is that a healthy and supportive interaction between a deacon or candidate and his home parish and pastor is extremely important to the deacon, his family, the parish, the diocesan Church, and its order of deacons. Nonetheless, having recently faced the prospect of losing a priest as parochial vicar with no guarantee of a replacement, I have taken steps to begin with the parish pastoral and finance councils a discussion of what a deacon's ministry is and how it might be expected to function in our parish as part of a general realignment of ministerial personnel that is undoubtedly on the horizon. I believe it is more responsible at this point to leave to my successor the decision about proposing a candidate, while using the rest of my tenure to introduce a gradual preparation of the parish for that future possibility.

Such a preparation is vitally important, because I believe that the identity of the deacon and a proper understanding of his role in pastoral service are still far from being commonly agreed upon among Catholics, even among priests and by many Church leaders. Confusion on the part of the laity is a major problem for the diaconate, while a priest's lack of enthusiasm for the deacon's role, or even his denial of any valid role for the diaconate, can be destructive to the deacon, his family, and the Church community; it is also an affront to our understanding of holy orders.[4] Some priests do not appreciate the difference between a deacon's vocation and their own, or the similarities between them. Years ago, while serving as a high school chaplain, I attended a Serra Club dinner at which the guest speaker was a Christian Brother assigned to the same school. After delivering an interesting talk about his vocation—which, from having lived and worked alongside religious brothers for the first time, I had recognized as different from my own—Brother was asked by a well-meaning Serran, "Why didn't you go 'all the way' and become a priest?" Brother's face hardened as he tried patiently to explain again how he had experienced his call to religious life.

Many deacons face a similar situation among Catholics who do not know what to make of someone who is an ordained clergyman and wears sacred vesture in his ministry, but who usually earns his living from secular employment, is most often married, most often has children, dresses like the laity when not "doing ministry," rarely lives on church property, and is not called "Father." Uncertainty from the laity is at least understandable, but to face such uncertainty from priests, brothers in ordained ministry, and fellow-collaborators with deacons under the direction of the bishop is especially disheartening. The first requirement is to understand that the diaconate is a distinctive order within the threefold sacrament of holy orders. The distinction is not total, but it is important.[5]

I believe that every parish community ought to "feature" the services of an ordained deacon, not primarily as a matter of having sufficient numbers of personnel for ministry, but because every believer deserves to "receive" the sacrament of holy orders in the sense of benefiting, in a real and visible way, from the service of each order—bishop, priest, and deacon. In a fundamental sense, of course, we do benefit from them, but that can often seem abstract: it is better when the relationships are recognized and felt. If, as Church documents indicate, the diaconate is essential to the life of the Church,[6] then it seems to me that every viable church community should feature the visible and active presence of a deacon among its ministerial personnel. For me, a deacon's ministry has more to do with its sacramental role in strengthening the life of the Church than it does with the personnel equation; that is, who is going to do what. We need deacons *not* primarily because of something they uniquely can "do" but because of what they "are" or represent in all that they "do." The deacon is a living, breathing reminder of the essential character of charity as a mark of the Church community and of each Christian.[7] His ministerial activities give expression to that reminder and offer models that encourage in others a consistent commitment to charity.

I have long feared a marginalizing of the deacon's proper role as a result of the dynamics of utilizing an available deacon as the "substitute of choice" for increasingly less available priests in many of the latter's familiar ministerial functions. Priests, particularly pastors, should be careful not to draft deacons into serving primarily as substitutes for them, not least because it tends to suggest a "temporary" quality to the deacon's role: for example, if we had a sufficient number of priests, would the Church then not "need" deacons?

I believe the Second Vatican Council's call for the diaconate's restoration as a permanent order[8] spoke to the reality that something vital was missing from the Church's experience. I do not mean that "diaconal service" was missing, for the Church has always been blessed with individual believers and groups (religious communities, for instance, and associations like the St. Vincent de Paul Society) who have manifested in public ways the charity of Christ and modeled it for imitation by the faithful. But what restoring the diaconate has done is to reintroduce an "icon" of diaconal service to the official ministerial structure of the Church, the essential framework that "orders" the Body and sacramentally nourishes the ministerial witness of the entire community of faith.[9] The diaconate that existed for centuries in the Latin Rite of the Western Church in an almost vestigial form (as the step immediately before ordination to priesthood) is now empowered to stand before the Church again in an authoritative way, fulfilling its mission to call the community of believers to faithful obedience to Christ's command, "Love one another as I have loved you."[10]

The deacon's vocation is different from that of the priest—not in the sense that it is any less real or authentic, or that priesthood is a template that, with certain adaptations and deletions, reduces to diaconate[11]—but in the sense that the focus of the deacon's vocation is a specialized sensitivity to the physical and social needs of people and to ways in which the resources of the Church, both personal and material, can be called forth and organized to meet those needs. I see it as a matter of emphasis: the three orders that constitute the sacrament of holy orders—episcopate, presbyterate, and diaconate—serve the Church by sustaining its essential identity.[12] That identity arises from the infusion of divine grace in the souls of its members, in the virtues of faith, hope, and charity. I see each order with a particular orientation to one of these virtues, not to the exclusion of the others, and not in a three-step movement from least to most comprehensive, but in an interdependence that reflects both individual distinctions and an integral unity among them, in service to the grace that sanctifies believers and binds them to God and to one another. In this view, the bishop's distinctive mission is to care for the virtue of faith, articulating it and holding the local Church to the rule of faith in communion with the universal Church. The priest has a special mission to nurture hope, primarily through celebrating the sacraments of Eucharist and reconciliation; gathering groups of the faithful in obedience to Christ's command, "Do this in remembrance of me";[13] and encouraging confidence in the Lord's promise to bring all things to their fulfillment. The deacon's distinctive mission is the virtue of charity, as he embodies and expresses Jesus' challenge to his followers that we should do for one another, and for all the world, what he did for us.[14] Washing his apostles' feet was a vivid demonstration of Jesus' expectation that we must put ourselves at the service of others, an example of what he ultimately did by laying down his life on the cross. In pastoral practice, the orders work in harmony to promote the fidelity of the Church to her mission, their interdependence respecting the hierarchical principle springing from the Headship of Christ: deacons and priests are subordinate to the authority of the bishop, which binds them in an exercise of fraternal unity in service to the One Body of Christ.[15]

With his distinctive focus, a deacon looks at things with a different kind of vision, recognizing a need and wanting to do something about it, not as an instinctive helper (or not *just* as a helper), but as a disciple of Jesus, recognizing in every other person a sister or brother deserving of the reverence we would pay Christ himself. The more a deacon's actual ministerial activities reflect his fundamental character as an "icon" of Christ's charity, the stronger will be the community's understanding of the deacon's identity and of his role as a source of guidance and nourishment in fulfilling their own vocations as disciples.

The Church sees the deacon's broad mandate of service expressed in a threefold division of his time and energy among the ministries of word, worship, and charity.[16] When I was responsible for assisting the development of "ministry agreements" to govern deacons' assignments, I urged not a "three equal parts" division, but one closer to a 25 percent/25 percent/50 percent breakdown of responsibilities. It is easy, especially in the context of parish life, for ministries of worship and word to absorb too much of a deacon's time and energy. When asked to help in almost any capacity, especially by the pastor or another priest, a deacon will rarely refuse. And, because his responsibilities typically are shouldered along with those of marriage, parenthood, and secular employment, the Church often (and wisely) limits a deacon's "official ministry" to a certain number of hours weekly (recognizing, of course, that he is always an ordained minister). Putting the ministry of charity first and devoting 50 percent of his time and energy to it, a deacon can maintain the right balance and respect his essential identity. Ministries of word and worship—preaching, catechizing, assisting at liturgies, distributing holy communion, participating in marriage preparation, presiding at baptisms and weddings, wakes and burial services, and so on—would comprise together the remaining 50 percent of the deacon's overall ministry commitment.

Strictly maintaining the percentages may be artificial, but it is the discipline that is important: unless we the faithful can "see" (either directly or through the lens of his activities in word and worship) the deacon's hands-on involvement in fundamental acts of charity, like the corporal works of mercy, then the message that the deacon conveys will not be as clear as it should be. The deacon's active participation in the ministries of word and worship gives the community access to the "sign" of his involvement in direct charitable service, where specific persons benefit from the deacon's presence. By exercising and nourishing his own strongest instincts, his ministry of charity helps the deacon to hold his focus and to speak with authority of the needs that must be addressed by God's People in ever-widening circles, from the family, neighborhood, and local community to the larger society and beyond, ultimately embracing the global community.[17] But a deacon needs help in observing this discipline, and the most important person in that process—aside from a married deacon's wife and family—is usually the priest.

A pastor or priest, already stretched in trying to meet multiple demands, must curb the habit of having recourse to the deacon for a wide array of ad hoc involvements that, though legitimately serving real needs, are capable of being undertaken by others. Respecting the distinctive character of the deacon's role, the priest should recognize that its aim is the building-up of the Church in charity. That should be the primary standard by which a deacon's effectiveness is evaluated. This should be what the bishop and the priest hold the deacon accountable for—the vitality, breadth, and authenticity of the Church's charitable works in Christ's name. That does not mean that the deacon has to initiate or direct or even take part in every charitable endeavor in his immediate sphere of influence, but he should in some way "serve" all of them, as at least a friendly and supportive monitor or advocate, affirming people's instincts for doing good and encouraging the stretching of that energy to encompass an ever-greater range of good works. Then the deacon's presence at the altar and in liturgical rites, his preaching and teaching activities, will resonate with greater clarity and authority, strengthening the link between response to God's word in worship and response to it in the world.[18]

The priest must find fraternal ways of holding the deacon to this primary expectation of his ministerial identity, first by making it the quality that a priest seeks to notice or evaluate in assessing a potential candidate's vocational aptitude for the diaconate. A perceptive priest interested in promoting sound diaconal ministry should be able to discern the essential elements of a diaconal vocation in a prospective candidate early in a man's life. And, especially if an immediate response to that vocation is not possible or prudent because of existing circumstances in the man's life (family, job situation, or other pressing responsibilities), the priest should at least notice and affirm those essential elements by encouraging volunteer involvements that can keep the man's diaconal character alert and in good working order until it might be formally committed. This would also involve spiritual guidance and support, addressing the "deacon" who is already being formed by God's grace within the prospective candidate. Knowing another's talent and potential for ministry imposes a responsibility for helping to develop it: the priest who sees "deacon" in another has a sacred duty to assist him in bringing it to maturity for the service of God's People.[19]

With one who is a candidate for diaconal ordination, and with one already ordained, the priest has a responsibility to reinforce the understanding of the deacon's primary focus in the ministry of charity. By getting to know the distinctiveness of the deacon's vocation, the priest serves as an invaluable collaborator in his ministry. This knowledge should include a sense of the interplay of elements in the deacon's life from which he derives both energy and stability—not only his basic spiritual orientation, but also the dynamics of marriage, parenthood, family life, secular job, and community involvement. Here the priest needs in many ways to be a learner, trying to understand the power of these influences in the deacon's experience, rather than looking to impose a sense of ministerial identity or spirituality that, for the deacon, may be artificial.

The introduction of married men to the ranks of Latin Rite clergy as deacons is a reality that has not yet been fully appreciated for the positive resource it is. Deacon-and-wife couples already share an experience of grace in the sacrament of matrimony; how a deacon taps that spiritual reservoir is something most priests, as celibates, need help to understand. The priest who ministers with or counsels a deacon or candidate will also have to be patient with a range of complications that arise from the different worlds in which the deacon or candidate lives and thrives. In particular, the rhythms of a deacon's life will not always be easily integrated with, or accommodating to, the structured routines that define parochial life. Yet most deacons, as well as their wives and families, make Church and ministry a priority that they strive to honor, mostly with success. Sensitivity to, and understanding of, the pressures a deacon faces will be among the forms of support a deacon most appreciates from a priest.

It is important for the priest to recognize the extent to which, like his own, a deacon's life is changed by his ordination. Deacons and wives describe the sometimes difficult choices they have to make, as well as the awkwardness of dealing with confusion on the part of family members, longtime friends, and colleagues—and all this while the deacon, his wife, and their family try to adjust to a different and often very demanding set of priorities that inevitably reorder previous commitments and relationships. This extends to a deacon's fellow parishioners, who may place him in uncomfortable situations as he appears now as an insider who renders "the Church" both *more* accessible and, perhaps, *too* accessible. The well-selected deacon should be able to deal properly with these stresses and tensions, particularly if his personality is not inflated by his clerical status or threatened by criticism. The priest can count on an instinctive loyalty from the deacon, but should allow the deacon leeway as he tries to respect both his former peers among the laity and his brother, the priest.

A priest must understand the degree to which a deacon's relationship with the Church and its other ordained and vowed personnel may expose him to the human dimension of the ecclesiastical reality in ways that may be puzzling or even disillusioning. The deacon may be confronted with evidence of personality flaws and of discrepancies between talk and practice that seem to border on hypocrisy. The priest, precisely as a priest, must relate to the deacon with deep sensitivity, realizing—most likely from his own experience of the same realities—the unique kind of pain and confusion that one who sincerely resonates to ideals will suffer in these circumstances. And, because the deacon's well-being also affects others, such as a wife and family members, the priest must exert a truly pastoral compassion in offering guidance and perspective that, in dealing honestly with the causes of such pain, also encourages movement toward healing and reconciliation.

As noted above, as a pastor now approaching the end of his term and conscious of the inability of the archdiocese to supply priests in the numbers we have been used to, I have explored ways of positioning the parish to find alternatives. The matter of seeking either to recruit a candidate for diaconal formation or to request the assignment of an already-ordained deacon has come up. I have had to explain to the parish pastoral council how I believe a deacon might most effectively serve the parish, and that has led me to review my understanding of the deacon's distinctive contribution. The temptation to see the deacon generally as a minister able to provide certain services that priests have provided up to now is just that—a temptation—and one that is not easily resisted. Of course, the presence of an ordained deacon would ease the burden to be expected when the parish faces a reduced number of assigned priests. That will require serious adjustments, both for the priest(s) and for parishioners. A deacon adds flexibility to the corps of Church personnel, to be sure. But I hope a pastor would not succumb to the temptation simply to replace a priest with a deacon, to the extent that a deacon could assume functions previously provided by a priest.

What, then, are some scenarios depicting how a deacon might *fruitfully* function in this parochial setting? In sacramental preparation, for example, should a deacon simply be assigned to "take his turn" leading the pre-baptism session for parents and godparents? Or, because a deacon is an ordinary minister of baptism, should the preparation be entrusted to him entirely? Might he be better utilized in the process by having him address the diaconal dimension of the Christian life and by talking with the parents about ways in which family life can awaken in a baptized child, even from a young age, a sense of responsibility for service rooted in charity? Since a deacon would most often be a parent himself, he, perhaps in company with his wife, would be well situated to lead this type of discussion.

In preparing children for first communion, should not the deacon be part of the formation process, again from the perspective of stressing the link between accepting the Lord's Body and Blood in the Eucharist and sharing his love with others through acts of compassionate service?[20] Before confirmation, should not the deacon be a resource and model for candidates whose formation includes service projects meant to help them explore how to identify and respond to human needs in the parish or community? In preparing the engaged for marriage, a deacon or deacon-and-wife couple could find an ideal ministry to share: in our culture, the engaged need inspiration and support in trying to envision their future married life as *exclusive* between the spouses but not *exclusionary* of others. Should not a deacon address with them the suggestions in the formulas for the final blessing in the Rite of Marriage? For example, "May you always bear witness to the love of God in this world, so that the afflicted and the needy will find in you generous friends." Or, "May you be ready and willing to help and comfort all who come to you in need. And may the blessings promised to the compassionate be yours in abundance."[21]

Another temptation for the priest is to value the deacon for the expertise he is often thought capable of bringing from his secular career to administrative aspects of Church life. The history of the diaconate shows an ancient link between the diaconate and the administration of the Church's material resources, primarily for the relief of the poor. But, rather than simply depute a deacon with accounting skills or managerial experience to oversee

Church administration, should we not utilize those gifts in a distinctively diaconal manner? For example, deacons often are expected to serve ex officio on parish or diocesan pastoral or finance councils.[22] Would not such bodies be more faithful to their missions if a deacon were to monitor their discussions and recommendations from the perspective of whether human needs are being adequately addressed? After all, the deacon has been entrusted in a special way with the "care of the soul" of the local Church in terms of its vitality in Christian service. The deacon will be most effective in this responsibility if he undertakes it from a stance of encouragement and suggestion. He will need to know that the bishop or pastor accepts and shares this sense of his role as a deacon, as a voice for those who have none, and as an embodiment of the lesson contained in Jesus' parable of the Last Judgment: "As you did for one of the least of my brethren, you did it to me."[23]

The deacon's whole ministry—its focus rooted in charity and given expression in the ministries of word and worship—is directed toward fostering the growth of the Church in faithful obedience to Jesus' command of mutual love.[24] With regard to liturgical preaching, I believe that the primary emphasis in a deacon's preaching should be promotion of the virtue of charity. If that is the central focus of his ministry, he should always be seeking ways to expand the community's sense of responsibility for carrying out Christ's mandate of charity. I believe that a deacon, in meditating on the scriptures, "sees" or "hears" different opportunities for highlighting the call to serve those in need. It would be a real contribution to the life of the community if, every time we heard a deacon, we came away with an insight into possibilities for responding to a need that his natural sensitivity, strengthened by the grace of orders, has helped us to recognize or feel with greater intensity and with the idea that some practical remedy is within our reach.

As much as, or perhaps even more than, deacons themselves, priests are positioned to have an enormous impact on the success of the Church's integration of the diaconate in its pastoral life. I say this because of the priest's role at so many points of significance for both the diaconate and for the individual deacon. As one responsible for the overall health of a parish—the basic communal unit where Catholics are formed, nourished, and connected with one another—a pastor or parochial vicar can secure the diaconate's future by understanding it and encouraging its authentic exercise within that setting. As the one who is sought most often for counsel by a prospective candidate for the diaconate, a priest can aid the discernment of a diaconal vocation and sharpen the focus of the man considering such a commitment. As a fellow minister, a priest can be a resource for assisting the deacon in negotiating the transition into a life of public ecclesial service.

The growth of the restored diaconate remains vulnerable, despite its impressive numbers, subject to competing claims on its identity in the maelstrom of forces trying to resolve the pastoral challenges facing the contemporary Church. I believe that the priest, during these times especially, is the most important friend a deacon and the diaconate can have. This is not to suggest that priests should be uncritical of the actual performance of deacons or reluctant to pose questions challenging the assumptions behind some expressions of diaconal ministry. Indeed, the priest needs to be the kind of committed friend who will be courageous enough to say what should be said, even if there is no inclination on the part of others to hear it.

The priest must also be brave enough to admit that the diaconate represents a force that, to some extent, will redefine our experience of priestly ministry in a Church in which many are gifted for service. Committed to living his own proper ministry faithfully and authentically, the priest can promote a flowering of many forms of ministry. He should recognize in the diaconate, participating in the threefold sacrament of holy orders, a ministry especially deserving of his respect and support, restoring to the Church's lived experience a resource for nurturing an essential element of her identity, something willed by Christ himself to equip her for faithfulness in proclaiming his kingdom of charity, justice, and peace.

# PART THREE
# The Spiritual Dimension

# The Spiritual Formation Path

## The Vision and Hope of the Director

## *David Dowdle*

Of the many gifts the *National Directory* holds for formation programs across the country, articulating an ever-developing theology of the diaconate is one of the greatest. From the *theology* of the order, the *spirituality* of the order can begin to emerge. The theology and spirituality of the order then begin to form boundaries for the identity of the deacon that help applicants and aspirants to discern, candidates to grow and develop, and deacons to more fully become icons of Christ the Servant.

No *Directory*, however, can reveal *all* the possibilities that lie within each of the four paths of inquiry, aspirancy, candidacy, and post-ordination. Personal growth, identity change, transformation, and conversion are constitutive elements of each path in *any* formation program. The director of formation needs a vision to see the potential that exists within each path in order for the overall program to be strengthened and improved, according to the norms and standards provided by the *Directory*. The vision that the director has will then better be able to draw from each participant in the formation process the gifts that God has in store for those who seek to serve his Church.

Many directors have trouble quantifying the spiritual formation path. Observable ministerial skills can be evaluated, but how does anyone measure spiritual growth? Unlike the intellectual path, there is no paper-and-pencil test that will result in a pass/fail outcome. While knowledge of theology can be a prerequisite and an essential element of spiritual growth, in and of itself knowledge is *not* an indicator of a life lived deeply in the Spirit. Relational skills, whether between husband and wife or minister and parishioner, can be observed, taught, or critiqued with a degree of objectivity. For instance, it is possible to describe the parameters that determine what "fair fighting" is in a marriage. Many directors cannot ask how to describe a similar dynamic in a spiritual relationship, other than by way of analogy to a human relationship. After all, we only "know" the human side of the divine-human relationship.

Hospital chaplains are certified by an arduous process involving supervision, peer feedback, and patient interaction. Many who feel called to become a hospital chaplain have great difficulty in meeting the standards necessary to become a *certified* hospital chaplain. Is it possible to be as rigorous in "certifying" someone for ordained ministry as a deacon? How can growth in a spiritual relationship be certified? And does certification accomplish this?

Elements of each path lend themselves to a checklist approach in trying to quantify what the formation program teaches and what the candidate has learned. Was this theology course taught or not? Did the candidate complete three soup-kitchen visits or not? At least on the surface, the yes/no answers of the checklist approach provide a starting point when comparing programs between dioceses or when a particular program engages in self-study. It can lead to curriculum changes, impact the calendar, affect financial and personnel resources, and bump up against time restraints and other limitations. The checklist can also give a sense of progress to the participant: "I am one third of the way done."[1]

A checklist approach may indeed be a starting point. But in regard to the spiritual dimension of diaconate formation, I suggest that the director needs a vision for the entire formation process in order to see why certain elements even make it to the list in the first place and what is hoped for as a result of including them. I will try and articulate what each director needs to "look for" in the spiritual dimension of the aspirancy and candidacy paths. By refining how the director can look for spiritual realities beyond the items on the check list, the process that is formation is more likely to yield what is hoped for by the *National Directory* and its emerging theology: deacons configured to Christ the Servant.

# Inquiry and Application Phase

Who applies to diaconate formation programs? By and large, it is men who are in midlife, chronologically and spiritually, and who may be either married or unmarried. (A whole untapped area for reflection is how living a married vocation influences spiritual formation. If seminary formation is the assumed model, then it assumes the candidate to be celibate/unmarried. What changes in spiritual formation should be made for the married candidate?) Whether a man is married or not, the director needs to "look for" where each individual is at in the process of spiritual maturity.

If the applicant is in the very beginning of midlife (mid-to-late thirties, early forties), he may very well still be in the ascendancy stage of development, needing to prove himself and his self-worth by "accomplishing" being ordained a deacon.[2] For this type of applicant, the formation process can be something to be survived or endured in order to attain the goal of being ordained. Becoming a deacon can be just the next mountain to be climbed and conquered, like acquiring an advanced academic degree or being the youngest man in the parish to become a Fourth Degree Knight of Columbus. This type of applicant needs to prove something, needs to have some kind of external validation that he is "good." His attitude may be that he deserves to be a deacon because he has earned it.

The applicant could also be moving out of midlife and into his senior years. He may have regrets about the price he paid to get where he is in life, sacrificing time with family and friends to be successful in business, and is now driven to make up for lost opportunities. Having achieved as much material success as his career will allow him, he now turns to the pursuit of deeper values and is often motivated by a desire to "give back." It is also possible that a man like this, driven by the need to give back will, ironically, continue to neglect his wife in order to pursue this dream. Becoming a deacon for this type of applicant is the conduit from which his generosity of time for others flows, especially if he is retired from full-time employment. He may see himself as having acquired some wisdom over the years, and he wants to utilize it for the benefit of others and, by doing so, enrich his relationship with God.

For the majority of those in midlife—somewhere between their early to mid-forties to their late fifties or early sixties—they are actively engaged in reexamining their life choices. Their marriages can be anywhere from good to great. (Some do come to formation programs hoping to make up what may be seriously lacking in their marriage. Using an inventory—or some other means—to help affirm that *only* strong marriages are accepted in a formation program is critical for both the spouse and the formation program.) These men are probably not going to get too many more promotions at work. Perhaps they are about to become empty nesters, or perhaps grandchildren are beginning to appear. Not that life is bad, but they begin to experience a desire for "more." Perhaps when they were younger, they had a desire to serve the Church as a priest, but they realized that marriage was their first, true vocation. They come to formation programs hoping that this "deacon thing" will lead them to greater intimacy with God (although they rarely, if ever, use that kind of language). They are willing to spend time and energy at growing in their faith, and they are secretly a bit proud that their pastor or others asked them if they had ever considered becoming a deacon.

One of the privileges of being engaged in formation ministry is meeting some truly wonderful people. There are no "bad" people who apply to formation programs. Quite the opposite: they are some of the best people from the parishes across the diocese. Most often these men are already leaders in their parish, and all they really want to do is to help other people and to do good things for Jesus. However, just because they are good people doesn't mean they should be deacons. That discernment is for a later time in the process. Right now, the question is what the director (and, by extension, the admissions and scrutinies board) should "look for" among the applicants. The director should look for men who are at various stages of spiritual development, who are somewhere on the continuum of midlife spirituality, and who are willing to have their faith challenged, deepened, and enriched in order to serve "the least, the last, and the lost."[3]

# The Aspirancy Path

Throughout the inquiry and aspirancy paths, particularly through the use of interviews and spiritual autobiographies, the director can begin to get hints of where the energy is coming from as an applicant pursues a vocation to the diaconate. In this initial stage of the formation process, what is the director supposed to "look for"? I suggest that the starting point is exploring the following assertion: *every religious vocation is rooted in human need.* A director will never find a response to that assertion if all that is looked at are biological data, sacramental records, personal references, and even ministerial experience, although each of those pieces may contain hidden clues to the bigger picture.

I have found over the years that when applicants tell their story, whether in an oral interview or in a written spiritual autobiography, they are remarkably candid and can be quite self-revealing. Was the applicant adopted? Did he go through a religious conversion (such as RCIA or AA)? Did he fail at a marriage relationship? What applicants often don't do is connect the dots from their individual story to their pursuit of a diaconal vocation. They may report that they enjoy teaching in a religious education program or being a lector at Mass, but they often miss that the human need they are trying to fulfill is tied, for example, to their grief for their father who died five years ago. They grieve the loss of his guidance in their life and miss the sound of his voice with its reassurance and fatherly protection. Ministry meets some of that need. They mistakenly hope the diaconate will fill the need completely.

In the aspirancy path, the director needs to determine if the aspirant has come as a teacher or as a learner to formation. Do they see themselves as a teacher, possibly even "complete," and spend much of the time that the group is together telling others "the truth," which is largely limited to *their* parish, *their* ministry, *their* experience? Or do they come as learners, open to seeing things differently and willing to suspend their own judgment or opinion long enough to see that they don't know everything, that they can learn more, that they need both confidence and flexibility?

I would often tell the aspirants that the skills, talents, and gifts that made them successful in their careers will be of absolutely no use to them in formation. When they first hear this, their reaction is anything from confusion to despair. You can almost hear them ask, "Then who, Lord, can be saved?" (Luke 18:26). The ones who are willing to ask themselves that question over and over again, who want to find others who might be able to help them find an answer, who are weak enough to try different ministries and different roles in the community, are usually the ones who will make good candidates for formation and ordination.

# The Role of the Spiritual Director

Being able to identify the *human* need that is driving the pursuit of a vocation is a necessary step, but it rarely can be identified at the beginning of formation. What does need to happen at the beginning is an initial relationship with a spiritual director. Ideally, this is a one-on-one relationship (rather than group spiritual direction, which may be the best a diocese can provide). Like any relationship, developing one with a spiritual director takes time. During the aspirancy path, since it is an initial relationship, there are several benchmarks that need to be made if the relationship is to serve the directee in discerning a vocation throughout the candidacy path.

Is there willingness or resistance to begin this relationship? To what degree is the directee capable of being honest in self-disclosing his life journey with the spiritual director? Is the directee skilled in reporting what happens in his personal prayer life? Can the director help the aspirant understand and appropriate the difference between praying with the Church (for example, Liturgy of the Hours) and private prayer? Does the aspirant have a balanced approach to the triple ministry of the deacon, or is he primarily focused on one aspect to the exclusion of the others? Is the directee willing to grow spiritually under the guidance of the director, which will require trust and vulnerability, or is he just meeting a requirement of the program by keeping his appointments?

The answers to these preceding questions are just some of the benchmarks that both the director and directee must hit before (or while) they are dealing with the fundamental discernment for the aspirancy: what is the man's need to be ordained a deacon? The *Directory* speaks clearly and quite accurately of how every vocation is a call from God. Not infrequently, applicants and aspirants will freely use this type of language about themselves: "I am called to the diaconate by God." During the beginning stages of formation, I rarely trust that the person who speaks this way knows what they are talking about. The reason is that, when you ask them to speak a little bit more about how or why they feel that God has called them to this ministry, they speak about *themselves* and not about God. Their responses are filled with things like "I've been involved with RCIA for ten years," or, "I get so much more out of ministry than I give to others," or, other "I" statements that are no doubt true, but also reveal that their focus is centered on themselves. (I wonder if the widespread availability of the *National Directory*, both in print and online, has been researched by applicants and provides the vocabulary for the responses about being called by God.) The *Directory* stresses the need for the applicant/aspirant to have this understanding of vocation but does not give any further indication of what exactly this means. Thus, some applicants "talk the talk" without demonstrating any insight into the deeper meaning of what is meant by being "called."

I rarely hear aspirants connect their vocation journey with trying to fill a "hole in the soul." Whether there are wounds from childhood (victims of abuse, still struggling with self-acceptance; or "children," trying to make up for disappointments they caused their parents); whether there is guilt from choices made while young adults (often involving drugs, sex, or the military); whether there is regret (from living for many years pursuing materialistic goals to the exclusion of any awareness of God in their life): aspirants who are in midlife are trying to correct their life map. They want to make better choices, holier choices, than they did when they were younger.

Quite often they are drawn inexorably into this correcting of their life's journey or rechoosing the priorities that characterizes their lives. Death, literal or metaphorical, is likely the driving force: They are numbed by years in the marketplace. A grandchild tragically dies. They bury their parents. They bury the dreams of their youth. Or publicity of the sexual abuse of minors by priests strips them of a naïve understanding of the institutional Church, and suddenly motivates them to "step up to the plate" and take an active role as part of the institutional Church they love.

# The Candidacy Path

As the candidacy path begins to unfold, so too does the importance of the role of the spiritual director. Those who generously serve in this capacity need to be proficient in spiritual direction, and they need the added depth and theological skill of a thorough understanding of what the vocation to the renewed diaconate is all about in the Church.

Being a spiritual director in a deacon formation program is quite different from being a spiritual director in a parish or campus setting. It is also different from being a spiritual director in the seminary. If the spiritual director does not have a clear theological understanding of *why* the diaconate is neither a gradation of lay ministry nor of priestly ministry (in other words, why the deacon is not "more than a lay minister but less than a priest"), the spiritual director will be of little help as the ongoing discernment of the deacon's vocation continues throughout the candidacy path. A huge area of silence in the *Directory* is the critical importance of forming spiritual directors to serve in deacon formation programs.[4]

*David Dowdle*

# The Spiritual Director's Vision
# of the Diaconate

The spiritual director needs to have a clear understanding of and appreciation for the separate sacramental and ministerial identity of the deacon. Before submitting names of qualified spiritual directors to the bishop for approval in the formation program, perhaps the director of formation needs a clear response from each potential spiritual director to the following question: "What is your passion for the diaconate?" This answer may help reveal how the spiritual director distinguishes the call of service to the diaconate, lay ministry, or priesthood.

Part of the training of spiritual directors for the formation program may include having the director of formation (or, where possible, the director of *spiritual* formation) give his or her vision for the diaconate. Spiritual directors will need to have prayed about and integrated their own vision of the diaconate before they are truly qualified to serve in this capacity for those in formation. It is impossible to pick up the early strands of a vocation to the diaconate in the beginning of a formation process unless the spiritual director has a clear understanding of some of the guideposts necessary. Herewith, a list of some, but obviously not all, of what the spiritual director needs to look for:

- If the deacon is "the Church's service sacramentalized,"[5] then ample evidence of a life lived in service to others should be obvious. But it is easy to mistake "busyness" for service. Just because a man devotes his discretionary free time to parish activities does not necessarily mean he is being of "service." He might simply like being in charge of committees or being perceived as the pastor's friend. Conversely, his career may intrinsically have a high degree of service as part of it—for example, teacher or police officer— but that doesn't automatically mean he is an excellent candidate for ordained ministry. What does he do with his time when he is *not* being paid?
- Most aspirants and candidates in the United States are

married. Where is there evidence of the aspirant's being of service in his marriage, to his spouse and children, or in his wider community?

- Attitudes of entitlement can come to the surface quickly. Ordination can be seen as something "owed" or "due" a man because he will have "earned" it by successfully completing a formation program.
- If the "ministry of charity and justice is most characteristic of the deacon,"[6] how is that ministry most characteristic of this aspirant or candidate? When an applicant needs to impress you with all his charitable activities, he tends to have little or no appreciation of what the Church teaches about *justice*.
- The aspirants and candidates I most enjoy being with are the ones who least *need* to be ordained deacons. Whether it is part of their spiritual tradition or not, theirs is an Ignatian approach to formation, wherein they are genuinely indifferent to being ordained. It is quite often not until the middle or end of the second year of candidacy when candidates (and wives, if fully participating) begin to trust the process enough to be able to say things like, "Even if they kick us out now, it will have all been worth it, we have grown so much." They have arrived at a heightened spiritual indifference.
- Conversely, the fear of rejection, of being found out as *not* being worthy of public ministry, of "failing" formation, of *not* earning the bishop's approval—all these will undermine any attempt at *real* conversion in the formation process. Fear will block openness. Being able to name this dynamic early in the spiritual-direction relationship might be key in moving past this common apprehension.

Spiritual directors who are grounded in the theology of the *National Directory* will be attentive to a balanced approach to the ministry of the deacon and will be less tempted to distort the formation process to their personal opinion of the ministry of the deacon. This doctrinal understanding of the diaconate has yet, in my opinion, to truly permeate an overriding vision and hope for the diaconate. It can begin with directors of formation not taking the *Directory* seriously enough and instead canonizing their own formation experience as being the template for all deacons in their diocese. The implementation of the *Directory* may simply require too much work to rethink an entire program that could be understaffed and/or under-resourced to begin with. The requirement of having a spiritual director is a direct result of the *National Directory*, yet it can be undermined by a lack of vision of the formation director or the spiritual director him- or herself. Let me give an example or two of how this looks in a program.

Say the spiritual director is also a pastor of a large, suburban parish. Twenty years ago, the parish had three priests: a pastor and two associate pastors. Now the pastor–spiritual director is the only priest, but he has a large lay staff to assist him in the administration of this busy parish, and they do quite well. That is, until it comes to actually celebrating weddings, baptisms, funerals, and the five weekend Masses. If, in his role as spiritual director, he allows himself to be driven by the pastoral need for help in presiding at liturgies, he may very well turn down the volume on those aspects of formation that emphasize evangelization and teaching. He may subconsciously determine a hierarchy of ministries for his directee that violates the spirit of the *triple munus* of the order. After all, he rationalizes, the parish has plenty of trained and qualified lay catechists that do an excellent job. There is no need for another member of the RCIA team, and there are other ways of recruiting parishioners to do sacramental preparation. What the parish needs is someone to do the ten to twenty-five baptisms after the five weekend Masses. (I have heard of more than one parish where all the baptisms are done by the deacons. I consider this kind of pastoral practice a threat to the identity of the deacon's vocation.) The pastor–spiritual director ends up emphasizing the deacon's ministry of the altar to the exclusion of the ministries of the word, of charity, and of justice based on his very real fear (as pastor) of being stretched too thin as the only ordained minister in the parish. He may end up forming a deacon who will never take his alb off.

The distortion of the three ministries can just as easily go another way. In this example, the spiritual director is pastor of a poor, urban parish. The human needs of the parishioners are crushing: they need assistance with food, clothing, and shelter. They need legal assistance of all kinds, from taxes (because they are often paid only in cash) to immigration law to legal protection from domestic violence. This pastor-spiritual director needs someone to organize the volunteers, relate to the local politicians and law enforcement agencies, walk the streets of the parish, and learn people's names and stories. The pastor–spiritual director also needs someone who has the time to work the food pantry, supervise the parish outreach program, and run the soup kitchen. Understanding church history, canon law, or Christology are not topics of daily conversation. The pastor–spiritual director may end up emphasizing the deacon's ministry of charity and justice to the exclusion of the ministries of word and altar. He may end up forming a deacon who will never put an alb on.[7]

Before submitting a spiritual director's name to the bishop to be approved for the formation program, the director of formation would do well to spend time forming the spiritual directors in the theology of the diaconate to help protect against these kinds of imbalances taking over the discernment process. If the spiritual director has an underdeveloped understanding of the theology of the restored diaconate, he will communicate that, consciously or unconsciously, to the directee. On the other hand, the fuller the understanding the spiritual director has of the vocation of the deacon, the more he will be able to help the directee to examine all aspects of the vocation that are necessary to freely petition ordination, if and when that time comes.

# Other Skills to Refine
# the Director's Vision

An interesting point of self-reflection for a director of formation might be to ask how and when he or she affirms participants and spouses or how and when confrontation occurs over the course of the program. Both are rich sources for uncovering what may be the core hidden values of the spiritual formation path. What do you praise? What do you fight against? Which are you more comfortable doing?

Many applicants, especially those who already have "the heart of a deacon," have a hard time identifying everything they are involved with that could be construed as part of a lifestyle that is focused on charity and justice. Serving others comes so naturally to them that they may not even recognize their activities as "service," because they are simply doing what they enjoy doing. The director needs to be a mirror for them, reflecting back all they are committed to that reveals someone who is already living a diaconal lifestyle.

At the same time, as long as human beings are involved in the ministerial enterprise, ego will be an issue. By midlife, no one comes without some kind of an awareness that there are always mixed motivations for getting involved in something. There is always a payoff of some kind. How is the motivation to be of service to others in creative tension with the need to be liked or respected by others? Cardinal George puts it succinctly: "The displacement of the ego necessary to serve faithfully and be content to be taken for granted as a servant is arrived at only through careful attention to spiritual development."[8]

# CHAPTER 9

---

# Themes for a Canonical Retreat

## The Spiritual Apex of Diaconal Formation

## *James Keating*

All diaconal formation, at least from inquiry through candidacy, culminates on the day of ordination. This day, however, only ends formation in its official preordination stages, since our formation in holiness continues until we die. All diaconal formation is ordered toward holiness and *not* simply attaining a new rank in the Catholic hierarchy or skill sets of competency. All such skills and competencies acquired in diaconal formation are to be rightly integrated into a heart desiring union with God. This desire, made manifest in the deacon's character, truly orients his ministry over the many years that lay ahead.

To prepare for ordination, the diaconal candidate is instructed to enter a retreat period (see *National Directory*, no. 236, as well as canon law, c. 1039, *Basic Norms*, no. 65). This five-day retreat is not an addendum to formation but its apex. During this retreat, the candidate is called to appropriate all he has learned during formation and host it within his heart. He is invited to listen most intently to the content of the retreat's conferences and integrate these with encounters he has had with Christ over the years of preparation. This retreat should be punctuated with silence and with the presence of the candidate's wife (if married), so he can be taken up into the fullness of love that has surrounded him and been given to him by God. This love is *not* meant simply for individual consolation; it is the food for the deacon's journey so he may not grow faint in doing the work of Christ.

As a further specification of the previous chapter on the spiritual formation of the deacon by Father David Dowdle, this chapter will explore the rich potential of the canonical five-day retreat preceding ordination. The hopeful result is that the diaconal candidates and their formators will consider their own disposition toward the retreat and its possibilities with due gravity. The following considerations are presented as *one thematic model* of such a retreat, one that is based upon the spirituality of the Ordination Rite, specifically the Prayer of Consecration, which is reproduced below. I could build a suitable canonical retreat upon many other foundations, such as the promises made to the bishop, a theology of ministry, or the deacon's relationship to priest and people. I chose *this* theme, however, because of the powerful call for conversion of character invoked within the Ordination Rite. In this way we can explore more deeply the call of the deacon to be a man of interior transformation and not simply one who performs ministerial acts.

# 1. Preparing for the Retreat

Ideally, the diaconal candidate should begin preparing for this canonical retreat by praying over the spiritual truths within the Ordination Rite itself. This could be done many months or weeks before but can also be used as a fruitful method of prayer in the days before the retreat begins. In his meditations, the candidate seeks to be with Christ, pondering the call Christ has given to him. To open himself to receive the call more fully, the candidate should speak with Christ on an intimate and personal level: Christ, I receive your call; from within this vocation, help me know you more deeply. Christ, I receive your call; over the years of service that lie before me, help me fully receive this vocation.

In so praying, the candidate becomes more open to the Holy Spirit, who wishes to drive the mystery of Christ more deeply into the deacon's heart. Pondering the rite before the retreat begins, the candidate prepares himself to be purified of residual concerns, anxieties, and doubts that might accompany him on retreat as a result of his own struggles and as an effect of the cultural matrix within which he lives and works. The diaconal candidate wants to always be aware that joy is released according to the proportion by which he receives his true vocation. Any interior preparation prior to the retreat will assist in deepening his capacity to receive the truth of his vocation in joy.

The essence of his vocation is expressed in the Ordination Rite, with particular direction found in the Prayer of Consecration. In this essay, I will meditate upon the portion of the Prayer of Consecration that follows below. This prayer and the themes it unfolds will guide my reflections and could serve as the content of the actual retreat conferences. Perhaps the candidate and his family could pray this Prayer of Consecration at home before he leaves for the retreat. In this way, each family member could pray for the success of the retreat and could support their father or husband as he goes away to be in prayer. It can also give the deacon candidate an occasion to express his gratitude to his family for all the years of sacrifice and support they have given to him throughout formation.

> **Bishop**: You established a threefold ministry of worship and service for the glory of your name. As ministers of your tabernacle you chose the sons of Levi and gave your blessing as their everlasting inheritance. In the first days of your Church under the inspiration of the Holy Spirit the apostles of your Son appointed seven men of good repute to assist them in the daily ministry, so that they themselves might be free for prayer and preaching. By prayer and the laying on of hands the apostles entrusted to those chosen men the ministry of serving at tables.

Lord, look with favor on this servant of yours, whom we now dedicate to the office of deacon, to minister at your holy altar.

Lord, send forth upon him the Holy Spirit, that he may be strengthened by the gift of your sevenfold grace to carry out faithfully the work of the ministry. May he excel in every virtue: in love that is sincere, in concern for the sick and the poor, in unassuming authority, in self-discipline, and in holiness of life. May his conduct exemplify your commandments and lead your people to imitate his purity of life. May he remain strong and steadfast in Christ, giving to the world the witness of a pure conscience. May he in this life imitate your Son, who came, not to be served but to serve, and one day reign with him in heaven.

We ask this through our Lord Jesus Christ, your Son, who lives and reigns with you and the Holy Spirit, one God, for ever and ever.

**R**. Amen.

Notice that the mission of the deacon underscores the type of moral character the ordinand is to possess, a character he is called to receive in grace. The only ministry recalled in the prayer is the one at the "holy altar." All the other themes focus upon the possession of the interior virtues a deacon needs to sustain him in service. As one begins the canonical retreat, it is good to rest with this powerful message. The Church understands the deacon's call to be one of becoming, first, *a certain kind of man* to which various activities, ministries, and services will then be entrusted. The virtues the bishop begs the Holy Spirit to bestow upon the deacon are the soil from which his service will grow. All the formation in theology, pastoral/field education, psychological/affective studies, and spiritual direction risks being reduced to *skills acquired by schooling* if the soil of the deacon's character is not well nourished by a love for holiness and a share in the life, death, and resurrection of Christ. In other words, *if he refuses to allow the Spirit to transfigure his character, the deacon risks becoming a mere ecclesial technician.*

Before the final retreat, the candidate must embrace the reality that Christ wants to re-create him into a new man: a man now dead to the world (lying on the floor of the cathedral) and alive to Christ (eager to receive the re-creation wrought by the Holy Spirit). Entering the canonical retreat, the candidate should be communicating to God that he is ready, not for new tasks, but for a new interiority. Ministries that perhaps the candidate cannot even foresee will flow from such a transformed heart; they lie dormant within him and are stirred into flame only by his will to cooperate in trust with God's ideas for his future. Since the grace of God will utilize the formation given in the deacon's formal training, these competencies will be the foundation upon which the Holy Spirit will build the man's true vocation. Only from *within* his studies can a deacon be weak before the Holy Spirit, not *in spite* of such studies. In this current culture, the deacon needs to submit to deeper spiritual and theological studies relevant to his unique vocation, not an academic sequence that "cuts corners." When the candidate rises from the cathedral floor, it is no longer his life. He is instead offered as a mission for the Father to use as he sees fit in fostering the kingdom on earth.

All formation up to this point of the retreat is found echoed in Luke 13:6–9:

> Then he told this parable: "A man had a fig tree planted in his vineyard; and he came looking for fruit on it and found none. So he said to the gardener, 'See here! For three years I have come looking for fruit on this fig tree, and still I find none. Cut it down! Why should it be wasting the soil?' He replied, 'Sir, let it alone for one more year, until I dig round it and put manure on it. If it bears fruit next year, well and good; but if not, you can cut it down.'"

A man's reaching the point of ordination indicates that the Church saw fruit being produced in his formation process. This scripture from Luke underscores that the deacon candidate must enter the passing of time that is the process of formation. Such formation is not a biding of his time but a time of cultivation, of engagement with the nutrients of the formation process. Obviously, the source of the nutrients is the Vine (John 15:1). The gardener in Luke cultivates and prunes and waters, hoping for fruit to emerge from *within* the tree. As the candidate enters this final retreat, he asks, "Am I secure in my communion with the Vine? Do I receive my nutrients from him and him alone? Do I yield my interiority to him and ask for his Spirit, the Spirit of Life, so that I might give witness in public from a pure heart and bear fruit for the kingdom?"

Americans are very interested in being active and accomplishing set goals; we like to put another notch on our belt. So American deacons will assuredly *do a lot*. This retreat, however, with its focus on the Prayer of Consecration, casts our eyes in a different direction: *within*. This retreat, with the Prayer of Consecration as its center, is inviting the will not to act but to make a commitment to endure an interior life in communion with the mystery of Christ. Can the candidate endure the spiritual life, the interior life, that cultivates and gives life to his ministerial activities? The Prayer of Consecration makes it plain that the Church is not looking for another group of generous men, men who do good things: the Church has those in many quarters. Instead, the Church is looking for a group of *spiritual* men, men who live from the inside-out, who regularly offer their hearts to Christ as places for him to come into and live his mysteries. The deacon must learn to endure this coming of Christ and, after doing so, witness to the effect that such an interior life has on the larger life of Church and society.

This final retreat during diaconal formation presents a unique opportunity to the participants to affectively receive in Christ all that the intellect has discovered during theological studies. In other words, the retreat is the time to appropriate fully what was labored over intellectually. The retreat invites the man to prayerfully ask God for the insight and strength to *become* the deacon he is called to be.

# 2. The Prayer of Consecration as the Heart of the Retreat

## Waiting on the Table of the Lord and the Call to Imitate Christ

The Prayer of Consecration indicates that the deacon is to serve **at** *the table of the Lord*. This table is the altar of Christ's own sacrifice. As Christ emptied himself and welcomed death, the deacon is called to empty himself and let the Father "raise" him. To be raised by the Father is to recognize that the work accomplished in such a new life is effected not *by* the deacon but *in him by Christ's Spirit*. Any ministry the deacon enters is thus cooperatively his, but it comes as a gift, and its power orders the recipient of such gifts toward God. The deacon is eager to have his gifts so ordered because, previous to his ordination, he was healed or is being healed of any disproportionate need to be needed. He stands at the table concerned about what Christ is concerned about, not what satisfies *him*, per se. Such freedom is attained by any candidate who truly enters the formation process. The deacon, then, stands at the Lord's table, the place of Christ's own self-giving, and in freedom desires to allow that mystery to enter and define him. He stands at the table, not exercising the priesthood of Christ, but sharing in the *diakonia* of Christ. The deacon is rendered available to both Christ and the needs of others so that *Christ's own self-gift is given* in diaconal service. The deacon becomes eager to say, "I have to give myself *in Christ's own self-gift*. The *power is* Christ's; the *cooperation* with such power *is my gift* to him and his Church."

To serve tables is not restricted to a popular idea of the deacon being always in the physical presence of materially deprived citizens in a manner that will best serve their needs. To serve tables in imitation of Christ also alludes to the deacon's kenotic ministry of letting the word speak through him, as symbolized by his ministry of the word at the Eucharistic Liturgy. The deacon is entrusted with the word of God upon his ordination. He is not entrusted with a soup spoon. The word that he is entrusted with must work its way into his heart in a way that makes him vulnerable to its power, fashioning in him the mind of Christ. This is a suffering that a deacon undergoes in his formation, as we are all normally more hospitable to sin than to grace. Mutually interpenetrating in the heart of the deacon are the word he receives and the poor he receives. Both are a fire that burns and purifies his ego in defiance of its relentless intrusion. Wherever the deacon ministers, and to whomever he brings the word, his own purification is being accomplished. The deacon brings not his own word, like a pompous intellectual, but a word that has burned its way into his heart, a word that is not his own, a word that has changed and is changing him from within. He delivers this word, which is not of his own making, with reverence and care because it bears the power of the Son and issues from the mouth and heart of God. In the power of the Son, the deacon imitates the Son.

In this understanding of waiting tables, the deacon prayerfully attends to his post at the altar of the Eucharist, not praying the prayers of the priest, but praying the prayers of the Church and his own prayers. Primarily, he carries prayers of intercession silently in his heart, spoken in the name of the Church at the Prayers of the Faithful (the General Intercessions). In the deacon, the Lord desires to be with his people *in their need*. The deacon cooperates in bringing a word of hope to all as he goes about his service in the middle of the secular culture of work, health care, law, education, labor, and more. As Christ descends upon the deacon at ordination, he is also descending upon the culture. In this way Christ continues to wait on the tables of human need through the deacon's receptivity to Christ's life, death, and resurrection. In this cooperation with grace, the deacon extends the presence of Christ so that, in and through the sacrament of orders, Christ presides still, in time, at the *liturgy of charity*. The deacon possesses no unique power by virtue of ordination but possesses a mission in being sent by the bishop; he *evokes from others* the power that is theirs by baptism.

Further, the Prayer of Consecration speaks of the deacon *imitating Christ*. To live such a life is impossible without a movement from within to yield to Christ's Spirit. This yielding is the prerequisite for any imitation. Any imitation of Christ is only the fruit of such yielding, a yielding that is truly a mystery. In this mystery the deacon gives himself *in Christ's own self-gift* to the Church. He is caught up in Christ and lives out this intimacy in a discerning manner: he makes his actions the fruit of prudence aimed at service to the Church.

This habit of yielding to the Spirit from within produces virtue within the deacon born of a deepening intimacy with Christ. Not everything Christ shares within the heart of a deacon is meant for public knowledge in preaching, counseling, or teaching. Some communication between the deacon and Christ is personal, for his own consolation and edification. The *character* of the deacon, however, is *never* veiled and is *always* present. Two graces are given to the recipients of the deacon's ministry as he serves the Church in manifold ways: a glimpse into the *diakonia* of Christ in the *actual service* rendered by the deacon and a glimpse into the effects of such divine indwelling as seen *in the character* of the deacon himself. In this way the deacon's presence ministers healing in both his *doing* and his *being*. To imitate Christ is to be regularly turning to the Father and listening intently.

Most vitally, this deacon welcomes Christ's movements and stirrings within his own conscience, prompting him to bear the power of the paschal mystery into the deepest cracks and crevices of popular and economic culture. Here among the laity, as one who *lives their life*, the deacon assists the laity to *endure the word* in its coming in truth, as he is also attempting. To endure the coming of the word is to beg God to give the strength to receive the truth and, once received, to give witness to it.

To serve in such a way is the rhythm of the deacon's mission, a rhythm that positions him to assist at the mystery of the altar and to assist in the mystery of developing lay holiness. Facilitating both mysteries to their end—rightful praise and worship of God—is the dignity and meaning of a deacon's being present in both spheres. These spheres are not separate but joined in and through the mystery of Christ's kenosis, his pouring himself out for and among human beings. In some simple but real way, the presence of an ordained man embedded in secular culture carries a grace from and at the service of this mystery of Christ's own pasch.

The deacon serves the table of the Lord and imitates Christ as a sacramentalized service. The deacon *is a mission*[1] that he carries from the altar to the larger Church, laboring in the culture to bring forth an image of Christ in our time. The presence of an ordained minister in the secular world assists the laity in receiving their own call to sacramentalized service: one that grows out of baptism and their participation in the Eucharist.[2] The sacramental configuration of the deacon to Christ, the servant, *permanently* identifies the deacon and characterizes his place in the Church. The deacon stands at the altar to be impressed with the mission of the Christ so that, in imitation of him, he may go out to bear that mission in service. The canonical retreat leads the deacon candidate to welcome this permanent configuration.

## The Witness of a Pure Conscience

Further on in the Prayer of Consecration, the bishop invokes God to give the deacon the *strength in Christ* to witness to the world a *pure conscience*. On the canonical retreat, the candidate wants to pray specifically to receive this strength from the Holy Spirit. Throughout the spiritual history of the Catholic Church, the saints have given regular testimony that, when a man is called to service in the name of the Church, he is oftentimes tempted to infidelity, despair, or cynicism. The many years of formation have hopefully instilled within the deacon candidate the interior resources from which to draw strength to enact his calling, so as to struggle against these and other temptations. Primarily, the conscience is made pure by its participation in the mystery of Christ, a participation that entails an ever-renewed commitment to prayer, despite any feelings to the contrary. The conscience is the love-imbued mind discerning questions about right and wrong behavior. This mind is not a separate faculty within the deacon's spiritual life. The conscience is the core of a person who receives the love of Christ and welcomes that love as the agent of change in all his or her thinking. All conversion passes through the love-imbued mind, the mind that has pondered the mystery of Christ and received its truth and love, by way of reason and affect.

The concept of purity carries with it a mistakenly narrow view of its meaning as being associated solely with the sexual life. More richly, however, it points to a mind that is filled with the fruits of intimacy with Christ. The impure conscience is the vain conscience, one that gives no thought of God and God's ways but rather strives for "independence." A man, on the eve of his ordination, wants to flee from any false understanding of independence, such as that which is articulated in political and academic circles. For many, independence means a false liberation from sources of truth outside one's own affections or ratiocinations. However, the deacon desires to have communion with the truth-bearing sources of the Church. *Communion is independence* for the cleric, communion with Christ and Church. For the pure mind to displace the vain mind, the deacon clings to his paradoxical freedom; he is only free when he is bound! Unlike some strains of political ideology, the deacon *wants* to associate with Christ *in obedience*. The deacon does not want to flee from associating with the Church of Christ in the spiritual and moral life; he only wants to flee from sin.

No deacon is ordained to share his own ideas. What makes the deacon a spiritual leader in his diocese, and not simply a humanitarian, is the ascetical feature of his ecclesially formed heart. The asceticism that each deacon is invited into consists in coming to suffer the indwelling of God's word as *his only word*. This is experienced as a suffering because persons favor their own preferences to the objective truth that is Christ.

This is not to say that the deacon cannot be creative or pose questions regarding scripture or Church teaching. It simply means that all creativity and all questions are to serve the end of truth and not vanity. Having the word of God as his only word means that the deacon is more disposed to be *questioned by* the word than to *pose questions*. In the Prayer of Consecration, the bishop invokes the Spirit, asking him to make the deacon steadfast in Christ. Fidelity to Christ, who is the Word, is the privileged mark of the deacon's character. It only becomes a burden to be steadfast and true to Christ if sin obscures his view of truth, orienting his affections toward the ego or ideologies of the current age. The pure conscience does not cling to personal preferences when the truth comes to be known. During the canonical retreat, praying for purity—the resting of the mind in communion with Christ—is sure ground upon which to establish a vocation of selfless service.

# 3. The Ordination Retreat and the Deacon's Care of the Chalice

The deacon serves at the table of the Lord as one who cares for the Blood of Christ. He is entrusted with the cup at the minor elevation and with the distributing of holy communion. He is also entrusted with the purifying of the sacred chalice and other vessels when the Liturgy of the Eucharist concludes. The deacon's piety has an invigorating source in his meditations on the self-offering of Christ upon the cross—shedding his blood out of love for the world—and in obedience to his heart listening to the Father. During the canonical retreat, the ordination candidates might want to allow the previous themes from the Prayer of Consecration (service at the table, the invitation to imitate Christ, and the call to possess a pure conscience) to coalesce with this powerful theme from diaconal piety: the deacon is linked to the Blood of Christ. The Letter to the Hebrews states it this way, "How much more will the blood of Christ, who through the eternal Spirit offered himself without blemish to God, purify our conscience from dead works to worship the living God!" (9:14). Liturgically, it is the Blood of Christ that purifies the conscience. The life of God, in other words, washes over and in and through the love-imbued mind orienting it toward the truth, which is the mystery and person of Christ. This Blood, this life of God, has been symbolically entrusted to the deacon. As St. Lawrence the deacon (d. 258) was entrusted with the treasures of the Church of Rome in their temporal form, so *all* deacons are entrusted with *the* treasure of the Church in one of its sacramental forms: the Cup of Salvation.

This treasure is not for hording, however: it is meant to flow into the heart and intoxicate the conscience with an attraction toward the holy. As Pio Cardinal Laghi once described:

> Since you are Deacons, by virtue of your service so close to the altar where Christ's sacrifice is consumed and where the bread is transformed into the Body of the Lord and the wine into his Blood, and since you are called to touch the Body and Blood of Christ with your hands and distribute them to the faithful, you have the unique opportunity to become like Christ, the "deacon" who made himself "everything for everyone," and to receive from him support, firmness and perfection.[3]

By virtue of the deacon's status as one who serves at the altar, he is called to imitate him whose Blood he consumes and distributes. It is an imitation that leads him to fill his own conscience with the mystery of the cross and resurrection, a mystery he then serves, in turn, at the altar of daily work, commitment, and sacrifice. The deacon holds the Blood, consumes the Blood, and then publicly confesses that he lives by the Blood that is given to him in the Spirit, the Spirit who broods over the sacrifice of the Holy Eucharist.[4]

Within the canonical retreat, it is crucial for the deacon candidate to embrace this mystery of his relationship with the sacrificial Blood of Christ, Christ's own life given for all. Christ's *gift* upon the cross can bestow upon the deacon candidate a symbolic entryway into intimacy with the One who called him to serve in his name. This gift is shared at the very table of sacrifice at which the deacon is invited to serve. The candidate will want to adhere to the retreat facilitator's invitation to appropriate a deeper configuration of vocation. Here, utilizing the Prayer of Consecration and the mystery of the deacon's affiliation with the Blood of Christ, he can gain access to the paschal mystery by way of the diaconal vocation. This mystery is, of course, the font for all who desire intimacy with Christ, but the deacon must approach it with a unique supplication: "Lord, how might I minister your life-blood in the Church and as a healing agent in the culture? Lord, help me to be filled with your life, so that I might be an envoy of life and hope to the culture."

Here we see the reality of *kenosis*, the deacon's sharing in the self-giving of Christ, mingled with the power of the Eucharist and the deacon's participation in this same liturgy.[5] The vocation that the deacon is called to enter, and to invite others to enter by way of his service, is the mystery of Christ shedding his own blood, a mystery of self-emptying even unto death, a mystery that no human can enter unless and until that very same mystery of Christ has come to make its home in the conscience, in the heart. During the ordination retreat, the candidate would do well to let this self-emptying of God in Christ visit him at the Eucharist. Within this encounter the deacon wants to cry, "Live this mystery again in me so that I might bring hope to those who live in the darkness of sin, suffering, and seclusion." Remembering that the Prayer of Consecration establishes the ordination of a deacon upon what God wants to do to *the character of the man* and not upon a commission to go about and be busy, the candidate would do well to let this kenotic mystery enter him in silence so as to bring him to *interior change*, a change of heart, a transformation that will give birth to peace, a peace out of which will flow all future ministry.

The purpose of diaconal formation is to create an opportunity for a man to be moved by God into a new life. This new life is characterized by the deep belief that God is thinking about the candidate's own needs so that now *he* is free to think about the needs of others. This is the blood that flows through the deacon, the blood of a new life of freedom, a divine freedom received according to the man's capacity to trust in faith. To submit to formation is to submit to the power of the Spirit, who effects a new interiority, a conscience born of the Blood of Christ, born of cooperation with grace, a grace that kills the fat and relentless ego and gives way to a secured peace. It is an interior peace, not built upon his own capacities but built upon his own self-gift to be used by God in His work of saving others from sin.

# Conclusion: The Ordination Retreat and Being Grafted onto the Mission of the Church

Finally, the canonical retreat should be an opportunity to allow the Spirit to search the deep places of the soul and raise up within the candidate a true knowledge of his own gifts, gifts he now puts at the disposal of the Church. Keeping in mind the Prayer of Consecration, the deacon should see that these gifts will be the energies that produce external acts, beyond the acts themselves. Each candidate, as a result of years of spiritual direction, should be a man comfortable with dwelling in his soul. As a result of such living, he is familiar with the graces given by God. What particular grace does the candidate think God is going to release in his ministry? What gift does the candidate desire? The candidate is invited to ask God to complete the good work he has already begun in this time of formation. He wants God to continue purifying him of sinful affections and releasing him to love what is good and true and holy. In this deepest of desires, to be a holy deacon, the candidate glimpses the true end of his vocation: to be a man who shares in the life of God for the healing and benefit of the Church and culture. With a burning desire for holiness, the candidate is now ready to be ordained because he has died and his life is now hidden with Christ in God.

# PART FOUR

# The Intellectual Dimension

# The *National Directory* and the Educational Formation of Deacon Candidates

## *Michael J. Tkacik*

## The *Directory* and the Ecclesiology of the Second Vatican Council

The United States Conference of Catholic Bishops' *National Directory for the Formation, Ministry, and Life of Permanent Deacons in the United States* (hereafter, the *Directory*) situates the Second Vatican Council's restoration of the permanent diaconate (*Lumen Gentium*, no. 29) against the backdrop of the Council's wider ecclesiological vision. This vision deposits that the Church is missionary by nature (*Ad Gentes*, no. 2) and a communion (*Lumen Gentium*, nos. 13, 17) of God's people (*Lumen Gentium*, nos. 9, 15–16) on pilgrimage (*Lumen Gentium*, no. 48; *Gaudium et Spes*, nos. 11, 21, 39, 43–44, 57, 62) within the world, serving as a sacrament of Christ (*Lumen Gentium*, no. 1; *Gaudium et Spes*, nos. 21, 42, 45). Such ecclesiological contextualization of the diaconate is due, in part, because the diaconate is deemed by the bishops to be *the driving force for the Church's service toward Christian communities and as a sign or sacrament of the Lord Christ himself* (*Directory*, no. 3). Deacons are in microcosm what the Church is in macrocosm—sacrament of Christ—and are uniquely able to build community within the Church and inspire service among the faithful.

# The Uniqueness of the Deacon

These unique ministerial possibilities of the deacon flow from the fact that deacons are members of the clergy by ordination and yet are frequently employed in the secular sphere:

> This combination of an ordained minister with a secular occupation and personal and family obligations can be a great strength, opportunity, and witness to the laity on how they too might integrate their baptismal call and state in life in living their Christian faith in society. (*Directory*, no. 56)

> The deacon may have a particular advantage in bringing this message to the laity because he lives and works in the secular world. The deacon, because of his familiarity with the day-to-day realities and rhythms of the family, neighborhood, and workplace, can relate the rich tradition of Catholic social teaching to the practical problems experienced by people. He also may serve to link the Catholic Church to other Christian communities, other faith traditions, and civic organizations to address pressing social needs and to foster a collaborative sharing of material resources and personnel in response to those needs. The deacon, as a servant of the Church's ministry of charity and justice, helps the faith community to understand and carry out its baptismal responsibilities. (*Directory*, no. 67)

Therefore, the deacon, if well-formed, can do much to facilitate and foster the wider ecclesiological vision proffered by the Second Vatican Council.

*Michael J. Tkacik*

# Deacons and the Laity

A principal way in which deacons facilitate the realization of Vatican II's ecclesiological vision is by actively promoting the lay apostolate (*Directory*, no. 57).

> In his preaching and teaching, the deacon articulates the needs and hopes of the people he has experienced, thereby animating, motivating, and facilitating a commitment among the lay faithful to an evangelical service in the world. (*Directory* 58)

One of the most significant teachings accentuated by the Second Vatican Council focuses on the central role that the laity plays in the Church's efforts to serve as a sacrament of Christ to the world (see *Apostolicam Actuositatem*; also *Lumen Gentium*, nos. 31–35). Baptism makes all of the lay faithful sharers in the priestly, prophetic, and kingly ministries of Jesus (*Lumen Gentium*, no. 31). This trifold dignity has implications for the laity *ad intra* (within the inner life of the Church) and *ad extra* (in the Church's apostolate of justice in the world). *Ad intra*, the laity are empowered by baptism for greater participatory roles in the sacramental life of the Church (*Sacrosanctum Concilium*, nos. 7, 11, 14; *Lumen Gentium*, nos. 10, 34) and are guided by the Spirit in matters of faith as members of the *sensus fidelium* (*Lumen Gentium*, no. 35). *Ad extra*, the laity are empowered by baptism to live a life of holiness within the world (*Lumen Gentium*, nos. 33, 36; *Apostolicam Actuositatem*, nos. 2, 7), exercising their apostolate via infusing and impregnating the secular realm with the values and spirit of the gospel (*Apostolicam Actuositatem*, no. 5).[1]

As the *Directory* indicates, the USCCB (United States Conference of Catholic Bishops) envisions that, given their unique status, identity, and function within the ecclesial community, deacons have an indispensable part to play in bringing the laity to an understanding of their baptismal dignity and the implications that such dignity has for their roles in the Church and in the Church's mission to the world (*Directory*, no. 252). The deacon plays a significant part in the faith formation of the laity and thus in advancing the ecclesial vision of the Second Vatican Council.

The Church and its adult faithful have a mission in and to the world: to share the message of Christ to renew and to transform the social and temporal order. This dual calling to evangelization and justice is integral to the identity of the lay faithful; all are called to it in baptism. Accordingly, faith formation seeks to help each adult believer become more willing and able to be a Christian disciple in the world.[2] The affinity between the lived experience of the laity and that of deacons (frequently married/family men with secular occupations), coupled with the increasing roles of the deacon within the Church's sacramental economy (which, for the majority of the laity, is their primary point of contact with the Church), heightens the ability of and the need for deacons to educate and motivate the laity to live out their baptismal dignity and apostolate.

# Diaconal Formation

If the diaconate is, indeed, linked to the missionary dimension of the Church via the trifold diaconal ministries of word, liturgy, and charity carried out in daily life (*Directory*, no. 85), then the renewal of the permanent diaconate must involve a formation process that illuminates these ecclesiological understandings of the Church, the laity, and the Church's mission to the world, and the roles and responsibilities deacons have in bringing these to realization (*Directory*, nos. 3, 43, 107).

> The establishment or renewal of diaconal ministry within a diocesan Church needs to be conceived and established within an overall diocesan plan for ministry in which the diaconate is seen as an integral component in addressing pastoral needs. (*Directory*, no. 257)

> The diocese should provide appropriate structures for the formation, ministry, and life of deacons. (*Directory*, no. 60)

It was precisely to secure this end that the USCCB produced the *Directory*:

> The specifications published in the *Directory* are to be incorporated by each diocese of the conference when preparing or updating its respective diaconal formation program. (*Directory*, no. 14)

In order to form deacons in a manner that would, in turn, enable them to facilitate the Church's mission, the USCCB identified four constitutive dimensions of diaconal formation: human, spiritual, intellectual, and pastoral (*Directory*, no. 104). Consistent with Vatican II's *Declaration on Christian Education* (*Gravissimum Educationis*), true education is deemed by the bishops as aiming at the formation of the human person so as to enable one to contribute to the good of society.[3] Catholic education is understood as fostering dialogue between the Church and the world, contributing to the betterment of culture and the renewal of the Church.[4] These aims of education—forming persons, edifying the common good, promoting dialogue between the Church and the world— echo the *Directory's* aims for diaconal ministry.

## The Human Dimension

Development of the human dimension of diaconal formation requires that—

> formation processes need to be structured so as to nurture and encourage the participants to acquire and perfect a series of human qualities which will permit them to enjoy the trust of the community, to commit themselves with serenity to the pastoral ministry, to facilitate encounter and dialogue. (*Directory*, no. 109)

As diaconal formation programs are developed and implemented, complementary and collaborative relationships among the various parties involved in forming deacon candidates— parish community, diocesan administrators, educators, and others

—will need to be created and fostered to ensure that the human dimension of formation is being actualized in each of these pertinent areas and loci of future diaconal ministry.

## Spiritual Formation and Aspirancy

Inherent in the spiritual dimension of diaconal formation is the cultivation of attitudes, habits, and practices that will serve as the foundation for lifelong spiritual discipline (*Directory*, no. 110), as well as spiritual guidance that illuminates specific traits of diaconal spirituality (111). The objectives of spiritual formation are directed toward edifying the deacon's prayer life; deepening his commitment to God, to the Church, to married or celibate life, and to the world; acquainting him with the spiritual tradition of the faith; and empowering him to incarnate spirituality in his day-to-day encounters (113).

Such maturation in spiritual development presupposes that the diaconal candidate has first received assistance in discerning his vocational call to the diaconate via an aspirancy period (*Directory*, nos. 182, 186).

> Discernment is an essential spiritual process in determining the presence of a vocation to the diaconate, as well as the capacity to live it fully after ordination. The spiritual dimension of formation, therefore, should assist the participant in assessing the depth and quality of his integration of personal, family, employment, and ministerial responsibilities. Further, it should assist his growth in self knowledge, in his commitment to Christ and his Church, and in his dedication to service, especially to the poor and those most suffering. (*Directory*, no. 114)

> During this period of discernment, the aspirant is to be introduced to the study of theology, to a deeper knowledge of the spirituality and ministry of the deacon, and to a more attentive discernment of his call. This period is also a time to form an aspirant community with its

own cycle of meetings and prayer. Finally, this period is to ensure the aspirant's regular participation in spiritual direction, to introduce him to the pastoral ministries of the diocesan Church, and to assist his family in their support of his formation. (*Directory*, no. 187)

In all, the aspirancy period ought to be marked by helping the candidate to discern his call, develop the skills needed to mediate Christ to others, cultivate a Christ-like disposition, and engage in theological reflection (*Directory*, nos. 189, 191, 196–97).

Here at our home institution, Saint Leo University in Florida, we work together with our diocesan partners to create an aspirancy period that strives to foster these objectives. As the *Directory* points out, prayer, discernment, spiritual direction, and exposure to ecclesial tradition are integral dimensions of the aspirancy period. The university and our diocesan partners work together to ensure that the candidates are afforded each and every one of these dimensions. We created a first-year curricular track devoted to the history, theology, and spirituality of the diaconate, which is offered with, and in a manner meant to complement, the *ad intra* formation processes of our diocesan partners. Together, we are creating an aspirancy period and process consistent with that envisioned by the *Directory*; that is, one that grounds the candidates in tradition, nurtures their spiritual development and discernment, and exposes them more deeply to the history, theology, and nature of the diaconate. Conducted in such a manner, the aspirant and diocese are both able to better discern the candidate's call to be a deacon.

## Intellectual Formation

Given the importance of, and the demands involved in, the deacon's role in helping to promote community within the Church and bring to realization the Church's missionary task of being a sacrament of Christ to the world, the bishops paid extensive attention to the intellectual formation of deacons:

The *National Directory* and the Educational Formation

An increasingly educated society and the new roles of leadership in diaconal ministry require that a deacon be a knowledgeable and reliable witness to the faith and a spokesman for the Church's teaching. Therefore, the intellectual dimension of formation must be designed to communicate a knowledge of the faith and church tradition that is "complete and serious," so that each participant will be prepared to carry out his vital ministry. (*Directory*, no. 118)

Such an intellectual formation demands that the academic study of theology be a primary and rigorous dimension of the formation process (*Directory*, nos. 118, 218). As Deacon Charles Bobertz observes: "The fact is that it takes more and better theological education than ever before to authentically present the church in the modern world."[5] Therefore, programs of theological study must equip deacons with the understanding of, and ability to communicate, the essentials of the faith in their sacramental roles and within their own sociocultural context. Additionally, a familiarity with Catholic social thought, an ecumenical sensitization, and a missiological disposition ought to also characterize such programs of study (*Directory*, nos. 119, 121, 131, 132, 144, 146, 149–52).

The intellectual formation is accentuated in the *Directory*, for it is deemed vital to preparing diaconal candidates for their pastoral service and it is the means by which they receive the knowledge and skills needed to successfully fulfill the trifold diaconal ministry of word, sacrament, and charity (*Directory* 120). To ensure this end, the bishops identify core content that is to comprise programs directed toward the intellectual formation of deacons. Such content includes scripture, patrology, Church history, fundamental theology (revelation and method), dogmatic theology (Christology, pneumatology, and anthropology), ecclesiology, morality, spirituality, sacramentology, canon law, ecumenism, and evangelization (*Directory*, no. 124). In light of this core content, the bishops charge those responsible for preparing the academic component of the candidate with determining a course of study that complies with this content prior to ordination, as well as a course of study that will further develop this content after ordination as part of a structured post-ordination program for continuing education and formation. (*Directory*, no. 125)

This articulation by the bishops in the *Directory* regarding the intellectual formation of deacon candidates served to inform the master of arts degree program in theology here at Saint Leo University, for our graduate theology program was created as a means to serve the Church in the process of diaconal formation. Having the *Directory* as a guiding template enabled us to develop a program and curriculum capable of meeting the intellectual needs of future deacons, as envisioned by the bishops. Toward this end, our curriculum was developed to ensure adequate exposure to the content fields outlined by the bishops in the *Directory*. The *Directory* and its appendices can serve any program as a tool when considering curricular development intended for diaconal formation.

## Pastoral Formation

In addition to candidates being competent intellectually, the bishops desire them to be pastorally prepared to put their knowledge into praxis via daily building up the Church (*Directory*, no. 130). Pastoral formation is intended to complement spiritual and intellectual formation via concretizing the charism of *diakonia* (*Directory*, nos. 126, 129).

Additionally, pastoral formation

should strengthen and enhance the exercise of the prophetic, priestly, and servant-leadership functions—deriving from his baptismal consecration—already lived and exercised by the participant in diaconal formation. In each path in formation, they must be taught how to proclaim the Christian message and teach it, how to lead others in communal celebrations of liturgical prayer, and how to witness to the Church in a

159

Christian service marked by charity and justice. The demonstration of pastoral skills is a crucial element in the assessment of fitness for ordination. Therefore, the qualities to be developed for these tasks are as follows: a spirit of pastoral responsibility and servant-leadership; generosity and perseverance; creativity; respect for ecclesial communion; and filial obedience to the bishop. (*Directory*, no. 127)

To help ensure that deacon candidates are pastorally prepared for their ecclesial service, Saint Leo University and our diocesan partners frequently integrate praxis-orientated exercises into our courses. As illustrative, when a course on sacraments is offered, not only are the historical and theological aspects of sacramentology presented, but experiential exercises are also integrated with them. This allows the candidates to develop a sense of sacramental presidency and pastoral sensitivities. Homiletics is often a freestanding course in its own right, incorporating assignments pertinent to developing and writing homilies, as well as providing occasions for candidates to enhance their public speaking abilities and delivery.

# Assessment of Candidates

The bishops insist that candidates demonstrate competence in each of these areas prior to ordination (*Directory*, no. 125). Assessing such competency opens up a plethora of possibilities for intra-ecclesial relations between the various persons or parties involved in the formation process (*Directory*, nos. 154, 185, 220–25), thereby promoting solidarity and communion within the ecclesial community. In a manner that preserves student rights and confidentiality, and in concert with prearranged agreements, Saint Leo University faculty, to the extent desired by and solicited from diocesan partners, assess not only the academic and classroom performance of deacon candidates, but also have periodic meetings with, and provide written evaluations of, the candidates to our partnering diocesan deacon directors. These meetings, discussions, and written evaluations are both a built-in dimension of the assessment process of the candidates, and trust-building measures that do much to foster the communion and communication between diocesan partners and the university.

# University-Diocese(s) Collaboration and Catholic Culture

The *Directory*, teachings of the Second Vatican Council, and the USCCB's own pastoral message on Catholic education all view cooperation between the Church and colleges or universities as indispensable to the health of the Church and her mission in society.[6] As expressed in *Ex Corde Ecclesiae*:

> A Catholic university enables the Church to institute an incomparably fertile dialogue with people of every culture...by offering the results of its...research....A Catholic university will be able to help the Church respond to the problems and needs of this age....A Catholic university...is also a primary and privileged place for fruitful dialogue between the Gospel and culture.[7]

> Every Catholic university...has a relationship to the Church....It participates most directly in the life of the local Church....At the same time, because it is an academic institution,...it participates in and contributes to the life and mission of the universal church.[8]

Hence, an additional benefit of collaboration and partnerships between dioceses and Catholic colleges and universities in the formation of deacons is that such collaborations can serve as a vehicle whereby the directives aimed at the preservation and perpetuation of Catholic culture via Catholic colleges and universities proffered in *Ex Corde Ecclesiae* might be implemented.

The *National Directory* and the Educational Formation

We at Saint Leo University are blessed by our partnerships with our various diocesan partners, for they significantly contribute to the university's efforts to preserve, perpetuate, and express its Catholic and Benedictine mission and values. We currently find ourselves at a time when the university is confronted with the daunting challenge and task of preserving and perpetuating its Catholic and Benedictine charism(s) without the sizable presence of Benedictine religious men and women the university once had. As other Catholic institutions increasingly find themselves in similar situations, an added benefit of university-diocesan partnerships in diaconal formation may prove to be the manner in which such partnerships serve to preserve and perpetuate the Catholic culture of the university.

# Pedagogical Models

The manner in which the intellectual and pastoral formation of deacons is conducted has also been addressed by the bishops. Given the candidates' maturity, life experiences, competencies, and expertise, the bishops say:

> The intellectual dimension of formation "should make use of the methods and processes of adult education.... [The participants] should be invited to draw and reflect upon their adult life and faith experiences (*Directory*, no. 122).

> Therefore, the formation faculty and staff should structure an intellectual process that includes an invitation to each participant to reflect on his adult life and experience in the light of the Gospel and the Church's teaching (*Directory*, no. 123).

Through calling for pedagogical methods that respect deacon candidates as adult learners, the bishops' vision of diaconal education echoes their pastoral plan for adult faith formation as outlined in their own *Our Hearts Were Burning Within Us*.

At Saint Leo University, we design courses with the candidates specifically in mind. We strive to acknowledge and integrate their personal and professional lives, life experiences, and ecclesial situation into our pedagogical strategies and methods.

# Continuing Education for Deacons

In addition to an extensive formation process, the bishops call for the continued education of deacons subsequent to their ordination (*Directory*, no. 253):

> The intellectual dimension of diaconate formation does not end with ordination but is an ongoing requirement of the vocation.... The intellectual dimension of post-ordination formation must be systematic and substantive, deepening the intellectual content initially studied during the candidate path of formation. Study days, renewal courses, and participation in academic institutes are appropriate formats to achieve this goal. (*Directory*, no. 248)

> With the approval of the diocesan bishop, a realistic program for the continuing education and formation of each deacon and the entire diaconal community should be designed taking due account of factors such as age and circumstances of deacons, together with the demands made on them by their pastoral ministry. (*Directory*, no. 47)

Such continuing education and formation is to be at the center, not periphery, of the Church's ongoing commitment,[9] inclusive of contemporary social and cultural developments;[10] that is, provided so as to ensure ongoing conversion and growth (*Directory*, no. 239), and "to provide the deacon with ample opportunities to continue to develop and integrate the dimensions of formation into his life and ministry" (*Directory*, no. 241).

The *National Directory* and the Educational Formation

Deacons are entitled to a period of time each year for continuing education and spiritual retreat. Norms should be established in each diocese regarding suitable length of time for these activities and the manner in which the deacon shall receive financial assistance for his expenses either from the diocese, from the current place of ministerial service, or from a combination of sources. (*Directory* 97)

Here at Saint Leo we have tried to respond to the continuing educational needs of deacons by working with our diocesan partners to provide deacons with periodic workshops, retreats, and educational weekends. For example, we have worked together to provide workshops on canon law and educational weekends on topics such as Islam and the contemporary implications of the Second Vatican Council. We are also developing online modules, which may also serve the continuing educational needs of deacons.

# The *Directory*, Diaconal Formation, and Catholic Education

The vision of diaconal formation proffered by the USCCB in the *Directory* provides a substantive template for diaconal formation via simultaneously incorporating the best of Catholic educational principles and values and applying them to the diaconal formation.

Catholic education is an expression of the mission entrusted by Jesus to the Church....Through education the Church seeks to prepare its members to proclaim the Good News and translate this proclamation into action. Since the Christian vocation is a call to transform oneself and society...the educational efforts of the Church must encompass the twin purposes of personal sanctification and social reform in light of Christian values.[11]

In their pastoral message on Catholic education, *To Teach As Jesus Did*, the USCCB specifically identifies *diakonia* as one of the dimensions of Catholic education. This dimension of education, like the diaconate itself, is rooted in revelation (*didache*) and is intended to direct one to service of the ecclesial fellowship (*koinonia*) and service unto the world.[12]

Implementation of the *Directory* allows for diverse manifestations of diaconal formation programs: freestanding diocesan structures, diocese-university partnerships, seminaries, collaborative and distance-learning models (*Directory*, nos. 261–65). However, given the depth of vision for diaconal formation that the bishops proffer, the manifold dimensions of diaconal formation, and the accentuated emphasis that the bishops place on the intellectual dimension of formation, the diocese-university partnership has clear and distinct advantages.

> The college/university-related model incorporates one or more parts of formation from diocesan staff and resources, while one or several parts of formation, such as the intellectual and/or pastoral, are provided and supervised by a Catholic college or university, usually located within the diocese. In these situations, diocesan coordinators carefully and comprehensively integrate the components of formation. Similar to the college/university model is the model that involves a graduate school of theology (*Directory*, no. 261).

As indicated above, here at Saint Leo University, we are privileged to be enjoying a number of diocesan partnerships whereby our theology department is working in collaboration with a number of diocesan bishops and their diaconate offices in implementing the USCCB's vision of diaconal formation as outlined in the *Directory*.[13] The nature of our collaborations reflects the bishops' envisioned college-university partnership described in the *Directory* as one of the potential models for implementing the *Directory*. As stated previously, in order to faithfully mirror this model and to accommodate the directives of the *Directory*, we have developed a curriculum intended to specifically address the needs of diaconal aspirants and candidates, and proffer a plethora of continuing education scenarios and options for deacons postordination.[14] The curriculum was developed in lieu of the *Directory*, its vision for diaconal formation, and the basic standards it outlines. The mission, goals, and objectives of Saint Leo University's Graduate Theology Program read as follows:

> The master of arts in theology is designed to expand the professional knowledge and skills of those engaged in or preparing for pastoral leadership and service, as well as for all who seek advanced theological and pastoral education. The curriculum offers a flexible adult learning model for both professional lay ministers and for candidates to the permanent diaconate, as well as for others involved in religious education, RCIA, youth ministry, spiritual direction, sacramental preparation, and other ministries.[15]

Together and in consultation with our partnering/collaborating diocesan deacon directors, we frequently meet with one another in order to revisit and discuss the curriculum and programs so as to ensure that the needs of the deacon candidates and the wishes of the bishops are being met. When and where adjustments or modifications are needed to ensure the best diaconal program possible, we work with our diocesan partners to make such amendments. Such partnerships and collaboration with the dioceses reveal the following:

> The department of theology is a vital resource to the Catholic community outside the University....Its scholarship can provide support and pastoral ministry to the church....Theologians can render special assistance to bishops, whose role, like theirs, includes the development...of Christian truth.[16]

## Diaconal Formation and Expanding Diocesan-University Relations

In this light, one can see how such collaborative work has not only yielded quality formation programs for deacon candidates, but has also done much to edify relations between the university and our diocesan partners. Collaborating and partnering in the formation and education of deacons has lent itself to additional collaborations and partnerships—this book and its collection of essays being but one of them! Additionally, for example, Saint Leo faculty have been invited by our home bishop, Robert Lynch, to participate in his three-year *Living Eucharist* initiative and to serve on the diocesan advisory committee charged with considering proposals for the renovation of the cathedral. Such expanded relations between dioceses and the university have done much to edify all parties involved and have provided a model of inter-ecclesial solidarity that is life-giving and worthy of emulation.

# Conclusion

The *National Directory* is a gift to the Church. Not only does it serve as a template outlining a vision for the education of deacons; it also provides a vision of university-diocesan partnerships and collaborations that have great potential for creating relationships of mutual and reciprocal edification for both dioceses and universities. Such solidarity can do much to preserve and perpetuate Catholic culture and bring to realization many of the ecclesial relationships called for at the Second Vatican Council. In the very process of forming those who are to sacramentally realize the *diakonia* of Christ, universities and dioceses are, themselves, via their collaboration and partnerships, manifesting *diakonia* to one another, as well as to society.

PART FIVE

# The Pastoral Dimension

# CHAPTER 11

━━━━━━━

# The Deacon as Preacher

## *Marshall Gibbs*

In the beginning was the Word, and the Word
was with God, and the Word was God. He was
in the beginning with God. All things came into
being through him, and without him not one
thing came into being. What has come into being
in him was life, and the life was the light of all
people. The light shines in the darkness, and the
darkness did not overcome it.

John 1:1–5

"In the beginning was the Word…"

In the beginning, God spoke all that is into existence. The
spoken word is a central concept in the Judeo-Christian tradition.
It is the source of understanding among people; it is the source of
common knowledge among people. While all our senses play an
integral and vital part in our understanding and perception of all
that is, verbal communication sets us apart from all other species
and makes possible the establishment of common understandings and traditions that become a part of our life experiences, to
and from which we relate the collective journey of our salvation
and our humanity. The opening hymn in the Gospel of John puts
all this into perspective through the Word, who is God incarnate
communicating with humankind through a vocal medium.

# The Deacon as Preacher

"So God created humankind in his image, in the image of God he created them; male and female he created them" (Gen 1:27). It is reasonable, then, that from the beginning most understanding and reason came from the minds of humankind in the form of verbal communication, perhaps primitive at first, but later more sophisticated and intellectual, until this verbal communication formed the oral tradition that later became the living image of a God that formed in the hearts and minds of humankind: finally converted to a written language in which were transcribed the stories, poetry, songs, and prayer destined to become the canon of scripture, from which the contemporary Christian community is asked to form a more uniform image of the Judeo-Christian tradition.

The foregoing suggests that nearly all rhetorical dialogue is a form of preaching; all extended explanation of concept employs the act of preaching; rhetoric designed to change minds and hearts, even if only to lighten pocketbooks, is preaching, too. This all sounds a bit heretical, but in reality it is empirically how most humans function. Humans spend most of their waking hours in dialogue with one another, attempting to convince others to change their minds, attitudes, perspectives, and in many cases their lifestyles, in accord with the proponent's ideas and value system.[1]

Deacons in the Catholic Church live in the real world. Through their experience of the world, they know that not every question has an answer. Most deacons seem to know wherein the mysteries of life reside, rather than the answers to all the mysteries.[2] Their life experience is an experience of constant secular dialogue. Most of their experiences are the same experiences that the nonordained are experiencing, and for which the nonordained are constantly searching for a voice. The nonordained find themselves "preaching" to their spouses, their siblings, their children, their coworkers, and anyone else who will listen. Their lived experiences are the source of their preachings, little parables that often begin with the words, "In my experience...." Storyteller Eudora Welty, observed that those who preach "cannot illumine the parables in their listeners' lives if they cannot find the significance of those same events in their own lives." She refers to this as the "continuous thread of revelation." In quoting Welty, Thomas Troeger notes that, "in finding the 'continuous thread of revelation,' we discover those experiential analogies by which our listeners can make sense of their own lives."[3]

⚬⚬⚬

Most dioceses now include homiletics as part of the formation experience of the diaconate, although this has not always been the case. As a result of the often uneven experience of homiletic formation around the country, there are locations in which some deacons find themselves preaching only rarely, if at all. This reality is further complicated by certain magisterial texts which *appear* to relegate Sunday preaching exclusively to the priest celebrant. This is an unfortunate misreading of the documents themselves.

The opening sentence of the introduction to *Fulfilled in Your Hearing* very clearly states that "the proclamation of the Gospel of God to all" is the primary duty of the priest.[4] The document then goes on to explicate the word *proclamation*, indicating that the word "can cover a wide variety of activities in the church. A life of quiet faith and generous loving deeds is proclamation: the celebration of the Eucharist is the proclamation of the death of the Lord until he comes. But a key moment in the proclamation of the Gospel is preaching."[5]

It is very clear from *Fulfilled in Your Hearing* and from the *General Instruction of the Roman Missal* that the Sunday celebrant is the primary, but not the only, preacher: "The homily should be given by the priest celebrant himself. He may entrust it to a concelebrating priest, or occasionally, according to circumstances, to a deacon."[6] Preaching to the Sunday assembly, then, should be considered a special privilege, a privilege which requires the deacon to possess a well-disciplined formula of homiletic preparation and training. It follows that the deacon must also be prepared as a celebrant to preach at baptisms, wakes, communion services, and other liturgical events. It also follows from the aforementioned quote from the *General Instruction of the Roman Missal* that for all of these occasions the deacon must be formed and trained in homiletics.

All of the above begs the question as to *why* some deacons experience discrimination relative to preaching assignments and others do not. Is it a question of education or perhaps their gift of rhetoric and/or charism? Is it a concern about their formation, especially their homiletic academic formation, coupled with a praxis that comes with guarantees? Is there a genuine misunderstanding of the role of deacon, or simply a lack of trust in his ability to relate to the lived experience of the assembly in his preaching? There may be a number of issues and concerns and they are probably not mutually exclusive.

Empirically, a key issue is a lack of understanding of the role of the deacon as it has evolved through the centuries, with emphasis on the last forty years since Pope Paul VI issued *Sacrum Diaconatus Ordinem*, providing norms for the restoration of a permanent diaconate in the Latin Church. Because of the relative disappearance of permanent diaconate for more than a millennium, bishops and presbyters had nothing by which to gauge the diaconate, its nature, and its exercise. This has resulted in a variety of approaches and interpretations of the diaconate around the world. With such a diversified approach, it is not surprising that there are many differing visions of the order of deacon: thus the conundrum with preaching. In most cases the bishops have granted faculties to preach and left it to the discretion of the presbyterate as to who and when the deacons will preach and by what criteria the decisions will be made.

# History of Preaching and the Diaconate

> And the twelve called together the whole community of the disciples and said, "It is not right that we should neglect the word of God in order to wait on tables. Therefore, friends, select from among yourselves seven men of good standing, full of the Spirit and of wisdom, whom we may appoint to this task, while we, for our part, will devote ourselves to prayer and to serving the word." What they said pleased the whole community, and they chose Stephen, a man full of faith and the

Holy Spirit, together with Philip, Prochorus, Nicanor, Timon, Parmenas, and Nicolaus, a proselyte of Antioch. They had these men stand before the apostles, who prayed and laid their hands on them. The word of God continued to spread; the number of the disciples increased greatly in Jerusalem, and a great many of the priests became obedient to the faith.

Acts 6:2–7

## From the Beginning

The concept of servant, especially suffering servant, and especially applied to Christ by Christian scholars, has its root in Isaiah 53, dating to 700 BC. While Hebrew scholars see these scripture references as indicating the suffering servant as the people of Israel, the text indicates the people as *diakoneo* or servant people. And Christian scholars see this same text as a foretelling of the Christ as *diakoneo*. By the time Matthew writes his Gospel, Jesus is the suffering servant who "came to serve, not to be served." Thus Christ is the original deacon from the Christian perspective.[7]

Early Christian writers introduced the idea of the "deacon" as an ordained order, within the context of Acts chapters 6 through 8. According to the text, the Seven were ordained by the laying on of hands in the early Church to serve at table, to preach, and to otherwise spread the gospel message. They emulated Christ the Servant, who went about as servant to all, most especially the marginalized, both within and without the Church communities. The author of the *Didascalia* compared the deacon "to Christ for two reasons. First, their service is that of Christ the *diakonos* washing his disciple's feet; second, their service is that of Christ the mediator, reporting men's needs to the Father. If then our Lord did this, will you, O deacons, hesitate to do the like?"[8] In the New Testament, preaching was a vital ingredient of liturgy and word. These deacons, "strengthened by sacramental grace, have as their service for the People of God, in communion with the bishop and his college of presbyters, the *diakonia* of liturgy, word, and charity."[9] The word *diakonia* comes from the Greek *diakoneo*, meaning "service," or "one who serves." However, as evidenced above, it would be a mistake to interpret the deacon literally as one who is employed to do only household jobs such as cooking, cleaning, and serving meals. In fact, many commentators have noted that a major early need filled by the deacon was "a keeping of accounts" or records detailing the distribution of food and other necessities to the community.[10]

The call to service as preacher is particularly clear in Acts 6:8–15 and 7:54–60, where Stephen was stoned to death because of his bold teaching and preaching of the good news. Of the original seven, Philip is equally notable for his powerful preaching, which proclaimed Jesus and, according to Acts 8, effected signs of exorcisms and cures. Philip's ministry took him throughout Samaria and along the road from Jerusalem to Gaza, spreading the gospel message, where as many as would hear it were converted and baptized. Following the tradition of the Church, then, the deacon is called to exercise a *diakonia* in the proclamation and preaching of the word and in, so doing, actively participate with Christ in the revelation of God the Father.

Acts 6 through 8 portrays a ministry active in preaching, charity, and liturgy. Paul's First Letter to Timothy is also dated somewhere in the first century between AD 60 and AD 105. It is very precise in spelling out the qualifications of an ecclesial diaconate; for example, "serious, not double-tongued, not addicted to much wine, not greedy for gain; they must hold the mystery of the faith with a clear conscience" (1 Tim 3:8–9). It is notable that there is no mention of preaching in the context of the epistle, which may indicate that, while the diaconate in Timothy's church was alive and well, their pulpit access may have been a bit more limited than in the churches described in Acts.

The *Didache*, which is believed by many scholars to have been written in Antioch at about the same time as First Timothy, mentions teaching when referring to bishops and deacons.[11] Contemporary to the *Didache* are the writings of Ignatius of Antioch, who refers to the deacons as his "fellow servants" and occasionally refers to their call to a preaching ministry. Noteworthy in this respect is Ignatius's *Letter to the Philadelphians* wherein he makes it clear that deacons preach the word as helpers of the bishop, and his *Letter to the Church of Smyrna and to Polycarp,* wherein he constantly refers to the "bishop, with the presbytery and deacons, my fellow-servants."[12]

The diaconate emerged differently in the diverse communities of the first century. Needs varied and the bishops who ordained these men saw their functions through different lenses, depending on the specific needs of the people to whom they were ministering. Edward Echlin notes especially the writings in *1 Clement,* the *Didache,* and the *Shepherd of Hermas* as being uniquely different when referring to the order and the manner in which the duties of the deacons developed. He notes that the office in Rome proceeded more gradually than in many of the other churches. Nonetheless, Lynn Sherman estimates that in those early days of the diaconate at least thirty-four deacons were elected to the episcopacy of Rome. It is reasonable to assume that these men were elected and elevated to leadership positions, religious or secular, if they possessed the oratory skills necessary to convict, inspire, teach, and convert.[13]

The well-known legend of Lawrence, a deacon of Rome, offers many interesting insights. In AD 258, the great bishop of Rome, Sixtus, was arrested by soldiers of the emperor Valerian, along with his beloved deacons and subdeacons, and was beheaded. Valerian had issued an edict to the Roman Senate that all the Christian clergy—bishops, priests, and deacons—were to be arrested and executed.

Valerian offered to spare Lawrence's life if he would gather all the gold and silver of the Church together in one central place. The poor, the handicapped, and the misfortunate in the city were all being supported by a thriving early Christian community, which understood the gospel imperative. For three days, Lawrence went throughout the city preaching to them to come together. When Valerian arrived, Deacon Lawrence presented him with the true "gold and silver" of the Church! Filled with rage, the emperor decided that beheading was not punishment enough for this Christian deacon. He ordered Lawrence to be burned alive, in public, on a griddle. Witnesses recorded the public martyrdom, with the legend maintaining that Lawrence even joked with his executioners to turn him over because he was "done on this side." The deacon cheerfully offered himself to the Lord Jesus and, in joking with his executioners, preached to the very end.

The tradition records massive conversions to the Christian faith as a result of the holy life, death, and preaching of Lawrence's ministry and sacrifice. He was poured out, like his Master, Jesus Christ the Servant, in redemptive love, on behalf of others. To this day it is still said that all of Rome became Christian as a result of the faithful life, and death, of this one humble deacon. He was buried in a cemetery on the Via Tiburtina. On that spot, Constantine would later build a basilica in honor of the Deacon Lawrence.

A special devotion to Lawrence, deacon and martyr, spread throughout the entire Christian community. Early Christians had no doubt that those who had gone to be with the Lord continued to pray for those who still struggled in this earthly life. They saw in Lawrence a great example of how to live, and how to die, faithful to the gospel. Years later, St. Augustine would reflect on the heroism of this great deacon in a sermon preached on his feast day, emphasizing that his life and death were an example for all Christians to emulate.

There seems to be uniform agreement that all persons appointed to diaconal office were, above all, honest, as they assisted in the administration and distribution of money. In addition, they seem to have been expected to possess the charism of preaching. The *Didache* expressly exhorts, "Accordingly, elect for yourselves bishops and deacons, men who are an honor to the Lord, of gentle disposition, not attached to money, honest and well-tried; for they, too, render you the sacred service of the prophets and teachers. Do not, then, despise them; after all they are your dignitaries together with the prophets and teachers."[14]

Also notable is the inference in these writings that the early deacon was a constant and close companion to the bishop whom he assisted. Clement seems to have been most vocal in portraying the deacon's role as a ministry of worship and charity, which would seem to indicate that the early deacon was charged with presiding at liturgy, even if not in the act of consecration, which, from most accounts, fell to the office of bishop.

Both bishop and deacon were expected to preach to or exhort the faithful. Ignatius of Antioch became acquainted with one deacon named Burrhus, when he accompanied his bishop to Smyrna. Ignatius was so impressed with Burrhus that he prevailed upon his bishop Onesimus to reassign him to Smyrna and serve with Ignatius. Ignatius is quoted as saying, "Now, about my fellow-servitor Burrhus, whom God has made your deacon and endowed with every blessing. Might I ask you to let him remain here with me, which would do honor both to you and to your bishop" (Ign. *Eph.* 2).[15]

By the end of the first century, the "triadic ministry" of bishop, presbyter, and deacon was clearly a part of the churches in Syria and Asia Minor, and the duties of the deacon, according to the writings of the time, in many ways seem to mirror the diaconate of the twenty-first century within the context of liturgy, word, and charity. This triadic relationship apparently flourished until the fifth century when, according to most scholars, the gradual decline of the diaconate began.

By the middle of the second century, Justin was writing a series of apologetics that indicated the presence of deacons throughout the Christian Church performing the basic diaconal duties, including teaching and preaching. Justin was a convert to Christianity who attempted via written rhetoric to lessen the persecution of Christians under Vespasian.

According to Enright, in the third century, Origen of Alexandria "was quite clear that deacons were to engage above all in preaching God's word."[16] During the third and fourth century, a series of eight apostolic constitutions were published, which had the effect of contemporary canon law: setting forth the conduct expected of all holy orders and defining the order of liturgy. Some scholars attribute these constitutions to Clement of Alexandria, while other scholars remain unsure of the authorship and continue to debate the identity of their origin. Regardless, in these constitutions the deacon was assigned many of the duties of the contemporary permanent deacon, including teaching and preaching. In fact, these rather ancient documents are in many ways similar to the contemporary *National Directory for the Formation, Ministry, and Life of Permanent Deacons in the United States.*

Early in the fifth century, "the historian Philostorgius (d. 439) testified that deacons still preached."[17] By the end of the fifth century, the permanent diaconate was dwindling. The principle celebrant of the liturgy, the bishop, was finding himself stretched even thinner as the number of communities continued to grow, and so the presbyter found himself in greater demand, resulting in an expansion of that order in direct proportion to the growth of the new communities. The diaconate, likewise, found itself more involved in liturgical service to the point that the order became a training time or stepping stone to the priesthood. By the Middle Ages, the diaconate as a permanent order of ministry to service, altar, and word had become all but nonexistent.

There would be men during the interim years from the sixth century until the nineteenth centuries who would remain lifelong deacons.[18] They were few and far between. With the exception of a brief attempt at the Council of Trent to revive the permanent diaconate, the office of deacon remained essentially the same. The diaconate remained a transitional office until its permanency was restored by the Second Vatican Council.

## Council of Trent

From Nicaea to the Reformation—which, among other things, is credited as a primary trigger of the Council of Trent—there are a number of documents referring to deacons. Almost all of the writings deal with the duty and behavior of deacons and virtually none refer to deacons as preachers. "It is not often realized that the Council of Trent declared itself to be burning with the desire of restoring the pristine understanding of the ministry of deacons, laudably received in the Church from the time of the apostles."[19]

Prior to the Council of Trent, there was conversation and discussion advocating for the return of the permanent diaconate. There are a number of letters between bishops attesting to the need and detailing the duties and functions deemed desirable at the time. There was, however, apparently little mention of preaching, and the record seems to indicate that much of the conversation was negative in that regard. Edward Echlin indicates that during the council there was strong opposition to the deacon as preacher and cites the bishop of Calvi, the bishop of Gaudix, and the Italian bishop Bellomo as outspoken opponents of diaconal preaching.[20] Despite this, as late as the final sessions, a document was submitted to the council for consideration that *did* include preaching, and it is worth noting, in part: "When the bishop so directs it pertains to deacons to baptize and preach."[21]

In summing up the council's action relative to the permanent diaconate, Enright says, "Here we have a laying out of everything the deacon did during the early centuries, but although any number of Catholic reformers wanted such a restoration, the attacks upon the priesthood and the sacrificial view of the Mass by the Protestant reformers, among other reasons, prevented this once highly esteemed order from returning at the time."[22]

## Reimplementation of the Permanent Diaconate

The foregoing is not to say that there was no discussion taking place among clerics and academics during the Vatican II preconciliar period. As can be determined from surviving letters and documents, the concept of a permanent diaconate was definitely on the minds of some. The need seemed clear but the structure was far from unanimous, even to the point that disagreement existed as to whether this possible wisdom community should be ordained clergy or commissioned laity. On April 20, 1840, Frankfurt physician and author J. K. Passavant wrote the following to Melchior von Diepenbrock, cardinal and prince-bishop of Breslau:

> The priestly state is too sharply separated from that of the laity. Here, it occurs to me, the church can expand the sphere of activity of deacons, so that these men, who would be allowed to be married, could carry out in part the teaching office and other ecclesiastical functions, while the priest (who would therefore have to be senior) would exclusively administer the sacraments, especially confession. If in the considered opinion of

the bishops, then, several deacons (archdeacons) could be drawn from the best educated ranks of the so-called laity, then the church would have excellent ministers at her disposal. [ ] What institutions could be started up, set in motion…what tremendous possibilities![23]

Josef Hornef tells us that Diepenbrock responded very positively to the above on April 23, 1840, citing Passavant's letter as a clear understanding of how the Church might be restructured and calling his ideas "an act of love toward mankind."[24] Hornef went on to recognize the contribution of French priest Dom A. Grea, who in 1885 proposed the restoration of "an ordained diaconate having an expressly charitable character."[25]

From the above we can see that as early as the 1840s, the preconciliar idea of a restored permanent diaconate was emerging in Germany.[26] By 1934, the periodical *Caritas* carried several articles promoting the concept and even going so far as to suggest the activities to be carried out by those men who might enter the order. There is little indication that liturgical preaching was ever considered or discussed in the time period between the Council of Trent and the Second World War. However, it is noteworthy that canon 1342 in the 1917 *Code of Canon Law* grants deacons the faculty of preaching. In practice, Echlin asserts, very few deacons actually preached and it must be remembered that they were transitional deacons who were coming from seminaries on the road to priesthood.

With the Second World War came the German concentration camps. Priests were incarcerated in forced labor and concentration camps wholesale. Cellblock 26 at Dachau was one of the larger and more infamous.[27] Among those priests were two men who spent much of their time discussing the possibilities for a new Church and for the need of a permanent diaconate: Father Otto Pies and Vicar Wilhelm Schamoni. Their attention turned to the possibilities for the Church of the future, a Church where they envisioned a critical shortage of priests and an ever-greater need for pastoral care. In response to these concerns, both men exchanged ideas concerning a possible restoration of the permanent diaconate. Interestingly, many of these discussions seemed to involve a need for more or better preachers, especially those who came from and spoke to the common man. There was additional concern for liturgical and pastoral assistance at the parish level and "that the priesthood should not be rendered easier. To the contrary the goal should be to strive for the 100 percent religious cleric."[28]

Schamoni's notes, saved from the collapse of the Third Reich, say:

> The question then arises as to whether or not it is right to leave pastoral care in the hands of a relatively small number of priests and their lay assistants. Archbishop Constantini had suggested that the work of a handful of missionary priests could be rendered more fruitful by ordaining an army of lay catechists to the ecclesial office of the diaconate. This suggestion needs to be examined to see if it is also applicable to our [present] European circumstances. Such a diaconate of married, employed, capable assistants, especially from the teaching profession—but also from all other professions and fields, and of course not bound to pray the daily office—would offer the following advantages:
>
> 1. Overworked and overburdened pastoral priests could be relieved of the catechesis of children and adults, which would then be entrusted to specially qualified individuals. Ecclesial office would lend a special sacredness and dignity to the missioning of these individuals.
>
> 2. Communities deprived of Mass despite [officially authorized] bination and trination would be afforded the opportunity for prayer services, liturgies of the word and communion services. The establishment of new communities and actual community life would be possible even with the most serious shortage of priests.
>
> 3. *The preaching of these deacons, who would be involved in the work-a-day world, would be particularly persuasive and down-to-earth. One perceives in current preaching that it is being done by individuals who are*

"*segregate a populo*" *["separated from the people"]* [emphasis added].

4. The Church has largely become a Church of authorities and officials. The feudal state and the civil servant state have rubbed off on her. *The diaconate would be an effective means to return Holy Mother the Church to a Church of the people* [emphasis added].

5. The Church has not succeeded in holding its ground among either the leading intellectual classes nor among those classes most easily led astray, the proletariat. In their own *milieu*, deacons *from* these classes *for* these classes could gain influence incomparably deeper than could any priest, since priests would never develop within this *milieu* the kind of rapport that deacons would have already established. One · could develop the diaconate into a means to win back the de-Christianized *milieu. An intelligent deacon from the working-class would, without any special theological training, be able to touch the heart of his worker colleagues with just the right words* [emphasis added].

6. Many vocations to the priesthood would result from the exemplary family life [of married deacons].

7. Deacons could hardly do any harm. If they do not keep their promise, the Church does not need to keep them, as opposed to what it unfortunately must try to do when dealing with the priests.

8. Converted protestant pastors could, as full-time deacons, be given a new, important range of activities.

9. The diaconate could be a bridge to the eastern churches.[29]

Writing later in 1953, Wilhelm Schamoni's vision for a permanent diaconate had subtly changed and then he wrote his often-quoted *Married Men as Ordained Deacons* in which he detailed his vision for the permanent diaconate, one might get the distinct impression that Schamoni saw a renewed diaconate as an answer to the already burgeoning priest shortage.[30]

## Second Vatican Council

"The conciliar bishops drew on this preconciliar material and endorsed a general structure of a theology of church."[31] The outcome was five major theological changes in the understanding of ecclesial ministry and leadership, especially as it effected the sacrament of holy orders, and "since the permanent diaconate in the Roman Catholic Church is an integral and *not* simply an accidental part of the sacrament of orders, the renewal of the permanent diaconate has itself reconfigured this sacrament."[32] In addition, the simultaneous restoration of the episcopacy to the sacrament of orders had major implications in the understanding of the sacrament. As discussed earlier, while the diaconate is officially a full and equal order, it is, from a practical standpoint, optionally dependent on the good graces of each independent bishop who may or may not elect to establish the ministry.

Responding to the vision of the council, Pope Paul VI issued *Sacrum Diaconatus Ordinem* on June 18, 1967, wherein he affirmed the concept of restoring the permanent diaconate:

> It is nevertheless "beneficial that those…who perform a truly diaconal ministry be strengthened by the imposition of hands, a tradition going back to the Apostles, and be more closely joined to the altar so that they may more effectively carry out their ministry through the sacramental grace of the diaconate." Certainly in this way the special nature of this order will be shown most clearly. It is not to be considered as a mere step toward the priesthood, but it is so adorned with its own indelible character and its own special grace so that those who are called to it "can permanently serve the mysteries of Christ and the Church"….
>
> All that is decreed in the *Code of Canon Law* about the rights and obligations of deacons, whether these rights and obligations be common to all clerics, or proper to deacons—all these, unless some other disposition has been made, we confirm and declare to be in

force also for those who will remain permanently in the diaconate.[33]

The new rites for the conferral of all three of the ordained ministries were authorized on June 17, 1968, in the apostolic constitution *Pontificalis Romani Recognitio*. Finally, on August 15, 1972, Pope Paul VI published new norms for the diaconate in the apostolic letter *Ad Pascendum*. By the spring of 1971, thirteen programs were in operation, with a total of 430 candidates. The first group of ordinations to the permanent diaconate took place in May and June of 1971.

The last thirty-five years have witnessed phenomenal growth of the order in the United States. There are presently nearly 17,000 permanent deacons serving in the 196 dioceses, of which, at last count, 170 had active diaconate formation programs; a few others were on hold as their programs were being redesigned to conform with the new *Directory*.[34]

# The Contemporary Diaconate through the Lens of the USCCB

As indicated above, Pope Paul VI officially restored the permanent diaconate in 1968. The bishops of the United States petitioned the Holy See in May 1968 to restore the diaconate in this country; that request was approved in August of the same year. The following November the Bishops' Committee on the Permanent Diaconate was established and the first formation programs were approved.[35] In 1971 and again in 1984, as experience with the diaconate expanded throughout the country, the bishops promulgated guidelines for formation.

Most recently, following new documents concerning the diaconate from the Holy See, promulgated in 1998, and following the continued expansion of the diaconate, the need for a more comprehensive and up-to-date national document on the diaconate became obvious to the bishops. Working with numerous diocesan consultation teams and assimilating the lived experience of numerous diocesan formation programs, the USCCB developed—and the Holy See affirmed—the *National Directory for the Formation, Ministry, and Life of Permanent Deacons in the United States*, promulgated in 2005.

In this directory, the United States bishops detailed their specific expectations to be implemented by August 10, 2005. William Ditewig makes it clear "that the *Directory* was not only written *by the bishops;* it was written *for the bishops*." He goes on to explain that "this fact is extremely important, and it can serve as a means of interpreting and understanding the *Directory*....We need to understand that the bishops are charging each other with the responsibility of catechizing the entire diocesan church on the nature and ministry of the diaconate."[36]

Philosopher George Santayana once observed, "Those who forget history are bound to repeat it." I think it would be impossible to discuss the preaching history of the diaconate in the Catholic tradition without maintaining an awareness of the history of the order and of the many similarities that exist between the order's history and the contemporary conditions of today's reinstated permanent diaconate.

I will now identify the similarities during the discussion of the 2000-year history of the order, especially as they pertain to both the preaching activities and the general *diakonia* exercised by contemporary permanent deacons. Human beings, being just that, have a tendency to repeat old habits without regard for the potential outcomes that may occur, even though those outcomes may be highly predictable when considered in light of past occurrences.

Perhaps it is the concept of recapturing the essence of first-century Christendom—often verbalized as a vision of catechists and scholars who have attempted to translate and implement their understanding of the documents of the Second Vatican Council—that has prompted formation decisions that made the newly reestablished permanent diaconate mirror in many ways the formation of the Seven in Luke/Acts and subsequent patristic writings. This may be especially true in the area of homiletics.

The bishops see a diaconate totally formed to function as evangelizers and teachers as ministers of the word; as witnesses and guides as ministers of charity; and as sanctifiers as ministers of liturgy. In paragraph 35, the *Directory* calls upon the deacon to properly proclaim the gospel and preach the homily in accord with the provisions of canon law.

The *Directory* is very clear regarding the *diakonia* of the word. Paragraph 80 declares that:

> Deacons are ordained *"to proclaim the Gospel and preach the Word of God"* [emphasis added]. They "have the faculty to preach everywhere, in accordance with the conditions established by [Canon Law]." "Deacons should be trained carefully to prepare their homilies in prayer, in study of the sacred texts, in perfect harmony with the Magisterium, and in keeping with the [age, culture, and abilities] of those to whom they preach." Further, "by their conduct…by transmitting Christian doctrine and by devoting attention to the problems of our time…[deacons] collaborate with the bishop and the priests in the exercise of a ministry which is not of their wisdom but of the Word of God, calling all to conversion and holiness."[37]

William Ditewig has been very specific in calling attention to Paragraph 40 of the *Directory* :

> In every case it is important that deacons fully exercise their ministry, in preaching, in the liturgy, and in charity to the extent that circumstances permit. They should not be relegated to marginal duties, be made merely to act as substitutes, nor discharge duties normally entrusted to non-ordained members of the faithful. Only in this way will the true identity of permanent deacons as ministers of Christ become apparent and impression avoided that deacons are simply lay people particularly involved in the life of the church.[38]

# Conclusion

And so, as a result of all that has gone before, on their day of ordination, deacons stand before their bishop, fully vested in alb, stole, and dalmatic. Each goes to the bishop and kneels before him. The bishop places the Book of Gospels in the newly ordained deacon's hands and says,

> Receive the Gospel of Christ
> Whose herald you now are.
> Believe what you read,
> Teach what you believe,
> And practice what you teach.[39]

The concept of "herald of Christ" is deeply rooted in scripture, including the Old Testament. A herald is a messenger, one who carries tidings for the king. A herald of Christ is *God's* messenger, one who proclaims the glorious truths about the Christ, the King of Kings. The prophet Isaiah was one of the major prophets in the Hebrew scripture who heralded the coming Messiah; the angels in the New Testament birth narratives were heralds that pointed the way to the babe in Nazareth; John the Baptist was the herald who pointed to Jesus as the long awaited Messiah; and today's deacons, among other ministers of the word, also serve as heralds who point the faithful to Christ as Sacrament of God the Father, the good news as depicted in the gospels. Avery Dulles, in his seminal book *Models of the Church*, expounds extensively on the role of the "Church as herald," as sacrament of Christ. He calls the entire Catholic community to be heralds of Christ; to be proclaimers who constantly preach God's word to the world with integrity and persistence.[40] Within that context, the deacon becomes a professional herald who is given the education, training, and charge to carry out that mandate. Richard McBrien called this proclaiming an ecclesiastical event that causes Church to happen: "a kerygmatic community which holds aloft, through the preached Word, the wonderful deeds of God in past history, particularly his mighty act in Jesus Christ."[41]

The Deacon as Preacher

In the New Testament, preaching is a vital ingredient of liturgy and word. Preaching has the ability to advance the catechesis and conversion taking place in the assembly, or conversely, to muffle the responses of the assembly, effectively acting as a switch that turns off the process. In other words, all preaching has the capacity to both build up and tear down the liturgical experience of the assembly. It is an awesome responsibility.

In the *Constitution on the Sacred Liturgy* (*Sacrosanctum Concilium*), the Second Vatican Council made abundantly clear the place and importance of preaching in the Liturgy of the Word in the celebration of the Mass:

> The sacred liturgy does not exhaust the entire activity of the Church. Before men can come to the liturgy they must be called to faith and to conversion: "How then are they to call upon him in whom they have not yet believed? But how are they to believe him whom they have not heard? And how are they to hear if no one preaches? And how are men to preach unless they be sent?" (Rom 10:14–15)[42]

Recalling, again, the episode recorded in Acts, we see that the apostles, overwhelmed by the sheer number of new converts, laid hands on the Seven so that they could extend the ministry to the otherwise-neglected members of the community. And so it was that these seven men became ministers of word, liturgy, and charity; bringing the new "Way" to the newly converted by relating their own personal lived experiences of the Christ as they preached, served, and worked among the people. "And so the apostolic preaching, which is expressed in a special way in the inspired books, was to be preserved by a continuous succession of preachers until the end of time."[43] Because of its ability to relate to the experience of those whom they served, the deacons' service in the early Church established a tradition among the orders that has been passed down through the ages.

It seems obvious from the above that a major part of the deacons' formation must be devoted to scripture and hermeneutics. Through the process of *lectio*, the deacon prayerfully connects God's word as handed down in scripture to the contemporary lives of the faithful as they ponder the retelling of the stories. The deacon also learns to construct contemporary stories that parallel the ancient stories that form the basis for the faith, as told by the authors of both the Hebrew and Christian scriptures. These illustrative narratives serve to expand and clarify the teachings and give contemporary meaning to the ancient texts.

Again, we refer to the bishops of the Second Vatican Council to glean an indication of the importance of the scripture stories and their place in the ministry of preaching. All scripture is story, told variously in narrative, song, poetry, prayer. And yet all scripture is not the whole story. Each of the storytellers tells an important part of the story, which makes moral, ethical, or significant points. The faithful are left to determine what else might have happened, what might have been left out of the story that could have made the message clearer. They are free to allow the stories to remind them of similar times and similar outcomes. They are free to imagine a different experience. Thus the deacon preacher himself can share his imagination, as well as his lived experience, with the faithful, inviting them to become a part of his story and allowing himself to be a part of theirs.

> Since the sermon is part of the liturgical service, the preferred place for it is to be indicated even in the rubrics, as far as the nature of the rite will allow; and the ministry of preaching is to be fulfilled with exactitude and fidelity. The sermon, moreover, should draw its content mainly from scriptural and liturgical sources. Its character should be that of a proclamation of God's wonderful works in the history of salvation, that is, the mystery of Christ, which is ever made present and active within us, especially in the celebration of the liturgy.[44]

The bishops summarize:

> By means of the homily the mysteries of the faith and the guiding principles of the Christian life are

expounded from the sacred text, during the course of the liturgical year; the homily, therefore, is to be highly esteemed as part of the liturgy itself.[45]

All of the above requires that the deacon be well formed in the practice of homiletics and dedicated to spending the time necessary to carry out the ministry of preaching.

Again, empirically, many deacons relate a unique life experience rich in the worldview of the secular marketplace and especially knowledgeable in the understanding of marriage and family to the scripture pericope being proclaimed. Because of this unique life experience, the majority of deacons preach through a lens focused on secular experiences in many ways similar to and identifiable with the people in the pew.

For the most part, then, the deacon has lived most of his life in the secular world. Most deacons are parents, husbands, and often, the principal source of income for their families. In many cases the deacon has graduate degrees and life experience that are very diverse from his religious parish life. His lived experience provides a source of pertinent understanding from which he can draw similarities from the great stories found in scripture, enabling him to unpack these readings in a unique and personal way. Just as Jesus preached his message of good news through the use of parables, stories that graphically illustrated the central theme being conveyed, so too, these deacons can rely on the stories of their unique lived experience to convey these universal gospel truths in contemporary terminology. These men are, for the most part, well educated, disciplined, selfless individuals dedicated to serving others, especially through their *diakonia* of the word as they live the sentiment attributed to St. Francis of Assisi: "Preach the gospel always. When necessary, use words."

CHAPTER 12

# The Deacon's Ministry vis-à-vis the Laity and Parish Life

## John R. Alvarez

## A Perspective on the Ministry of the Deacon

History informs us that there has never been only one way to serve as a deacon.[1] Present circumstances reinforce what history avers. In today's Church, diaconal ministry continues to be expressed in a broad variety of roles. Whether expressed in the role of a mentor, helper, teacher, spiritual companion, preacher, parish administrator, liturgist, director of diaconal formation, a leader of the diaconal community in a local church, or a parish life coordinator, sharing responsibility for the life of a parish with a nonresident pastor—the current ministry of the deacon continues to be adaptable and diverse, but in continuity with its historical and theological roots. As a result of the broad range of roles possible in diaconal ministry, adaptability and flexibility seem to be basic prerequisites for anyone considering the diaconate. The dynamics of a Church serving the needs of the modern world without being consumed by it require the men accepting the radical call to diaconal service to remain informed, adaptable, and teachable, while maintaining a meaningful spiritual life. The Second Vatican Council, in its "Pastoral Constitution on the Church in the Modern World" (*Gaudium et Spes*), observed that the Church bears the responsibility to creatively and seriously engage the modern world.

> The Church has always had the duty of scrutinizing the signs of the times and of interpreting them in the light of the gospel. Thus, in language intelligible to each generation, she can respond to the perennial questions which men ask about this present life, and the life to come, and about the relationship of the one to the other. We must therefore recognize and understand the world in which we live, its expectations, its longings, and its often dramatic characteristics.[2]

As a result of this collective call to know and influence the world at large (as well as the smaller domains of our communities, parishes, and families), change becomes for the deacon an integral part of his daily reality, even at a time of life when most individuals are usually least inclined to wrestle with change or a challenging role. This is perhaps one concrete way in which the deacon expresses and lives the *kenotic* dimension of his service to God's people.

In addition to being diverse in the ways it may be expressed, diaconal ministry is fundamentally focused on serving others with the mind and heart of Jesus. Thus the "downwardly mobile career" that is diaconal ministry, as Cardinal Walter Kasper refers to it, embraces the humility and attitude that are key characteristics of sacramental service.

> Kasper seems to be saying,…there is no one way to be a deacon, but every way must be identifiable and recognizable as a form of service, inviting and empowering others to serve in such a way that communion with God and communion among people is advanced. That is pragmatically what it means to be church and what it means to be a deacon in the church.[3]

According to this view, diaconal ministry seeks to be an expression and instrument of the Pauline charism of communion.

As such, the deacon is a servant to communion in that everything he is and does, whether directly or indirectly related to his ministry, is ordered to building up God's community—the kingdom of God. As an instrument of communion, the deacon promotes the development and growth of Christian communities in their every manifestation—small Christian communities, formally organized ministry groups, children in faith formation and their families, and any group that wishes to gather to do God's work. Just as important, the deacon is an expression of communion in the manner in which he approaches building up God's community. By building community in ways that are consistent with St. Paul's model of developing community (cf. 1 and 2 Cor)—that is, with and through, rather than over, those he has promised to serve—the deacon helps build, nurture, and sustain the community of believers whom he serves.

> The entire diaconal ministry revolves around pastoral leadership, not in terms of positional authority…but in a sense of leading, inspiring, enabling, and modeling for other members of the church what servant-leadership can mean in living the demands of Christian discipleship in the contemporary world.[4]

In this way, the ministry of the deacon expresses concretely a new way of seeing and being for both the deacon and the people whom he serves. Instead of attempting to be the center of all activity and exercising leadership from a strictly pyramidal leadership framework, the deacon leads, inspires, and promotes the common good through his love and concern for those with whom he ministers. Consistent with the admonition of St. Polycarp to "…be merciful, and zealous, and…walk according to the truth of the Lord, who became the servant of all,"[5] the deacon adopts the approach of a guide, mentor, and advocate, rather than that of a task-oriented supervisor. The deacon helps, supports, and, when necessary, lovingly carries those to whom he ministers. This diaconal and, thus, *kenotic* approach to ministry provides to all a concrete model of leadership-in-communion; that is to say, the model of leadership for a deacon is relational, rather than power-based. It avoids institutional forms of author-ity and, instead, adopts a form based on love and moral author-ity. In the way that the deacon conducts his ministry, he communicates to the world what it looks like to live and work with the heart and mind of Jesus. In other words, "the service of the deacon is the Church's service sacramentalized."[6] As such, it is the deacon who calls forth the threefold baptismal dignity of the laity, and to help them understand and exercise the rights and responsibilities that accompany that dignity. In that regard, every deacon's perspective on his role as animator of communi-ties should be influenced by St. Paul's closing admonition to the community at Corinth:

> Finally, brothers and sisters, farewell. Put things in order, listen to my appeal, agree with one another, live in peace; and the God of love and peace will be with you. Greet one another with a holy kiss. All the saints greet you. The grace of the Lord Jesus Christ, the love of God, and the communion of the Holy Spirit be with all of you. (2 Cor 13:11–13)

One significant potential consequence of the view of the dea-con as animator of communion is that it supports a balanced and nuanced understanding of diaconal ministry on the part of the deacon, the rest of the clergy, and the laity as well. How the major constituencies with whom he interacts perceive the ministry and roles of the deacon will affect his perception of himself and his role in the Church and, in turn, will influence his behavior.

> Role identity emerges from ongoing social interactions and others' expectations. The more others associate an individual with a particular role, the more the role merges with the self-concept. This role-person merger drives future actions as the individual strives to behave consistently with the identity.[7]

Although others' perceptions of us do not affect who we are ontologically, it clearly influences our perceptions of ourselves and, thus, our behavior. So, it is important that the deacon, on a practical level, continues to develop his understanding of diaconal ministry. It is equally as important that those with whom he ministers maintain a balanced and accurate perspective about diaconal ministry. If not, there is the potential that others' confused expectations for the deacon, borne out of an incomplete or even incorrect understanding of diaconal ministry, will have consequences for both the deacon and the Church. The deacon's perspective of his ministry will be adversely affected by others' misperceptions of his role in the Church, which can have its negative consequences in confusion about roles, in unnecessary conflicts, and, most important, in missed opportunities to serve God's people as we are called by him to do. Moreover, we risk turning the noble ministry of the deacon into a theologically precise, Neoplatonic construct that is incompletely understood and wholly unappreciated, and that lacks a concrete example of it in the world. Accordingly, the potential of this ministry will be largely unrealized to the detriment of the Church and God's people.

One characterization of the diaconate and diaconal ministry that appears to continue to have substantial currency is the notion of the deacon as a "bridge." This metaphor for the deacon's ministry has a long history. For example, references to the deacon as "messenger" and "prophet" of the bishop as well as the "ear, and eye, mouth, heart, and soul" of the bishop can be found in the third-century document *Didascalia Apostolorum* and suggest the notion of the deacon as a bridge. In light of the close theological and working relationship between the bishop and deacon that diaconal ordination establishes and later presumes, such characterizations of the deacon's ministry are apt. It is the deacon who, in collaboration with the shepherd of the local Church and his pastors, identifies who is being "neglected in the daily distribution" (Acts 6:1) and brings these needs to the attention of the loving and concerned shepherd. It is also the ministry of the deacon to become a concrete sign of the Good Shepherd's and the local shepherd's concern, love, and care for all the people of the local Church. The metaphor of the deacon as bridge captures those dimensions of the deacon's ministry. It speaks to both the deacon and those he serves of his role as one who facilitates by providing a direct route between those who serve and those who are served. On the other hand, metaphors, by their nature, are limited. As they clarify an idea, they also oversimplify it. As such, metaphors tend to be reductionistic and hence call for caution in how they are applied. To this point, Paul McPartlan identifies some of the challenges that such a characterization of diaconal ministry raises.

> The term *bridge* [as a description of the permanent deacon], however, also has some problems, which are important to identify. The deacon is spoken of as a bridge precisely to stress the connectedness of church and world, liturgy and life, pastors and faithful....The danger, however, is that the very image itself suggests a gap that needs to be bridged (and, moreover, that is not bridged unless there is a deacon)—that is not our basic view of things. Yes, there *was* a gap between the church and the world prior to Vatican II, but there should *not* have been; and if we call the deacon a bridge as a matter of course, we are in danger of implying that there is *of course* a gap between the church and the world, between the pastors and the faithful, and so on. As the International Theology Commission says, the idea of the diaconate as *medius ordo* (that is, bridge) "might end up by sanctioning and deepening, through that very function, the gap which it was supposed to fill." I would suggest that it is truer to the vision of Vatican II, particularly as set forth in *Gaudium et Spes*, to speak of the *seamlessness* or *solidarity* between the church and world, and to speak of the deacon as a splendid and very special sign of that seamlessness or solidarity.[8]

Used without a heavy dose of care, the characterization of the deacon as a bridge can create an opportunity for the ministry of the deacon to be misperceived as that of a mediator and translator between the hierarchy and the laity. Such a misunderstanding of the deacon's ministry could obscure the great potential and richness of the ministry to the detriment of the many who could be served well by it. Also, since bishops, priests, and the laity are able to communicate with one another adequately without having to resort to the services of a deacon-mediator, if not also translator, creating such an artificial role for the deacon could have the effect of relegating this honorable ministry to the historical trash heap of other ideas with unrealized potential. Precisely because the bridge metaphor for diaconal ministry has a long and honorable past, it seems that the potential for unwittingly extending its use beyond safe limits is more likely. Caution seems appropriate here to balance the two forces of the inherently reductionistic pull of a metaphor on the one hand, and the historically conditioned push to overextend the use of a popular construct on the other. Whatever metaphors we might use to describe the ministry of the deacon, a fundamentally important function of the deacon, as a servant of communion, is to read the signs of the times in service to God's people and the Church.

> [The deacon] sees the signs of the times close up every day, but, as an ordained minister of the gospel, he is particularly called to *read* the signs and to interpret them in the light of the gospel, so as to lead his Christian brothers and sisters, who are all charged with the same responsibility. Properly understood and lived, the diaconate should surely, therefore, be a leaven for the apostolate of the laity.[9]

It is in solidarity with, and out of filial love for, God's people that the deacon seeks to be a leaven for the apostolate of the laity.

# The Ministry of the Deacon with and to the Laity

It is notable that the centuries when the diaconate was effectively absent have also been centuries when the laity became increasingly passive in the liturgy and increasingly neglected in terms of a formal apostolate. There is a least a hint here again that a flourishing diaconate and a flourishing laity actually go together.[10]

As McPartlan here suggests, current experience alludes to a link between a functioning diaconate and an engaged laity. Current statistics tend to bear this out. For example, the Center for Applied Research in the Apostolate (CARA) reports that in 2007 there was a total of 15,407 permanent deacons in the United States, up from 7,204 in 1985.[11] The U.S. Bishops' Conference document *Co-Workers in the Vineyard of the Lord* reports that in 2005 there were a total of 32,795 lay ecclesial ministers in paid and volunteer positions in parishes in the United States.[12] CARA also reports that in 2006–2007 there were 20,240 individuals enrolled in lay ecclesial formation programs throughout the country.[13] Of course, none of these statistics imply a cause-and-effect relationship between the number of permanent deacons and the number of laity actively involved in ministry. Nevertheless, it seems valid to state that a substantial number of laity are involved in significant ministry in the Church at a time when the ministry of the deacon has been growing. The experience in the United States suggests that the early concerns about the permanent diaconate discouraging lay participation in the Church may have been overstated.

To the extent that the deacon understands that one dimension of his ministry is to be leaven for the apostolate of the laity, it seems reasonable to expect that the laity will respond by more fully, actively, and consciously participating in the life of the Church and in their spiritual life. This may be another good reason to want to encourage and promote a balanced and meaningful understanding of the ministry of the deacon. It is through the ministry of the deacon, although not exclusively so, that the laity are encouraged, helped, and inspired to claim and live their baptismal dignity. By what he says, by what he does, and by *how* he does it, and through his consistent mentoring of those with whom he serves, the deacon becomes a living example of loving service for all. As the deacon emulates Christ the Servant, with God's help, the laity are increasingly encouraged to respond in ways that will serve the kingdom of God more fully. After all, who can ignore for long the inexorable yet gentle urgings of Christ's loving call to serve?

> The participation of the lay faithful in the threefold mission of Christ as Priest, Prophet and King finds its source in the anointing of Baptism, its further development in Confirmation, and its realization and dynamic sustenance in the Holy Eucharist. It is a participation given to each member of the lay faithful *individually*, inasmuch as each is one of the *many* who form the *one Body* of the Lord....Precisely because it derives *from* Church *communion*, the sharing of the lay faithful in the threefold mission of Christ requires that it be lived and realized *in communion* and *for the increase of communion itself.*[14]

As a servant of communion and leaven of the apostolate of the laity, it is the deacon who should be among the very first to reach out to God's beloved, by words and deeds, to help the lay faithful to fully, actively, and consciously participate in the threefold mission of Christ as priest, prophet, and king. Of course, to be able to do that, the deacon's threefold ministry of charity, word, and liturgy must fully incorporate and reflect Christ's threefold mission, and he must have been formed to understand his role in this important mission.

Any hint of clericalism on the part of the deacon (or for that matter the laity) seriously runs the risk of jeopardizing the ability of the laity to take seriously, and to make their rightful claim to, their mission, which is Christ's own. Tkacik and McGonigle address briefly, yet comprehensively, the attitude about ministry that a power-centered clericalism inevitably engenders:

> Ministry in the Church is not seen as an inter-action of diverse gifts given by the Holy Spirit to all through baptism, but as a fixed arrangement by which some posses special powers (the clergy) and others are the recipients of the operative effects of these powers (the

laity). The ministry of leadership is not seen as service, but rather as divinely granted authority from above which must be accepted by the People of God.[15]

It is first the deacon that must grow beyond such a distorted view of ministry to one conducted and lived consistently with the mind and heart of Jesus. The deacon, who is called to serve as Jesus the Servant did, serves with a radical Christ-centrism. The early history of the diaconate illustrates the spirit of this type of service. As legend has it, when St. Lawrence the deacon was asked to bring the treasures of the Church to the emperor, he brought the poor and the marginalized of the local Church. This is the spirit of radical Christ-centrism in which the deacon serves. It is through this spirit of service that the ministry of the deacon can begin to help the laity see their role in the Church with balance and clarity. It is the ministry of the deacon to help the laity develop a modern ecclesiology so that they can become free to explore the many ways in which they can live the mission of Christ that is theirs to live. It is the ministry of the deacon to develop a life-giving, balanced perspective on the hierarchical nature of the Church so that he can help God's beloved live their lives as full sharers in the priestly, prophetic, and kingly mission of Jesus.

> The church can be said to be hierarchical, not in the sense of a chain-of-command or a pyramidal structure, but in the sense that the church possesses a "sacred order" (*hier-arche*). The church then can be called "hierarchical" in the sense that it is an *ordered* communion constituted by a great diversity of ministries and Christian activities that together build up the life of the church. This ordered communion is grounded in the sacrament of baptism.[16]

To be sure, responsibility, authority, and accountability are all part of life in the Church. An ordered and orderly communion could not exist without them. Nevertheless, at a very minimum it should be the deacon who exemplifies, in what he says and does, the highest, most life-giving articulation of how an ordered communion, founded by Christ, lives and behaves. As the deacon is an icon of Jesus the Servant and servant of communion, then his life within the ordered communion founded by Christ should—must—resound with a leadership based on relationships rather than power. As such, the deacon teaches that the Church is founded on the principles of relational rather than power leadership by the way he lives and conducts his ministry. And it is very important that the laity have access to this lesson, because it is in this way that they will become freer to claim and live their baptismal dignity. To that end, the ministry of the deacon can help the laity participate in the priestly, prophetic, and kingly mission of Jesus in very specific and helpful ways.[17]

## Participation in the Priestly Mission of Jesus

The lay faithful are sharers in the *priestly mission*, for which Jesus offered himself on the cross and continues to be offered in the celebration of the Eucharist for the glory of God and the salvation of humanity. Incorporated in Jesus Christ, the baptized are united to him and to his sacrifice in the offering they make of themselves and their daily activities (cf. Rom 12:1, 2). Speaking of the lay faithful the Council says: "For their work, prayers and apostolic endeavors, their ordinary married and family life, their daily labor, their mental and physical relaxation, if carried out in the Spirit, and even the hardships of life if patiently borne—all of these become spiritual sacrifices acceptable to God through Jesus Christ (cf. 1 Pt 2:5). During the celebration of the Eucharist these sacrifices are most lovingly offered to the Father along with the Lord's body."[18]

The construct of a "nonordained priest as priest" may seem foreign to some of the laity, especially to the generation of Catholics that predates the Second Vatican Council. For part of the history of the Church, the laity were involved minimally in parish life. So, to speak to the laity of a priestly mission, perhaps even to laity born after the Second Vatican Council, might seem to them as odd, if not also incredible. At a minimum, they might begin to conclude that they did not sign up to live their life doing "churchy" things, such as praying all the time, reading only Church periodicals, and giving up vacations and other "luxuries" of life. Yet their lives take on a radically meaningful character when they realize that the priestly life is theirs to live and to enjoy. It is the ministry of the deacon to help the laity recognize and appreciate this great gift—that the priestly life is a life of nobility, integrity, and wholeness—and within their reach. It is a life that everyone will want to live.

Central to the notion that the priestly mission of Jesus is an integral part of the lived ministry of the laity is life as prayer. *Too often, it seems, otherwise devout Catholic-Christians develop the notion that the day-to-day life they lead on earth is mostly a burden to be endured, rather than a life to be lived to the fullest.* A view more in harmony with our faith's perspective on the created order would, instead, lead us to recognize and honor the fact that, properly lived, our life is destined to be a prayer of praise and joy—one would hope a relatively long, joyful prayer. Every burden with which we struggle, every joyful moment in which we revel, every good deed we do, especially those done without even a thought—in short, every moment of our existence is a prayer to the God who created us and makes our moments possible. If more Catholics could realize the power that lies in the inherent sacredness of a Christian life, even when lived unevenly, they would experience more deeply the divine presence in their life, as well as the sacredness of all of creation. Our God, who is present in every molecule of creation, makes it a reflection of his love and solicitude for everything he created, but especially us.

Too often, it seems, we might ignore or fail to appreciate the nobility and integrity of our lives that result from our being created by a loving and eternal Creator. It is through the routine, and hence easily overlooked, events of our lives that we sing the praises of the One who created us in his image and likeness. This is our liturgy of life. The deacon, through his ministry to the laity, draws them to a recognition of and appreciation for their life as prayer. Through the deacon's example, as well as the lived example of his family, the laity can be drawn to a more complete and balanced understanding of how their lives can resonate with prayer in the routine events of their day.

In addition, aware of his role in the liturgy of the Church, as well as the liturgy of life, the deacon is able to draw others into the acceptance of life as prayer. To be sure, the deacon and the people he serves have different roles in the Liturgy of the Eucharist, yet it is through his participation with them in the liturgy of life that he is able to exemplify for the laity in the liturgy the extent to which every moment of our lives is a form of prayer.

> The renewal in the Eucharist of the covenant between the Lord and man draws the faithful into the compelling love of Christ and sets them afire. From the liturgy, therefore, and especially from the Eucharist, as from a fountain, grace is channeled into us; and the sanctification of men in Christ and the glorification of God, to which all other activities of the Church are directed as toward their goal, are most powerfully achieved.[19]

After all, it is in the liturgy that we bring our cares, concerns, and joys and offer them to God, who makes them holy and incorporates them into the very Body and Blood of his Son, Jesus Christ. In this way, the liturgy is a microcosm of the liturgy of life, and it is the deacon who helps establish a very visible and enduring connection between our daily lives and the liturgy. Finally, at those infrequent times in the deacon's life when he has the last say—at the dismissal at the end of Mass, for example—he sends forth the people he serves to live the liturgy of life, to live what they have just received, to enliven the world with the divine love to which they have a valid claim and for which they have an obligation to share.

## Participation in the Prophetic Mission of Jesus

Through their participation in the *prophetic mission* of Christ, "who proclaimed the kingdom of his Father by the testimony of his life and by the power of his word," the lay faithful are given the ability and responsibility to accept the gospel in faith and to proclaim it in word and deed, without hesitating to courageously identify and denounce evil. United to Christ, the "great prophet" (Lk 7:16), and in the Spirit made "witnesses" of the Risen Christ, the lay faithful are made sharers in the appreciation of the Church's supernatural faith, that "cannot err in matters of belief" and sharers as well in the grace of the word (cf. Acts 2:17–18; Rev 19:10). They are also called to allow the newness and the power of the gospel to shine out every day in their family and social life, as well as to express patiently and courageously in the contradictions of the present age their hope of future glory even "through the framework of their secular life."[20]

Anyone familiar with the fate of the prophets might blanch a bit over the prospect of taking on that role. From Amos to John the Baptist, those whose calling it has been to describe "the signs of the times"[21] to a people not open to such messages often led a life characterized by derision, threats, and, not infrequently, death. Yet, prophets (and saints!) we are called to be, within the circumstances of our life. Fortunately, it appears that God does not call too many of us to the radical call of the prophets of old. Instead, our call is to live a life that proclaims God's kingdom and the gospel of Jesus Christ in how we conduct our day-to-day existence. And it is the particular call of the deacon to make concrete that kind of call to the prophetic ministry of Jesus Christ.

Generally, the deacon participates in the type of life that most of the laity experience. Usually he is employed by an organization outside of the Church; and he faces the daily pressures of earning a living while trying to maintain his ethical standards. He must wear the many hats of an employee, provider, husband, father, possibly grandfather, and whatever roles he may have in the Church as a result of his ordination to the permanent diaconate. Just having to bear gracefully the many burdens that accompany the wearing of so many hats begins to speak eloquently and concretely to the laity about what it means to participate in the prophetic mission of Jesus Christ. Moreover, in the workplace, the managers and colleagues of the deacon eventually learn of his "outside activities." Invariably, two things occur: first, the deacon finds himself being consulted on personal matters by his colleagues and even managers, and second, the expectations for his ethical behavior increase significantly. The experience of deacons bears this out. In one such case, whenever a deacon's manager wanted to consult him on a personal or personnel matter she would tell him, "I need you to put on your collar" (metaphorically, of course). The manager trusted him enough to entrust him with confidential matters so that another might be helped. That type of witness to the Christian life not only brings the light of Christ to the workplace, but it also communicates to each person touched by that witness, whether Catholic or not, religious or not, what it means to be a loving, living Christian— that is to say, what it means to live according to the mind and heart of Jesus. It also reinforces the fact that work, properly understood, both honors and reinforces the dignity of humankind.

> If one wishes to define more clearly the ethical meaning of work, it is this truth that one must particularly keep in mind. Work is a good thing for man—a good thing for his humanity—because through work man *not only transforms nature*, adapting it to his own needs, but he also *achieves fulfillment* as a human being and indeed, in a sense, becomes "more a human being."[22]

When lives are touched by such a witness, it begins to leave a mark on the hearts and minds of people that can eventually become the indelible mark of God's love. And when that begins to occur, lives change for the better. Hope fills the heart and faith begins to blossom.

Perhaps, also, the Catholic laity begin to understand that they have a similar role to play. After all, the ministry of the deacon is not to become the most popular, star-studded Christian in an organization; it is to "walk the talk" by living the words of the gospel of Jesus Christ within the context of the lives that most individuals live. There is no greater testament to the gospel than a Christian life fully lived, and it is the deacon that, with God's help, does that. But that living testament of the gospel is not intended mostly for the benefit of the deacon. It is primarily intended for the world. So it seems necessary for the witness of a deacon to be perceived as achievable by the "regular" people. After all, if the deacon sets himself up as a "super Christian," he may be admired, he may be respected, he may even become the source of jealousy, but he will probably not become an instrument of growth for others. The way of the Christian will, instead, appear to be an impossible mission reserved for the most saintly or pious among us. Instead, it is through a life lived nobly and with humility that the deacon preaches prophetically to his primary constituency, the laity, so that they are encouraged and inspired to make the prophetic mission of Christ their own. And the deacon is uniquely positioned to do just that because he is a representative of Christ's Church that lives and works shoulder-to-shoulder with those whom he serves.

Of course, being a prophet in the workplace can place the deacon in difficult situations, but how he handles those complex situations can be a solid proclamation of the gospel to those who have not yet heard of it. For example, a deacon who was a senior manager in an institution was asked by his management to close a department and lay off everyone in it. The deacon could have refused, then been replaced by someone else who might be inclined to follow orders to the letter at the expense of the employees in the department. Instead, the deacon negotiated a fair severance package for each person, arranged to find alternative employment for them, and was able to give them several additional weeks of pay to ease the transition to the new job. That is the gospel in action and that is precisely how the prophetic ministry of the deacon helps others to learn how they can participate in it also. Living the life of a prophet can be difficult and threatening at times, but the deacon, through the witness of his life, can help those he serves to recognize that the light can shine in even the darkest moments. He can also help others discover the heart and soul of the prophet that lives within them.

## Participation in the Kingly Mission of Jesus

Because the lay faithful belong to Christ, Lord and King of the Universe, they share in his *kingly mission* and are called by him to spread that Kingdom in history. They exercise their kingship as Christians, above all in the spiritual combat in which they seek to overcome in themselves the kingdom of sin (cf. Rom 6:12), and then to make a gift of themselves so as to serve, in justice and in charity, Jesus who is himself present in all his brothers and sisters, above all in the very least (cf. Mt 25:40). But in particular the lay faithful are called to restore to creation all its original value. In ordering creation to the authentic well-being of humanity in an activity governed by the life of grace, they share in the exercise of the power with which the Risen Christ draws all things to himself and subjects them along with himself to the Father, so that God might be everything to everyone. (cf. 1 Cor 15:28; Jn 12:32)[23]

The deacon has been aptly described as a "sacrament of God's love."[24] He is to be for all a visible sign of God's love, as well as an instrument of that love. There is perhaps no more certain sign of God's love than to experience someone who is genuinely concerned about the well-being of all humanity and actively engaged in tending to the most pressing needs of God's beloved. It is the deacon whose ministry calls him to become that sign for all to see and to emulate. By doing that, the deacon inspires the laity to do likewise. Similarly, by virtue of his access to the resources of the Church, the deacon is able to bring to those most in need the help and the hope that will sustain them. By doing what he must do, the deacon not only becomes an instrument of God's preferential concern for the poor and the marginalized, but he also, and perhaps just as importantly, becomes a witness to the laity of their mission to serve those most in need among us. In that way, charity becomes a verb, rather than remaining an ideal beyond the reach of all but the most holy among us. No one person can serve the needs of everyone and no one person can "restore to creation all its original value." Thankfully, the role of the Messiah is taken. Nevertheless, in his exercise of leadership on behalf of God's beloved, the deacon is able to not only help those most in need improve their lot, but also to lead others to help by his example. After all, isn't that what the King of Kings did for us?

As noted earlier, in *how* he conducts his ministry, the deacon's leadership style is (or should be) relational. That is to say, he seeks to influence others through example and love, rather than resorting to institutional forms of authority. Although the ministry of the deacon does not have invested in it very much, if any, institutional authority, it is not uncommon for individuals outside of the church structures to grant them some deference by virtue of their ordained status. Regrettably, some deacons become tempted to fall into the trap of accepting this deference as a sign of institutional authority and then proceed to act as if the perception were reality. Often, the inevitable conflicts that such a clash between perceptions and reality create tend to diminish the deacon's effectiveness. Worse still, such an unhappy situation can tend to reinforce in the laity the notion that ministry in the Church is based on institutional power rather than on the more appropriate relational power. And nothing could be further from the intent of the kingly mission of Jesus Christ in which all the laity share. Jesus' authority came from his deep relationship with the Father. His was a kingship based on an inexorable connection to and an expression of God's love. Christians who not only have adopted the name of Jesus the Christ but also have made a promise to live according to the mind and heart of Jesus, are thus called to take on the kind of kingship that Jesus himself adopted. It is the ministry of the deacon to make this adoption concrete, visible, and approachable.

> The Church cannot serve as a sacrament of Christ to the world unless her members live their lives in such a way to reveal Christ to others. Acting as sacraments themselves, the faithful enable the Church to act as a sacrament. The awesome responsibility that this vision and self-understanding of what it means to be Church

bestows upon the laity cannot be overstated. We laity must respond to the challenge bestowed upon us by the Holy Spirit and live our lives within and outside of the Church in a manner that both reveals Christ, and claims as our own our rightful role in the Church's mission to the world and her own *ad intra* experiences as community.[25]

By quietly living the life of a king in the manner that Jesus did, the deacon inspires everyone whose life he touches to become a king in the same way. As a result, the world might sooner or later more actively seek to become part of God's kingdom on earth. That is the ultimate hope for humankind and the deacon's ministry works toward fulfilling that hope.

# The Ministry of the Deacon and Parish Life

The parish-based ministry of the deacon is extremely important in Kasper's view....He suggests that it would be a good idea to provide at least one deacon for every parish so that the sacramental nature of the parish might be complete. He writes: 'Each parish has to make sure that *diakonia* is realized. This means that faith and preaching, as well as the Eucharist and liturgy must be oriented to *diakonia*. Faith without *diakonia* is not a Christian faith. Preaching without *diakonia* is not Christian preaching. A non-diaconal parish celebrating the Eucharist may express its faith, but its faith remains dead; in the final analysis it cannot find God, as they miss the point that God reveals himself in the people, especially the poor.[26]

To be sure, everything said about the ministry of the deacon vis-à-vis the threefold mission of the laity applies to parish life. However, there are some additional dimensions of the deacon's ministry that are evident when one views that ministry through the lens of parish life. Cardinal Walter Kasper's perspective on the ministry of the deacon in the parish, quoted by Deacon William Ditewig above, identifies some of the additional dimensions of diaconal ministry. For one, the presence of the active and balanced ministry of the deacon in the parish both expresses and influences the faith of the parish. This is no small thing. The implications for the life of a parish are significant as well as life-giving.

Consider, for example, the likely long-term effects to a parish of a public ministry focused on the needs of those who can speak for themselves and those who cannot, based on a relational rather than a power model of leadership, and expressed in solidarity with the mission of the parish. Such a ministry would complement the ministry of the priests in the parish and inevitably become a source of inspiration for all. That can be, perhaps must be, characteristic of the ministry of the deacon in the parish. As parishes seek to evolve from a maintenance-centered perspective to a broader mission-driven existence, the ministry of the deacon, properly exercised, can be of invaluable assistance in the transformation of a parish.[27] Cardinal Kasper's suggestion that there should be a deacon in every parish seems to speak to those parishes who seek to extend their vision beyond that of daily survival.

> The intermediary function of the deacon is different from other intermediate structures that exist in the church between the bishop and the laity, such as councils and synods. As a unique representative of the bishop, the deacon could mediate the bishop's care and concern for the individual members of his flock in a personal manner.[28]

In this sense, the deacon validly and productively serves as a bridge in service to the people of the local Church. In another sense, the deacon's ministry in a parish can have an important catechetical dimension beyond the effects resulting from the obvious teaching activities in which a deacon might engage. In the manner in which he conducts his ministry, in the differences between his ministry and that of the priest that his presence makes apparent, in his solicitude for anyone who seeks the medicine of a patient and loving listener, the deacon teaches profound lessons about the mission of the Church and, hence, the parish and about the role of every person in that mission. To be sure, such lessons are not exclusively his to teach, but they are primarily his to impart.

In the daily operations of the parish the deacon may also have an important role to play. Not all deacons have the gifts necessary to administer the daily operations of a parish. Yet many do and, once again, their ministry can have an important, though not exclusive, role in this area.

> The church has been naturally—and rightly—reluctant to turn even its secular affairs entirely over to people whose primary experience has been in a worldly, perhaps for-profit environment. The church is not, after all, in a profit-making business, and it will always (in the interest of its mission) make at least some choices that a business would never elect. Here, too, however, there is a clear leadership role for deacons: we know both the church and its priorities on the one hand, and we have some insight into the benefits that strong management, good governance and leadership, and common sense have brought to institutions in the secular world. For deacons, using the insights and experience we glean from secular work is a challenging assignment to which our exciting, still evolving ambassadorial role is calling us.[29]

Historically, deacons have been given the responsibility of administering the goods of the Church.[30] The needs and experiences of the Church in modern times seem to support the wisdom of electing to remain in continuity with our past practices in that area. From a practical view, the deacon with the appropriate skills can be a valued assistant to the pastor in administering the daily operations of a parish, particularly a large one. However, it would be wise for pastors to consider more than the deacon's prior business experience before committing to such a role in the parish for the deacon.

For one, the deacon must possess a balanced ecclesiology. That is to say, he must understand the mission of the parish and the Church's mode of governance so that he is able to administer the goods of the Church in a way that is consistent with the mission of the Church in the modern world. Otherwise, the parish runs the risk of managing its important resources in ways that are incongruent with its mission. And such an unhappy situation will only add to the woes of the pastor, threaten the parish's ability to live out its mission, and obscure the *diakonia* of the faith of the parish. When the skills of the deacon are consistent with the needs of the parish in this regard, one possible result of the ministry of the deacon is that it will add years to the life of the pastor. On the other hand, when the mismatch between the deacon's skills and parish's needs is great, the administrative role of the deacon can have the unhappy and incongruous effect of shortening the life (or perhaps the tenure) of the pastor.

From a different perspective, the administrative role of the deacon, properly conducted, can become an instrument of growth for the people of the parish. Through his words and deeds, the deacon can teach the people of the parish what the Church holds to be important and, by implication, what their priorities might also be. For example, while it is certainly important to make prudent decisions about one's finances, one should be careful to not allow economic factors to consistently trump other or less concrete considerations. Parish operations would naturally exemplify how one might order one's priorities so that they are more consistent with those of the gospel. Parish life and operations must in appearance and fact exemplify gospel values, and so should the life of every Christian. It is, therefore, fair to expect that the deacon's administrative role would articulate these values so that all might learn how a Catholic Christian organization and people should conduct their daily lives. It is to all Christians to whom the responsibility falls to be a leaven for the world. The people of the Church are called to do that through their lived example. The deacon, through his ministry, serves as a reminder and example to all. Certainly the signs of the times seem to be telling us that humankind is starving for examples of a life well lived.

Finally, when the deacon shares his life, his work, and his struggles with those he serves, his ministry speaks eloquently about the call to serve, which also he shares with his brothers and sisters in the pews. To serve others meaningfully and consistently with the mind and heart of Jesus requires more than just a mechanical or perfunctory administration of care. It requires a sense of solidarity with the struggles of those we serve; it calls for an openness to the often difficult task of discerning needs from wants; it moves us to develop a genuine regard for the dignity and nobility of the person; it *demands* that we learn to see with the eyes of those who come to us for succor. That is the life's work of *every* Christian, and it is demanding work. Without having or exercising a monopoly on such work, the ministry of the deacon, by virtue of who he is and how he does what he does, facilitates for others their participation in the work of the kingdom, done with the mind and heart of the King. There is nothing easy, comfortable, or, perhaps, even "normal" about publicly and honestly sharing one's life with strangers, some of whom may be, at best, minimally attentive and, at worst, utterly indifferent to the sharing. Nevertheless, it is through the cross of this sometimes terribly challenging and difficult ministry that the deacon can encourage his brothers and sisters in Christ, who are his partners on this most important of journeys, to walk toward the light of new life that we encounter every time we hold out, in love, a helping hand to a stranger or to one of our own. If the deacon's ministry to God's beloved teaches anything, it teaches, "As you did it to one of the least of my brethren, you did it to me." (Matt 25:40)

# Notes

## Foreword

1. Paul VI, *Hodie Concilium*, AAS 58 (1966): 57–64.

2. *Lumen Gentium*, no. 11.

3. *Lumen Gentium*. no. 1; *Gaudium et Spes*, no. 40.

4. Congregation for the Clergy, *Directory for the Ministry and Life of Permanent Deacons* (hereafter, *DMLPD*) (Vatican City: Libreria Editrice Vaticana, 1998), no. 47.

5. Patrick McCaslin and Michael G. Lawler, *Sacrament of Service: A Vision of the Permanent Deacon Today* (New York/Mahwah, NJ: Paulist Press, 1986), 62–63.

6. Cardinal Roger Mahony, "Church of the Eucharist: A Communion for Mission," in *Origins* 33:42 (April 1, 2004), 723.

7. *Lumen Gentium*, no. 29, referring to the functions of the diaconate.

8. Walter Kasper, *Leadership in the Church: How Traditional Roles Can Serve the Christian Community Today* (New York: Crossroad, 2003), 40.

9. Ibid.

10. Kasper, 23.

11. United States Catholic Conference (USCC), *A National Study on the Permanent Diaconate of the Catholic Church in the United States, 1994–1995* (Washington, DC: USCC, 1996), 13.

12. Kasper, 27.

13. John Paul II, catechesis at the general audience of October 6, 1993, *Deacons Serve the Kingdom of God*, no. 6, in *Insegnamenti* XVI, 2 (1993), 954.

14. *DMLPD*, no. 49.

15. John Paul II, "Deacons: Apostles of the New Evangelization," February 19, 2000, no. 2.

16. Ibid., no. 3.

17. John Paul II, postsynodal apostolic exhortation *Pastores Gregis*, October 16, 2003, no. 49.

# Introduction

1. Congregation for Catholic Education, *Basic Norms for the Formation of Permanent Deacons* (Vatican City: Libreria Editrice Vaticana, 1998), Introduction 2.3.
2. See *Lumen Gentium*, no. 18.
3. *Gaudium et Spes*, no. 40.
4. See chapter 6 of my *The Emerging Diaconate: Servant Leaders in a Servant Church* (Mahwah, NJ: Paulist Press, 2007).
5. Ibid.
6. *Basic Norms*, Introduction 2.4 to 2.7.
7. *Lumen Gentium*, no. 24.

# Chapter 1

1. *Lumen Gentium*, no. 29.
2. Paul VI, *Sacrum Diaconatus Ordinem* (June 18, 1967), I/1.
3. One author points to an exchange of letters in 1840 between a physician and a priest-friend in Germany as an early indicator of the interest being expressed there and elsewhere in Europe. For an overview of the continental discussions on the possibilities of a renewed contemporary diaconate, see my *The Emerging Diaconate: Servant Leaders in a Servant Church* (Mahwah, NJ: Paulist Press, 2007).
4. April 28, 1968, Cologne, Germany; November 3, 1968, Rottenburg, Germany; December 8, 1968, Bamburg, Germany; December 8, 1968, Douala, Cameroon.

# Chapter 2

1. Rick Warren, *The Purpose-Driven Church* (Grand Rapids: Zondervan, 1995), and *The Purpose-Driven Life* (Grand Rapids: Zondervan, 2002).

2. United States Conference of Catholic Bishops, *National Directory for the Formation, Ministry, and Life of Permanent Deacons in the United States* (Washington, DC: USCCB, 2004), no. 105.

3. United States Conference of Catholic Bishops, "Guidelines for Doctrinally Sound Catechetical Materials" (*Origins*: CNS Documentary Service, vol. 20: no. 27, December 13, 1990), 430.

4. Congregation for Catholic Education / Congregation for the Clergy, *Basic Norms for the Formation of Permanent Deacons: Directory for the Ministry and Life of Permanent Deacons* (Washington, DC: USCCB, 1998), no. 66.

5. Pope John XXIII, "Address to the Council Fathers at the Close of the Council's First Session," December 8, 1962, in *The Pope Speaks*, vol. 8, no. 3 (1963), 399–400.

6. John R. Donahue, SJ, "The Parables of Jesus," in *The New Jerome Biblical Commentary*, eds. Raymond E. Brown, SS; Joseph A. Fitzmyer, SJ; and Roland E. Murphy, OCarm (Englewood Cliffs, NJ: Prentice-Hall, 1990), 1367.

7. Aristotle, *On Interpretation*, part 1, trans. E. M. Edghill, http://classics.mit.edu.

8. Andrew M. Greeley, "The Catholic Imagination and the Catholic University," in *America* 164 (March 16, 1991), 285–86.

9. *National Directory*, no. 105.

10. The reader is encouraged to reference the works from which the "Imaginary Conversation" was constructed. The following four titles are by Carl G. Jung: *Psychology and Alchemy* (Princeton, NJ: Princeton University Press, 1967); *Approaching the Unconscious* (New York: Dell Publishing, 1968); *Modern Man in Search of a Soul* (New York: Harcourt, Brace & World, 1933); and *Psychology and Religion* (Princeton, NJ: Princeton University Press, 1967). The "Imaginary Conversation" also drew from Choan-Seng Song, *Third-Eye Theology* (Maryknoll, NY: Orbis

Press, 1981); Raimundo Panikkar, *The Unknown Christ of Hinduism* (Maryknoll, NY: Orbis Press, 1981); David Bosch, *Transforming Mission: Paradigm Shifts in Theology of Mission* (Maryknoll, NY: Orbis Press, 1991); Maria Montessori, *The Discovery of the Child* (New York: Ballantine Books, 1990), and *The Absorbent Mind* (New York: Dell Publishing, 1984); Rudolph Steiner, *Spiritual Ground of Education* (New York: Anthroposophic Press, Inc., 1972), and *Practical Advice to Teachers* (New York: Anthroposophic Press, 1976); Paulo Freire, *Pedagogy of the Oppressed* (New York: The Continuum Publishing Co., Inc., 1989), and *A Pedagogy for Liberation: Dialogues on Transforming Education* (Westport, CT: Bergin & Garvey Publishers, Inc., 1987).

11. Robert McAfee Brown, *Unexpected News: Reading the Bible with Third World Eyes* (Louisville, KY: Westminster John Knox Press, 1984).

12. Thomas Merton, *Contemplation in a World of Action* (New York: Doubleday, 1973), 161.

13. Vatican II, *Gaudium et Spes*, no. 1.

14. Ibid.

15. *National Directory*, no. 105.

# Chapter 4

1. *National Directory*, no. 153.

2. Ibid., no. 155.

# Chapter 5

1. John Paul II, *Novo Millennio Ineunte*, no. 46.

2. *De Zelo et Livore* 12, in J. P. Migne, ed., *Patrologiae Cursus Completus: Series Latina* 4, 646. Cited henceforth as PL.

3. *De Bono Patientiae* 9, PL 4, 628.

4. *Christifideles Laici*, no. 32.

5. United States Conference of Catholic Bishops, *Co-Workers in the Vineyard of the Lord: Resource Document on Lay*

*Ecclesial Ministry* (Washington, DC: USCCB, 2005), 13.

6. *Lumen Gentium*, no. 10.

7. *Co-Workers in the Vineyard of the Lord*, 11.

8. See *Lumen Gentium*, no. 10, and *Presbyterorum Ordinis*, no. 2.

9. *Lumen Gentium*, no. 33.

10. Ibid., no. 12.

11. *Christifideles Laici*, no. 15.

12. Canon 225, §2.

13. See Markus Barth, *Ephesians: Translation and Commentary on Chapters Four to Six*, Anchor Bible (New York: Doubleday, 1974), 618.

14. F. R. Barry, *A Philosophy from Prison* (London: SCM, 1926), 151.

15. For a more in-depth treatment of the theology of marriage, see Michael G. Lawler, *Marriage and Sacrament: A Theology of Christian Marriage* (Collegeville, MN: Liturgical Press, 1993).

16. *Summa Theologiae, Supplement*, 34, 2, ad 2.

17. See *Origins* 17 (1987), 327–29.

18. United States Catholic Conference, *National Directory for the Formation, Ministry, and Life of Permanent Deacons in the United States* (Washington, DC: USCCB, 2005), nos. 31–40, 18–22.

19. *Sacrosanctum Concilium*, no. 7.

20. *Roman Pontifical*, the Rite of Ordination of Deacons.

21. I borrow the word *underside* from Jorg Rieger, *Remember the Poor: The Challenge to Theology in the Twenty-First Century* (Harrisburg, PA: Trinity Press International, 1998), 1–5.

22. See Augustine, In *Joannis Evangelio Tractatus* VI, 1, 7, PL 1428.

23. *Sermo* 340, 1, PL 38, 1483.

24. See *Lumen Gentium*, no. 10, and *Presbyterorum Ordinis*, no. 2.

25. *Lumen Gentium*, no. 29.

26. *The Rites of the Catholic Church* (New York: Pueblo Publishing, 1976), 541.

27. Ibid., 544.

28. *Sacrosanctum Concilium*, no. 59.

29. *Lumen Gentium*, no. 11.

30. *Familiaris Consortio*, no. 68.

31. Ibid.

32. Ibid.

33. See *National Directory*, no. 167; also see no. 66.

34. Center for Marriage and Family, *Time, Sex, and Money: The First Five Years of Marriage* (Omaha, NE: Creighton University Press, 2000).

35. *National Directory*, no. 66.

36. Karl Rahner, "Women and the Priesthood," in *Concern for the Church* (New York: Crossroad, 1981), 36.

37. See Aimé Georges Martimort, *Deaconesses: A Historical Study* (San Francisco: Ignatius Press, 1986); Roger Gryson, *The Ministry of Women in the Early Church* (Collegeville, MN: Liturgical Press, 1976); Gary Macy, *The Hidden History of Women's Ordination: Female Clergy in the Medieval West* (Oxford: Oxford University Press, 2008): Phyllis Zagano, *Holy Saturday: An Argument for the Restoration of the Female Diaconate in the Catholic Church* (New York: Crossroad, 2000); the Council of Chalcedon, c. 15, which refers to the ordination of women deacons and which decrees that a woman, who must be at least forty years of age, is to be ordained only after careful scrutiny. See also Norman P. Tanner, ed., *Decrees of the Ecumenical Councils* (Washington, DC: Georgetown University Press, 1990), 94.

# Chapter 6

1. Center for Applied Research in the Apostolate (CARA), *Profile of the Diaconate in the United States* (Washington, DC: CARA, 2006).

2. Ibid.

3. Carl C. Jung, *Two Essays on Analytical Psychology*, R. R. C. Hull, trans., Vol. 17 of *Collected Works* (Princeton, NJ: Princeton University Press, 1953).

4. Daniel J. Levinson, *The Seasons of a Man's Life* (New York: Ballantine Books, 1978).

5. Erik H. Erickson, *Identity and the Life Cycle* (New York: W. W. Norton & Company, 1980).

6. Jung, *Two Essays.*

7. Levinson, *The Seasons of a Man's Life.*

8. Carol Gilligan, *In a Different Voice* (Cambridge, MA: Harvard University Press, 1982).

9. *National Directory*, no. 153.

10. Jung, 131.

11. United States Conference of Catholic Bishops, *National Directory for the Formation, Ministry, and Life of Permanent Deacons in the United States* (Washington, DC: USCCB, 2005), no. 123.

12. Ibid., no. 126.

13. Bishops' Committee on the Permanent Diaconate, *Permanent Deacons in the United States: Guidelines for Their Formation and Ministry* (Washington, DC: National Conference of Catholic Bishops, 1984), 157.

# Chapter 7

1. Although I recognize the practical sense for a diocese to entrust direction of diaconal ministries to deacons, and indeed acquiesced in the decision by the archdiocese to replace me with a deacon, I believe there remains an argument for having a priest closely involved in this important work. In Newark, the position of vicar for deacons, held by a priest, seems capable of fulfilling this role of "objective authority" in serving both the archdiocese and the diaconate community, in collaboration with the deacon-director of the office and the formation process.

2. I believe, with many others, that not all individuals who *could* be deacons, in light of their clear talent for the ministry, as demonstrated in consistent and longtime patterns of "diaconal" service, *should* or *need* to become *ordained* deacons, which involves specific ecclesial expectations and obligations that an individual may be prudent *not* to assume.

3. The precise nature of a deacon's leadership role is beyond the scope of this article. For a discussion of this topic in greater detail, see, for example, William T. Ditewig, *The Emerging Diaconate: Servant Leaders in a Servant Church* (Mahwah, NJ: Paulist Press, 2007).

4. Cf. *National Directory for the Formation, Ministry, and Life of Permanent Deacons in the United States* (Washington, DC: USCCB, 2005), nos. 23–26, citing *The Catechism of the Catholic Church*, no. 1536.

5. Ibid., nos. 27–30.

6. Ibid., no. 24.

7. Ibid., no. 38.

8. Ibid., Preface, no. 3.

9. Ibid., no. 32.

10. John 15:12.

11. *National Directory*, no. 50.

12. Ibid., no. 24, citing Pope John Paul II, *Christifideles Laici*, no. 22.

13. 1 Corinthians 11:24.

14. *National Directory*, no. 32.

15. Ibid., no. 50.

16. Ibid., nos. 31–39.

17. Ibid., no. 38.

18. Ibid., no. 37.

19. Ibid., nos. 159–73.

20. Ibid., no. 33.

21. *Rite of Marriage* (1969), nos. 125 and 128.

22. Ibid., no. 51, citing *The Code of Canon Law*, c. 536.

23. Matthew 25:40.

24. *National Directory*, no. 36.

# Chapter 8

1. Please reread that statement before moving on. It seems to me it is trying to describe the process that leads to genuine humility, in the very best sense of that word, in an aspirant/candidate. It is a theological foundation for the confrontation necessary to challenge anyone who seeks ordination to the diaconate. It may be a kind of "vision statement" for the director of formation, assisted by the spiritual director, in helping applicants and aspirants to discern, candidates to grow and develop, and deacons to more fully become icons of the Christ the Servant.

Notes

*Editorial note*: Some newly appointed directors of formation at times confuse the *Directory*'s "Basic Standards for Readiness" for just such a checklist. Although it is understandable that, by outward appearance, the external formatting of the standards might seem to be a kind of checklist, experienced educators and formators understand that competencies are not achievable through a checklist methodology. This would do a disservice to the underlying purpose of the standards.

2. See NADD publication, *"Called, Formed, Sent,"* by Richard Rohr, originally presented to the NADD National Convention April 21, 2001, in Tempe, AZ.

3. This image was presented by Cardinal Roger Mahoney in an address to the NADD National Convention at Moraga, CA, June 2000.

4. It is beyond the scope of this chapter to fully explore the theological distinctions of each of these vocations. Much further discussion among those people currently trying to implement the *National Directory* is needed to expand paragraph 194 in chapter 5, "Aspirant Path in Diaconal Formation," and paragraph 216 in chapter 6, "Candidate Path in Diaconal Formation," which rely almost exclusively on the 1984 guidelines and their emphasis on vocation discernment as a response to the universal call of holiness.

5. John Paul II, "Papal Address to Permanent Deacons," Detroit, 1987. Accessed at www.deacons.net/Pope/PopeDetroit.htm.

6. Congregation for Catholic Education, *Basic Norms for the Formation of Permanent Deacons* (Washington, DC: USCCB, 1998), no. 9.

7. It is understood that a pastor (external forum) should never be the spiritual director (internal forum) of his own parishioner who is in formation. In wearing multiple hats, the "pastor hat" may influence the "spiritual-director hat" in forming a candidate who would be most helpful in meeting the pastor's real ministerial needs.

8. Francis George, OMI, "The Bishop and His Deacons: Reflections on the Directory for Deacons," in *Sacrum Ministerium*, Congregatio Pro Cleris, Annus IV, January 1998.

# Chapter 9

1. See James Keating, "Moral Life of the Deacon," in Keating, ed., *The Deacon Reader* (Mahwah, NJ: Paulist, 2006), 121.

2. John Paul II, Allocution to Permanent Deacons, *Origins* 17 (September 19, 1987): 327–29.

3. http://www.vatican.va/roman_curia/congregations/cclergy/documents/rc_con_cclergy_doc_19022000horam_en.html.

4. Archbishop Stafford in 2000 made a connection between a deacon's vocation as minister of the cup and the ancient vocation of confessor: http://www.vatican.va/roman_curia/congregations/cclergy/documents/rc_con_cclergy_doc_19022000_idf_en.html.

5. See William T. Ditewig, *The Emerging Diaconate: Servant Leaders in a Servant Church* (Mahwah. NJ: Paulist Press, 2007), esp. chapter 7.

# Chapter 10

1. See Michael J. Tkacik and Thomas McGonigle, OP, *Pneumatic Correctives: What Is the Spirit Saying to Church of the 21st Century?* (Lanham, MD: University Press of America, 2007).

2. United States Conference of Catholic Bishops. *Our Hearts Were Burning Within Us* (Washington, DC: USCCB, 1999), 24.

3. Leckey, Dolores R. *Rediscovering Vatican II: The Laity and Christian Education* (Mahwah, NJ: Paulist Press, 2006), 23.

4. Ibid., 24.

5. See Charles A. Bobertz, "Theological Education and the Diaconate," in *The Deacon Reader*, James Keating, ed. (Mahwah, NJ: Paulist Press, 2006), 148.

6. See Vatican II's *Declaration on Christian Education (Gravissimum Educationis)*; also the United States Conference of Catholic Bishops' *Pastoral Message on Catholic Education (To Teach as Jesus Did)* and *Pastoral Plan for Adult Faith Formation (Our Hearts Were Burning Within Us)*.

7. See Pope John Paul II, *Ex Corde Ecclesiae*, nos. 6, 31, 43.

8. Ibid., no. 27.

9. See United States Conference of Catholic Bishops, *To Teach as Jesus Did* (Washington, DC, 1972), 43.

10. Ibid., 48.

11. Ibid., 7.

12. Ibid., 14.

13. At the time of writing, Saint Leo University was partnering with the dioceses of St. Petersburg, Savannah, Orlando, and Richmond in the aspirancy and formation process of candidates to the diaconate.

14. As illustrative examples, we have integrated homiletics and the history, theology, and spirituality of the diaconate into our curriculum.

15. See Saint Leo University, *Graduate Academic Catalogue 2008–2009*, 61.

16. *To Teach As Jesus Did*, 80.

# Chapter 11

1. Robert Dykstra, *Discovering A Sermon: Personal Pastoral Preaching* (St. Louis, MO: Chalice, 2001), 25.

2. Ibid., 82.

3. Thomas Troeger, *Imaging a Sermon* (Nashville: Abingdon, 1990), 90–91.

4. Bishop's Committee on Priestly Life and Ministry, *Fulfilled in Your Hearing: The Homily in the Sunday Assembly* (Washington, DC: United States Conference of Catholic Bishops, 1982), 1.

5. Ibid., 1.

6. United States Conference of Catholic Bishops, *General Instruction of the Roman Missal* (Washington, DC: United States Conference of Catholic Bishops, 2003), 35.

7. See Owen F. Cummings, *Deacons in the Church* (Mahwah, NJ: Paulist Press, 2004), especially his chapter on Jesus as Deacon.

8. Edward Echlin, *The Deacon and the Church: Past and Future* (Staten Island, NY: Alba House, 1971), 47.

9. United States Conference of Catholic Bishops, *Ceremonial of Bishops* (Collegeville, MN: Liturgical Press, 1989), 151.

10. Lynn Sherman, *The Deacon in the Church* (New York: Alba House, 1991), 8.

11. *The Didache*, trans. James A. Kleist, ed. Johannes Quasten and Joseph Plumpe. Ancient Christian Writers: The Works of the Fathers in Translation (New York: Newman Press, 1948), 24.

12. St. Clement and St. Ignatius, *The Epistles of St. Clement of Rome and St. Ignatius of Antioch*, trans. James A. Kleist, Ancient Christian Writers, ed. Johannes Quasten and Joseph Plumpe, vol. 1 (Mahwah, NJ: Paulist, 1946).

13. Sherman, 14–17.

14. *The Didache*, 24.

15. Echlin, *The Deacon and the Church*, 19.

16. Edward Enright, "The History of the Diaconate," in *The Deacon Reader*, ed. James Keating (Mahwah, NJ: Paulist, 2006), 15.

17. Echlin, *The Deacon and the Church*, 76.

18. See Owen F. Cummings, *Deacons in the Church*.

19. Paul McPartlan, "The Permanent Diaconate: Catholic and Ecumenical Perspectives," Briefing 32 (2002), 14, http://www.catholicchurch.org.uk/briefing/0204/april.pdf.

20. Echlin, *The Deacon and the Church*, 102.

21. Owen Cummings, *Deacons and the Church* (Mahwah, NJ: Paulist, 2004), 51.

22. Enright, "The History of the Diaconate," 23.

23. Josef Hornef, "The Genesis and Growth of the Proposal," in *Foundations for the Renewal of the Diaconate*, ed. Bishops' Committee on the Diaconate (Washington, DC: USCCB, 1993), 6.

24. Ibid., 6.

25. Ibid., 7.

26. See William T. Ditewig, *The Emerging Diaconate: Servant Leaders in a Servant Church* (Mahwah, NJ: Paulist Press, 2007).

27. Hornef, 11.

28. Ibid., 9.

29. Wilhelm Schamoni, qtd. in Hornef, 9–11.

30. Wilhelm Schamoni, *Married Men as Ordained Deacons*,

1955, trans. Otto Eisner (Margate, Kent: The Thanet Press, 1953), 34–38.

31. Kenan Osborne, *The Permanent Diaconate: Its History and Place in the Sacrament of Orders* (Mahwah, NJ: Paulist, 2007), 4.

32. Ibid., 4–7. Osborne goes on to identify those five major theological changes as (a) the establishment of the mission and ministry of all baptized-confirmed Christians as a foundation of institutional Church ministry, (b) the reestablishment of the episcopacy as an official part of the sacrament of orders, (c) the redefinition of priesthood, (d) the reestablishment of the permanent diaconate, and (e) the official expansion of lay ministry into ecclesial dimensions of *tria munera* (proclamation, sanctification, assembling).

33. Pope Paul VI, *Sacrum Diaconatus Ordinem: General Norms for Restoring the Permanent Diaconate in the Latin Church*, Eternal Word Television Network, June 18, 1967, http://www. ewtn.com/library/PAPALDOC/P6DIACON.htm (accessed January 19, 2008). The internal quotations within the extract here are in the original.

34. William Ditewig, "The Diaconate of the Future," part 1, *Deacon Digest*, January 1, 2008, 10–11.

35. United States Conference of Catholic Bishops, *National Directory for the Formation, Ministry, and Life of Permanent Deacons in the United States* (Washington, DC: USCCB, 2005), 3.

36. William Ditewig, "The Diaconate of the Future," part 2, *Deacon Digest*, March/April 2008, 10–11.

37. United States Conference of Catholic Bishops, *National Directory for the Formation, Ministry, and Life of Permanent Deacons in the United States* (Washington, DC: USCCB, 2005), 38. The internal quotations within the extract here are in the original.

38. William Ditewig, "The Diaconate of the Future," part 4, *Deacon Digest*, July/August 2008, 10.

39. National Council of Catholic Bishops. *The Rites of the Catholic Church as Revised by the Second Vatican Council*, vol. 2 (Collegeville, MN: Liturgical Press, 1991), 59.

40. Avery Dulles, *Models of the Church* (New York: Doubleday, 1974), 76–88.

41. Richard McBrien, *Church: The Continuing Quest* (New York: Newman, 1970), 11.

42. *Sacrosanctum Concilium*, no. 9.
43. *Dei Verbum*, no. 8.
44. *Sacrosanctum Concilium*, no. 35.
45. Ibid., no. 52.

# Chapter 12

1. Owen F. Cummings, "Theology of the Diaconate," in *The Theology of the Diaconate: The State of the Question*, Owen F. Cummings, William T. Ditewig, and Richard R. Gaillardetz (Mahwah, NJ: Paulist, 2005), 28.
2. *Gaudium et Spes*, no. 4.
3. Cummings, *Theology of the Diaconate*, 28–29.
4. Ditewig, "Charting a Theology of Diaconate," in *Theology of the Diaconate*, 55.
5. *Lumen Gentium*, no. 29.
6. John Paul II, "Address to the Permanent Deacons," Detroit, September 19, 1987.
7. Marcia Finkelstein and Michael T. Brannick, "Applying Theories of Institutional Helping to Informal Volunteering: Motives, Role Identity, and Prosocial Personality, Social Behavior, and Personality," in *Social Behavior and Personality* 2007, 35 (1), 101–4.
8. Paul McPartlan, "The Deacon and *Gaudium et Spes*," in *The Deacon Reader*, ed. James Keating (Mahwah, NJ: Paulist Press, 2005), 69.
9. Ibid., 68.
10. Ibid., 72–3.
11. Center for Applied Research in the Apostolate (CARA), *Frequently Requested Catholic Church Statistics*. Retrieved January 2008 from www.cara.georgetown.edu.
12. United States Conference of Catholic Bishops, *Co-Workers in the Vineyard of the Lord: A Resource for Guiding the Development of Lay Ecclesial Ministry*, 2005, 13.
13. CARA, *Catholic Ministry Formation Enrollments: Statistical Overview for 2006–2007*. Retrieved January 2008 from www.cara.georgetown.edu.

14. John Paul II, *Christifideles Laici*, no. 14. Italics are in the original.

15. Michael J. Tkacik and Thomas C. McGonigle, *Pneumatic Correctives: What Is the Spirit Saying to the Church of the 21st Century?* (Lanham, MD: University of America Press, Inc., 2007), 84.

16. Richard R. Gaillardetz, "On the Theological Integrity of the Diaconate," in *The Theology of the Diaconate*, 82.

17. Chapter 3 of *The National Directory for the Formation, Ministry, and Life of Permanent Deacons in the United States* describes the four dimensions of diaconal formation that contribute to developing an ecclesiology and pastoral perspective in harmony with a ministry that promotes and supports the laity's efforts to claim and live their baptismal dignity. In that regard, the document speaks of the kind of ministry that will be required of the deacon in the third millennium. This document also provides actionable criteria for assessing the degree to which particular skills are present.

18. John Paul II, *Christifideles Laici*, no. 14. Italics are in the original.

19. *Sacrosanctum Concilium*, no. 10.

20. John Paul II, *Christifideles Laici*, no. 14. Italics are in the original.

21. *Gaudium et Spes*, no. 4.

22. John Paul II, *Laborem Exercens*, no. 9. Retrieved August 2008 from www.vatican.va/holy_father/john_paul_ii/encyclicals /documents/hf_jp-ii_enc14091981_laborem-exercens_en.html. Italics are in the original.

23. John Paul II, *Christifideles Laici*, no. 14. Italics are in the original.

24. Ray R. Noll, "The Sacramental Ministry of the Deacon in Parish Life," in *The Deacon Reader*, ed. James Keating (Mahwah, NJ: Paulist Press, 2005), 203.

25. Tkacik and McGonigle, 57.

26. William T. Ditewig, "Charting a Theology of Diaconate," in *The Theology of the Diaconate*, 60.

27. See Robert S. Rivers, CSP, *From Maintenance to Mission: Evangelization and the Revitalization of the Parish* (Mahwah, NJ: Paulist Press, 2005).

28. William S. McKnight, "The Diaconate as Medius Ordo," in *The Deacon Reader*, ed. James Keating (Mahwah, NJ: Paulist Press, 2005), 92.

29. Thomas Baker, "The Deacon and Work," in *The Deacon Reader*, 197.

30. William T. Ditewig, *The Emerging Diaconate: Servant Leaders in a Servant Church* (Mahwah, NJ: Paulist Press, 2007), 62–71.

# Bibliography

## Primary Sources

*Acta et documenta Concilio oecumenico Vaticano II apparando, Series prima (antepraeparatoria)*. Vatican City: Typis Polyglottis Vaticanis, 1960–61.

*Acta et documenta Concilio oecumenico Vaticano II apparando, Series secunda (praeparatoria)*. Vatican City: Typis Polyglottis Vaticanis, 1969.

*Acta Synodalia Sacrosancti Concilii Vaticani II*. Vatican City: Typis Polyglottis Vaticanis, 1970–78.

Bishops' Committee on the Permanent Diaconate. *Permanent Deacons in the United States: Guidelines on Their Formation and Ministry*. Washington, DC: United States Catholic Conference, 1971; rev. 1984.

Center for Applied Research in the Apostolate. "The Permanent Diaconate Today." Washington, DC: CARA, June 2000.

———. "Profile of the Diaconate in the United States: A Report of Findings from CARA's Deacon Poll." CARA Working Paper Series, Number 6. Washington, DC: CARA, April 2004.

———. "Catholic Ministry Formation Directory Statistical Summary: 2005–2006. Washington, DC: CARA, April 2006.

———. "Diaconate Post-Ordination Survey." Washington, DC: CARA, May 2006.

*Code of Canon Law: Latin-English Edition*. Washington, DC: Canon Law Society of America, 1999.

Congregation for Catholic Education. *Basic Norms for the Formation of Permanent Deacons*. Vatican City: Libreria Editrice Vaticana, 1998.

Congregation for the Clergy. *Directory for the Ministry and Life of Permanent Deacons*. Vatican City: Libreria Editrice Vaticana, 1998.

*The Documents of Vatican II, All Sixteen Official Texts Promulgated by the Ecumenical Council 1963–65.* Walter M. Abbott, ed. New York: Guild Press, 1966.

John Paul II. "The Heart of the Diaconate—Servants of the Mysteries of Christ and Servants of Your Brothers and Sisters." Allocution to the permanent deacons and their wives. Given in Detroit, MI, on September 19, 1987. *Origins* 17 (1987): 327–29.

———. Allocution to a plenary session of the Congregation for the Clergy. Given on November 30, 1995. *L'Osservatore Romano*, English Language Edition, n. 51/51, 20/27 December 1995: 5.

———. "Deacons Serve the Kingdom of God." Allocution on the permanent diaconate given at the general audience on October 6, 1993. *L'Osservatore Romano*, English Language Edition, n. 41, October 13, 1993: 11.

———. "The Deacon Has Many Pastoral Functions." Allocution on the permanent diaconate given at the general audience on October 13, 1993. *L'Osservatore Romano*, English Language Edition, n. 42, October 20, 1993: 11.

———. "Deacons Are Called to a Life of Holiness." Allocution on the permanent diaconate given at the general audience on October 20, 1993. *L'Osservatore Romano*, English Language Edition, n. 43, October 27, 1993: 11.

———. *Fides et Ratio.* Vatican City: Typis Polyglottis Vaticanis, 1998.

———. "Deacons as Apostles of the New Evangelization." Address to permanent deacons and their families during the Jubilee Day for Deacons on February 19, 2000. *L'Osservatore Romano*, English Language Edition, February 23, 2000.

Paul VI. *Hodie Concilium. AAS* 58 (1966).

———. *Sacrum Diaconatus Ordinem, motu proprio.* June 18, 1967. *AAS* 59 (1967): 697–704.

———. *Ministeria Quaedam, motu proprio.* August 15, 1972. *AAS* 64 (1972): 529–534.

———. *Ad Pascendum, motu proprio.* August 15, 1972. *AAS* 64 (1972): 534–540.

United States Catholic Conference. *A National Study on the*

*Permanent Diaconate of the Catholic Church in the United States, 1994–1995*. Washington, DC: United States Catholic Conference, 1996.

United States Conference of Catholic Bishops. *National Directory for the Formation, Ministry, and Life of Permanent Deacons in the United States*. Washington, DC: United States Conference of Catholic Bishops, 2004.

# Secondary Sources

Alberigo, Guiseppe, and Joseph A. Komonchak, eds. *History of Vatican II*. 5 vols. Maryknoll, NY: Orbis and Leuven, Belgium: Peeters, 1995–2006.

Barnett, James M. *The Diaconate: A Full and Equal Order*, rev. ed. Valley Forge, PA: Trinity Press International, 1995.

Beal, John P., James A. Coriden, and Thomas J. Green, eds. *New Commentary on the Code of Canon Law*. Commissioned by the Canon Law Society of America. Washington, DC: Canon Law Society of America, 2000.

Bernardin, Joseph. "The Call to Service: Pastoral Statement on the Permanent Diaconate." Chicago: Archdiocese of Chicago, 1993.

Borras, Alphonse. "Les effets canoniques de l'ordination diaconal." *Revue Théologique de Louvain* 28 (1997): 469–80.

Borras, Alphonse, and Bernard Pottier. *Le grâce du diaconat: Questions actuelles autour du diaconat latin*. Brussels: Editions Lessius, 1998.

Buechlein, Daniel M. "The Sacramental Identity of the Ministerial Priesthood: 'In Persona Christi.'" In *Priests for a New Millennium: A Series of Essays on the Ministerial Priesthood*. Bishops' Committee on Priestly Life and Ministry, 37–52. Washington, DC: United States Conference of Catholics Bishops, 2000.

Center for Marriage and Family. *Time, Sex, and Money: The First Five Years of Marriage*. Omaha: Creighton University Press, 2000.

Collins, John N. *Diakonia: Re-interpreting the Ancient Sources*. New York / Oxford: Oxford University Press, 1990.

Congar, Yves. *Lay People in the Church*. London: Geoffrey Chapman Publishers, 1965.

Cummings, Owen F. *Deacons and the Church*. Mahwah, NJ: Paulist Press, 2004.

Cummings, Owen F., William T. Ditewig, and Richard R. Gaillardetz. *Theology of the Diaconate: The State of the Question*. Mahwah, NJ: Paulist Press, 2005.

Ditewig, William T. *The Emerging Diaconate: Servant Leaders in a Servant Church*. Mahwah, NJ: Paulist Press, 2007.

———. *101 Questions & Answers on Deacons*. Mahwah, NJ: Paulist Press, 2004.

———. "The Deacon as Voice of Lament and Link to Thanksgiving and Justice." *Liturgical Ministry* 13 (Winter 2004): 24–28.

———. "The Once and Future Diaconate: Notes from the Past, Possibilities for the Future." *Church* 20:2 (Summer 2004): 51–54.

———. "Charting a Theology of the Diaconate: An Exercise in Ecclesial Cartography." In Owen F. Cummings, William T. Ditewig, and Richard R. Gaillardetz, *Theology of the Diaconate: The State of the Question*, 31–65. Mahwah, NJ: Paulist Press, 2005.

———. "The Contemporary Renewal of the Diaconate." In *The Deacon Reader*. James Keating, ed., 27–55. Mahwah, NJ: Paulist Press, 2006.

———. "The Kenotic Leadership of Deacons." In *The Deacon Reader*. James Keating, ed., 248–277. Mahwah, NJ: Paulist Press, 2006.

Donovan, William T. *The Sacrament of Service: Understanding Diaconal Spirituality*. Green Bay, WI: Alt Publishing Company, 2000.

Dulles, Avery. *Models of the Church*. New York: Doubleday, 1974.

Echlin, Edward. *The Deacon and the Church: Past and Future*. Staten Island, NY: Alba House, 1971.

International Theological Commission. *From the Diakonia of Christ to the Diakonia of the Apostles*. Historico-Theological

Research Document. Mundelein, IL: Hillenbrand Books, 2003.

John Paul II. *Christifideles Laici*. Boston: Pauline Books and Media, 1988.

———. *Ex Corde Ecclesia*. Boston: Pauline Books and Media, 1990.

———. *Familiaris Consortio*. Boston: Pauline Books and Media, 1981.

———. *Laborems Exercens*. Boston: Pauline Books and Media, 1981.

Kasper, Walter. *Leadership in the Church: How Traditional Roles Can Serve the Christian Community Today*. New York: Crossroad, 2003.

Keating, James. *The Deacon Reader*. Mahwah, NJ: Paulist Press, 2006.

Komonchak, Joseph A. "The Permanent Diaconate and the Variety of Ministries in the Church." *Diaconal Quarterly* III/3 (1977): 15–23; III/4 (1977): 29–40; IV/1 (1978): 13–25.

———. "The New Diaconate Guidelines." *Proceedings of the National Association of Permanent Diaconate Directors Convention in Baltimore, Maryland, April 28—1 May, 1986*. Chicago: National Association of Permanent Diaconate Directors, 1986: 5–9.

Lawler, Michael G. *Marriage and Sacrament: A Theology of Christian Marriage*. Collegeville, MN: The Liturgical Press, 1993.

Leckey, Dolores R. *Rediscovering Vatican II: The Laity and Christian Education*. Mahwah, NJ: Paulist Press, 2006.

McBrien, Richard. *Church: The Continuing Quest*. New York: Newman Press, 1970.

McCaslin, Patrick, and Michael G. Lawler. *Sacrament of Service: A Vision of the Permanent Diaconate Today*. New York: Paulist Press, 1986.

Mitchell, Nathan, OSB. *Mission and Ministry: History and Theology in the Sacrament of Order*. Wilmington, DE: Michael Glazier, 1982.

Rahner, Karl. "On the Diaconate." In *Foundations for Renewal of the Diaconate*, trans. David Bourke, 193–212. Washington, DC: United States Catholic Conference, 1993.

———. "The Theology of the Restoration of the Diaconate." In *Theological Investigations*, vol. 5, trans. Karl-H Kruger. New York: Crossroad, 1983, 268–314.

———. "The Teaching of the Second Vatican Council on the Diaconate." In *Theological Investigations*, vol. 10, trans. David Bourke. New York: Seabury Press. A Crossroad Book, 1977, 222–232.

Rahner, Karl, and Herbert Vorgrimler, eds. *Diakonia in Christo: Über Die Erneuerung des Diakonates*. Freiburg: Herder, 1962.

Rieger, Jorg. *Remember the Poor: The Challenge to Theology in the Twenty-First Century*. Harrisburg. PA: Trinity Press International, 1998.

*Rites of the Catholic Church*. New York: Pueblo Publishing, 1976.

Sherman, Lynn. *The Deacon in the Church*. Staten Island, NY: Alba House, 1991.

Shugrue, Timothy J. *Service Ministry of the Deacon*. Washington, DC: Bishops' Committee on the Permanent Diaconate, National Conference of Catholic Bishops, 1988.

Tanner, Norman P., ed. *Decrees of the Ecumenical Councils*. 2 vols. Washington, DC: Georgetown University Press, 1990.

Tkacik, Michael J., and Thomas McGonigle. *Pneumatic Correctives: What Is the Spirit Saying to the Church of the Twenty-First Century?* Lanham, MD: University Press of America, 2007.

Troeger, Thomas. *Imaging a Sermon*. Nashville: Abingdon Press, 1990.

United States Conference of Catholic Bishops. *Ceremonial of Bishops*. Collegeville, MN: Liturgical Press, 1989.

———. *Co-Workers in the Vineyard of the Lord: A Resource for Guiding the Development of Lay Ecclesial Ministry*. Washington, DC: United States Conference of Catholic Bishops, 2005.

———. *Fulfilled In Your Hearing: The Homily In The Sunday Assembly*. Washington: United States Conference of Catholic Bishops, 1982.

———. *General Instruction of the Roman Missal*. Washington, DC: United States Conference of Catholic Bishops, 2003.

—————. *Our Hearts Were Burning Within Us*. Washington, DC: United States Conference of Catholic Bishops, 1999.

—————. *To Teach as Jesus Did*. Washington, DC: United States Conference of Catholic Bishops, 1972.

Vorgrimler, Herbert, ed. *Commentary on the Documents of Vatican II*. 5 vols. New York: Herder and Herder, 1967–69.

Woestman, William H. *The Sacrament of Orders and the Clerical State: A Commentary on the Code of Canon Law*. Ottawa: St. Paul University, 1999.

Wood, Susan K. *Sacramental Orders. Lex Orandi* Series, ed. John D. Laurance. Collegeville, MN: The Liturgical Press, 2000.

Zagano, Phyllis. *Holy Saturday: An Argument for the Restoration of the Female Diaconate in the Catholic Church*. New York: Crossroad, 2000.

# Contributors

**John R. Alvarez** is a deacon of the Diocese of St. Petersburg in ministry at St. Paul Catholic Church in Tampa, Florida, a large, multicultural parish that serves over 4,900 families. He serves as the parish administrator and director of liturgy. He holds a diocesan assignment as the director of formation in the diaconate formation program and is also on the faculty of the diocesan lay pastoral ministry program. One of his major areas of interest is ministry leadership; he is currently collaborating on a book about the critical dimensions of ministry leadership.

**William T. Ditewig**, PhD, is a deacon of the Archdiocese of Washington, DC, and professor of theology at Saint Leo University near Tampa, Florida. Former executive director of the Secretariat for the Diaconate at the United States Conference of Catholic Bishops, he served on the writing team of the *National Directory for the Formation, Ministry, and Life of Permanent Deacons in the United States*. He has a BA in philosophy, MAs in education and in pastoral theology, and his PhD in theology from the Catholic University of America. A retired commander in the United States Navy, he is a prolific author and lecturer on ecclesiology and the diaconate.

**David P. Dowdle** was ordained a deacon in 1978 and a priest in 1979 for the Archdiocese of Chicago. Among his various assignments, he served as the director of spiritual formation for the diaconate formation program for the archdiocese before being named pastor of a large parish in the western suburbs of Chicago.

**Marshall Gibbs**, DMin, is a deacon of the Diocese of Orlando and currently serves as director of deacon formation for the diocese. He earned his doctorate in preaching from the Aquinas Institute of Theology, St. Louis, Missouri.

**Stephen J. Graff**, MDiv, PhD, is a deacon of the Diocese of Rochester, New York. He was the editor for the formation sections of the *National Directory* and has written extensively in the areas of ministry formation, standards, assessment, and field education for such groups as the Inter-Organizational Council, the National Association for Lay Ministry, the National Association of Diaconate Directors, and the Bishop's Committee on the Diaconate

Since 1984, **Ann Healey**, PhD, has served as director of deacon formation in English and in Spanish for the Diocese of Fort Worth. She has served on the National Association of Deacon Directors as regional representative, secretary, and president. She also served on the writing committee for the *National Directory for the Formation, Ministry, and Life of Permanent Deacons in the United States*. She is a spiritual director and a certified chaplain in the National Association of Catholic Chaplains.

**James Keating**, PhD, is director of theological formation at the Institute for Priestly Formation at Creighton University in Omaha, Nebraska. He is the editor of *The Deacon Reader* and author of *A Deacon's Retreat*, both by Paulist Press.

**Theodore W. Kraus**, PhD, is currently pastor of Santa Maria Church in Orinda, California, in the Oakland Diocese. Msgr. Ted has served as president of the National Association of Deacon Directors. He has been associated for twenty years with diaconal communities as director of formation, member of the formation faculty, and spiritual director. He was also appointed by the USCCB's Committee on the Diaconate as the project director for the preparation of the *National Directory for the Formation, Ministry, and Life of Permanent Deacons in the United States*. He is a frequent retreat director and presenter on the diaconate throughout the United States.

**Paul J. Langsfeld** is a priest of the Archdiocese of Washington, for which he was ordained in 1977. He has served in parish ministry, on the staff of the Congregation for the Clergy in Rome, as vice rector of Mount St. Mary's Seminary in Emmitsburg, Maryland, and as rector of the Pontifical College Josephinum in Columbus, Ohio. Msgr. Langsfeld has been committed to the formation of permanent deacons throughout his ministry.

**Michael G. Lawler**, PhD, is professor emeritus of Catholic theology at Creighton University and former director of Creighton's Center for Marriage and Family. He received his training in theology at Dublin, Oxford, Rome, and St. Louis. A prolific lecturer and writer, he has published twenty-one books and some 150 scholarly essays. His books include *Marriage and Sacrament*, *Christian Marriage and Family*, and *Marriage in the Catholic Church* (all from Liturgical Press); and *What Is and What Ought to Be* (Continuum). His latest book, coauthored with Todd Salzman, is *The Sexual Person: Toward a Renewed Catholic Anthropology* (Georgetown University Press).

**Timothy J. Shugrue**, a priest of the Archdiocese of Newark, served for ten years as the director of its Office of the Permanent Diaconate, where he was responsible for revising the archdiocesan guidelines for diaconal formation. As an officer of the National Association of Permanent Diaconate Directors, he served as a consultant to the Bishops' Committee on the Permanent Diaconate and is the author of the committee's monograph, "The Service Ministry of the Deacon." Msgr. Shugrue is presently a parochial vicar at St. Michael's Parish in Cranford, New Jersey.

**Michael J. Tkacik**, PhD, is associate professor of theology at Saint Leo University in Florida. He holds a BA in religion and philosophy from Auburn University, an MA in theology from Providence College, and a PhD in systematic theology from Duquesne University. His primary teaching interest and area of research is the sacramentology and ecclesiology of the Second Vatican Council. Michael has been involved in the intellectual formation of deacon candidates for fourteen years—both at his current institution and at his former institution, Providence College in Rhode Island. He lives north of Tampa, Florida, with his wife and three sons.

# green press
## INITIATIVE

Paulist Press is committed to preserving ancient forests and natural resources. We elected to print this title on 30% post consumer recycled paper, processed chlorine free. As a result, for this printing, we have saved:

7 Trees (40' tall and 6-8" diameter)
2 Million BTUs of Total Energy
713 Pounds of Greenhouse Gases
3,433 Gallons of Wastewater
208 Pounds of Solid Waste

Paulist Press made this paper choice because our printer, Thomson-Shore, Inc., is a member of Green Press Initiative, a nonprofit program dedicated to supporting authors, publishers, and suppliers in their efforts to reduce their use of fiber obtained from endangered forests.

For more information, visit www.greenpressinitiative.org

Environmental impact estimates were made using the Environmental Defense Paper Calculator. For more information visit: www.papercalculator.org.